Cost-Benefit Analysis of Environmental Health Interventions

Cost-Benefit Analysis of Environmental Health Interventions

Edited by

CARLA GUERRIERO

Department of Economics and Statistics
University of Naples Federico II & Centre
for Studies in Economics and Finance,
University of Naples Federico II, Naples, Italy

ELSEVIER

ACADEMIC PRESS

An imprint of Elsevier

Academic Press is an imprint of Elsevier
125 London Wall, London EC2Y 5AS, United Kingdom
525 B Street, Suite 1650, San Diego, CA 92101, United States
50 Hampshire Street, 5th Floor, Cambridge, MA 02139, United States
The Boulevard, Langford Lane, Kidlington, Oxford OX5 1GB, United Kingdom

Notices
Knowledge and best practice in this field are constantly changing. As new research and experience broaden our understanding, changes in research methods, professional practices, or medical treatment may become necessary.

Practitioners and researchers must always rely on their own experience and knowledge in evaluating and using any information, methods, compounds, or experiments described herein. In using such information or methods they should be mindful of their own safety and the safety of others, including parties for whom they have a professional responsibility.

To the fullest extent of the law, neither the Publisher nor the authors, contributors, or editors, assume any liability for any injury and/or damage to persons or property as a matter of products liability, negligence or otherwise, or from any use or operation of any methods, products, instructions, or ideas contained in the material herein.

British Library Cataloguing-in-Publication Data
A catalogue record for this book is available from the British Library

Library of Congress Cataloging-in-Publication Data
A catalog record for this book is available from the Library of Congress

ISBN: 978-0-12-812885-5

For Information on all Academic Press publications
visit our website at https://www.elsevier.com/books-and-journals

Publisher: Candice Janco
Acquisition Editor: Scott Bentley
Editorial Project Manager: Susan E. Ikeda
Production Project Manager: Sojan P. Pazhayattil
Cover Designer: Christian J. Bilbow

Typeset by MPS Limited, Chennai, India

Working together
to grow libraries in
developing countries

www.elsevier.com • www.bookaid.org

Dedication

To all our family members (two and four-footed)

Contents

List of contributors

Zaid Chalabi
Institute of Environmental Design and Engineering, Bartlett School of Environment, Energy and Resources, University College London, London, United Kingdom; Department of Public Health, Environments and Society, Faculty of Public Health and Policy, London School of Hygiene and Tropical Medicine, London, United Kingdom

Frank George
World Health Organization, Regional Office for Europe, European Centre for Environment and Health, Bonn, Germany

Carla Guerriero
Department of Economics and Statistics, University of Naples Federico II, Naples, Italy; Centre for Studies in Economics and Finance (CSEF), Naples, Italy

Paolo Lauriola
Italian National Research Council, Institute of Clinical Physiology, Unit of Environmental Epidemiology and Disease Registries, Italy

Giovanni Leonardi
London School of Hygiene and Tropical Medicine, United Kingdom

Stéphane Luchini
Aix-Marseille Univ., CNRS, EHESS, Centrale Marseille, AMSE, Marseille, France

Marco Martuzzi
World Health Organization, Regional Office for Europe, European Centre for Environment and Health, Bonn, Germany

Antonia Pacelli
Department of Economics and Statistics, University of Naples Federico II, Naples, Italy

Stefano Papirio
Department of Civil, Architectural and Environmental Engineering, University of Napoli Federico II, Napoli, Italy

Francesco Pirozzi
Department of Civil, Architectural and Environmental Engineering, University of Napoli Federico II, Napoli, Italy

Andrea Ranzi
Centre for Environmental Health and Prevention, Regional Agency for Prevention, Environment and Energy of Emilia-Romagna, Modena, Italy

L.E. Loria Rebolledo
Health Economics Research Unit, University of Aberdeen, Aberdeen, United Kingdom

Dean Regier
Cancer Control Research, BC Cancer and School of Population and Public Health, University of British Columbia, Vancouver, Canada

Rainer Schulz
University of Aberdeen Business School, University of Aberdeen, Aberdeen, United Kingdom

Verity Watson
Health Economics Research Unit, University of Aberdeen, Aberdeen, United Kingdom

John S.F. Wright
Institute for Public Policy and Governance, University of Technology Sydney, Sydney, NSW, Australia

Ariana Zeka
Brunel University London, United Kingdom

Acknowledgments

The authors wish to acknowledge the invaluable help, support, and advice of the following people, without whom this book would not have come to fruition: John Cairns, Sarah Willis, Monica Contestabile, Andy Haines, Riccardo Martina, Debby Stanley, Stefania Maddaluno, Fabrizio Bianchi, and Liliana Cori.

We also want to thank Andrea Accennato and Anne Wen for helping with the figures and text.

We are very grateful to the Colt Foundation and, in particular, to Jackie Douglas, who supported and attended the workshops "Cost—Benefit Analysis of Environmental Health Interventions."

Introduction

Carla Guerriero
Department of Economics and Statistics, University of Naples Federico II, Naples, Italy;
Centre for Studies in Economics and Finance (CSEF), Naples, Italy

Nature

There is a delight in the hardy life of the open.

There are no words that can tell the hidden spirit of the wilderness that can reveal its mystery, its melancholy, and its charm.

The Nation behaves well if it treats the natural resources as assets which it must turn over to the next generation increased and not impaired in value.

Conservation means development as much as it does protection.

Theodore Roosevelt

I.1 Introduction

Over the last two decades, increased industrialization and rising standards of hygiene have reduced the risks of environmental hazards associated with vector borne diseases, pathogens, and food contamination, but substantially increased risks associated with noncommunicable diseases contracted through exposure to toxic physical and chemical compounds (Prüss-Üstün and Corvalán, 2006).

There is mounting epidemiological evidence that the health consequences of physical (e.g., noise, vibrations) and chemical (e.g., lead, asbestos) hazards constitute a serious health threat. According to Prüss-Üstün and Corvalán (2007), environmental exposures are responsible for up to 24% of global diseases and 23% of global deaths. A prospective study "The Benefits and Costs of the Clean Air Act from 1990 to 2020" by the US Environmental Protection Agency (EPA) estimated the benefits of reducing fine particles and ground level of ozone pollution under the 1990 Clean Air Act amendments (EPA, 2011). In 2010 alone the study estimated that the 1990 Clean Air Act amendments prevented 160,000 cases of premature mortality, 13 million lost work days, and 1.7 million asthma attacks (EPA, 2011). A similar analysis conducted in Europe

"The Clean Air for Europe" quantified the potential health benefits of improving air quality in Europe between 2000 and 2020 (Watkiss et al., 2005). According to the study, the annual impact of particulate matter alone on human health accounts 3.7 million years of life lost and 700 annual infant deaths (using particulate matter exposure in 2000) (Watkiss et al., 2005). The issues of resource limitations, economic efficiency, and value for money comprise the essential criteria in which policy and regulatory decisions are made, and are critical to understanding the impact of proposed environmental, health, and safety regulations. By comparing the benefits and the costs of all available interventions, economic evaluation provides essential information to optimally use the limited budget (Hutton, 2000; OECD, 2006a,b).

National and international governmental bodies are required to perform economic evaluation to assess new regulatory interventions (Arrow et al., 1996; Atkinson and Murato, 2008). In 1993 President Clinton's executive order 12866 established that government and private parties should be fully informed about the costs and benefits of regulatory options (The White House, 1993). Similarly, the European Commission and the World Health Organization (WHO) strongly recommend the use of economic evaluation to demonstrate the economic return on investments in interventions and also to compare competing interventions (Atkinson and Murato, 2008; Hutton, 2000). In the United Kingdom, economic evaluation is part of the regulatory impact analysis, which is mandatory for appraisal of new regulations (HM Treasury, 2018).

Nevertheless, the use of economic evaluation to guide evidence-based decisions is still in its infancy and mainly applies to high-income countries. According to OECD (2018), there are large variations across sectors in the extent to which which cost—benefit analysis (CBA) is carried out. Overall there is still paucity of completed economic evaluations assessing either the cost-effectiveness or the cost—benefit of environmental health interventions (EHIs). Most of the published studies investigate interventions concerning occupational safety and health, and air pollution. There is limited evidence on the potential cost-effectiveness of other EHIs, such as ozone depletion and remediation of toxic waste sites (OECD, 2018; Hutton, 2000). A research reviewed the economic studies conducted in three environmental health areas: air pollution, water, sanitation hygiene, and vector control (Hutton, 2008). The review found a total of only 50 peer-reviewed economic evaluations, of which 16 were on vector control, 21 on air pollution, and 13 on water, sanitation, and hygiene.

Previous reviews found similar shortcomings in previous economic evaluations (Hutton, 2000, 2008; OECD, 2018). First, they highlighted a lack of agreement on the methods used to assess EHIs, which makes comparing the study results difficult. For instance, some economic evaluations fail to report key information such as the viewpoint adopted and the time horizon assumed for both the benefits and the costs. Other major weaknesses highlighted in previous reviews were differences in assessing potential benefits of interventions (quality-adjusted life year, child cases of diarrheal diseases, the value of saved lives, and productivity gains) and the lack of appropriate sensitivity analysis (Hutton, 2000; OECD, 2018).

I.2 Cost—benefit analysis of environmental health interventions

EHIs, such as congestion charge to reduce air pollution or toxic waste site remediation, are different from core healthcare interventions in many ways. First, together with human health improvements (mortality and morbidity risk reductions), they also introduce ecological improvements such as improvements to market products (e.g., harvest of food), increased real estate prices, increased tourism flows, and, as a result, they require the collaboration of different sectors outside the Ministry of Health (OECD, 2018; Watkiss et al., 2005; Hutton, 2008)

Second, compared to health service interventions, almost all EHIs are preventive interventions acting on the primary cause of disease (e.g., removing air pollution to prevent asthma attack vs treating an asthma with a bronchodilator) (Hutton, 2000, 2008). Given their preventive nature, they may take some time before being effective (e.g., the main bulk of the benefits of remediating a contaminated site will be observed only after several years).

The third main difference between health service interventions and EHIs is that the latter is associated with greater uncertainty. EHIs may affect large population but only bring small risk reductions that are difficult to gauge with certainty. In addition the relationship between many pollutants/hazards and health are also not yet well established.

Different economic analysis can be performed to provide evidence on the cost and the effectiveness of interventions affecting human health (Hutton, 2000, 2008). If the intervention has only health benefits, cost-effectiveness and utility analysis are the most common forms of economic evaluation (Prüss-Üstün and Corvalán, 2006).[1] Given the wide range of benefits associated with EHIs, CBA is preferable to other forms of economic evaluations because it allows utility gains and losses not related to health to be included in the decision-making process. Another key advantage of CBA over other economic evaluation methods (e.g., cost-effectiveness analysis and cost utility analysis) is its capacity to determine the optimal scale of the policy and determine whether interventions should be undertaken at all (Watkiss et al., 2005).

CBA can be used

1. to determine acceptable levels of risk defined as the risk level that maximizes the difference between total social cost and benefits, or in other words, where the marginal social benefits associated with the risk reduction are equal to the marginal social costs(MSCs) of pollution abatement;
2. demonstrate the economic return of investment;
3. compare the cost-effectiveness of competing interventions;
4. allocate limited resources efficiently; and
5. retrospective CBA can be used to complement ex ante CBA.

I.3 Rationale for the book

In the last decades, there has been a substantial increase of willingness to pay studies, using either revealed or stated preference, to assign a monetary value to the costs and benefits of EHIs. However, as mentioned in the previous section, a similar trend has not been observed for CBAs of EHIs. One of the main reasons for the lack of CBA studies is the absence of a common transparent methodology specifically outlined for EHIs. Using an interdisciplinary approach, this book provides a practical guide to the CBA of EHIs.

The specific objectives of the book are to

1. gain sufficient understanding of the concepts and the methods of CBA of EHIs,

---

[1] Cost effectiveness analysis compares the cost of an intervention with the health outcomes, e.g., life years saved. Cost utility analysis assesses the cost-effectiveness of an intervention converting the health outcomes averted in terms of common utility index such as quality-adjusted life year (QALY) or disability-adjusted life year (DALY). For further details on different economic evaluations methods, see Chapter 11, Case study: a realistic contaminated site remediation and different scenarios of intervention.

2. provide a clear conceptual framework that enables the readers to engage with different steps necessary to conduct a CBA of EHIs, and
3. enable readers from different disciplines and areas of expertise to engage with CBA practitioners about a planned analysis.

The book is complemented with a practical case study (see Chapter 12: Case study: a realistic contaminated site remediation and different scenarios of intervention), illustrating step-by-step how to conduct a CBA of remediating a toxic waste site in Mexico. This book is intended for a wide audience including policy makers, advanced undergraduate students, and postgraduate students in health economics, environmental epidemiology and engineering (e.g., environmental engineering, transportation engineering), private-sector operators (e.g., consultancy services), and NGOs willing to perform CBA of their interventions. No prior knowledge is necessary, but elements of welfare economics, mathematics, and statistics may be required to understand some contents.

I.4 The economic foundations of cost–benefit analysis

The objective of this section is to provide a brief overview of the fundamental economic theory underlying CBA of environmental health interventions. The concept of market is used in economics to describe any situation in which there is an exchange of goods between consumers and producers (Varian, 1992). The objective of economic analysis is to assess how the agents' (consumers and producers) interactions add up to determine the quantity exchanged on the market and the price at which each unit of good is sold. A simple representation of a single-good market is presented in Fig. I.1. The market diagram illustrates consumers' and producers' behaviors which are represented by the demand (*D*) and supply curve (*S*), respectively.

In perfect competition, consumers are assumed to purchase a combination of goods that maximize their utility given their budget constraint (Varian, 1992). The market demand curve shows the total quantity that consumers in the market are willing to pay for different price levels (the horizontal sum of all consumers' demand curves). As seen, the demand curve is downward sloping: as the price of the good increases a lower quantity will be exchanged in the market. The rational for a downward slope is based on the assumption of a diminishing marginal utility: the additional benefit of each additional unit is valued slightly less than that realized by the previous unit. The market supply curve, *S*, shows the

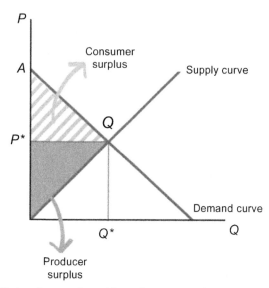

Figure I.1 Equilibrium in a market with perfect competition.

horizontal sum of the producers' marginal cost of the good. The supply curve is upward sloping because economists generally assume that, due to inputs scarcity, the cost of producing any additional unit is greater than the cost of producing the previous one (firms operating in the short run are constrained by fixed factors of production, which ultimately result in increasing marginal cost) (Varian, 1992).

In a competitive market economy, the intersection between S and D determines the equilibrium price $P^\star$ and the quantity of a good exchanged in the market $Q^\star$ (Varian, 1992). Assuming that the competitive market sets the price of the good at the price $P^\star$ then consumers pay $P^\star \mathrm{x} Q^\star$ to producers. In Fig. I.1 the net benefits for the consumers is given by the triangle $AP^\star O$ which corresponds to the area blow the demand curve and above the price line. This area, also referred as consumer surplus, is the sum of all individuals' willingness to pay for a good over and above that required by the market. The concept of consumer surplus is essential for CBA as it allows to quantify how much the society is willing to pay for a policy change. Specular to the concept of consumer surplus, there is the economic notion of producer surplus, which in Fig. I.1 is represented by the area below the price line and above the market supply curve (triangle $P^\star O Q^\star$). Producer surplus, also referred as net benefits to the producers, is given by the difference between what producers are willing to supply of a good and the price they actually receive (Varian, 1992).

Whenever there is no way to reallocate the goods so that someone is made better off without making someone else worse off, the Pareto optimality[2] is achieved. The economic condition of Pareto optimality ensures that the maximum social welfare (the sum of consumer and producer surplus) is achieved (OECD, 2007). This condition occurs when the market supply and demand curves reflect the society true Willingness to Pay (WTP) and MSC (Varian, 1992). If the market works perfectly, and a Pareto optimality is achieved without government intervention, there is no need to perform CBA. Only if there is a market failure CBA is necessary.

Five are the possible causes of market failure: the first one is the presence of a public good(s) (UK Treasury Book, 2018). Many aspects of the environment, for example, the cost of clean air, can be described as public goods. A public good has two characteristics:

1. *Nonrivalry*: This means that when a good is consumed, it does not reduce the amount available for others (e.g., benefiting from clean air does not reduce the air available for others).
2. *Nonexcludability*: This occurs when it is not possible to provide a good without it being possible for others to enjoy. For example, if you erect a dam to stop flooding—you protect everyone in the area (whether they contributed to flooding defenses or not).

In an unregulated market a public good is likely to be underprovided and exploited because its characteristics of nonrivalry and nonexcludability. A second possible cause of market failure is imperfect information:

---

[2] Pareto optimality or Pareto efficiency, named after the Italian economist and political scientist Vilfredo Pareto (1848–1923), is used in neoclassical economics alongside the theoretical construct of perfect competition, as benchmarks to judge the efficiency of real markets—though neither outcome is experienced outside of economic theory. Hypothetically, if there were perfect competition and resources were used to their maximum efficient capacity, everyone would be at their highest standard of living, or Pareto efficiency.

In practice, it is almost impossible to take any social action, such as a change in economic policy, without making at least one person worse off—which is why the concept of Pareto improvement has found a wider use in economics. A Pareto improvement occurs when a change in allocation harms no one and helps at least one person, given an initial allocation of goods for a set of persons. The theory suggests that Pareto improvements will keep enhancing value to an economy until it achieves a Pareto equilibrium, where no more Pareto improvements can be made.

buyers need to know the quality of the goods to judge the value they can provide while sellers need to know the reliability of the buyer. This information must be available to all, or there is asymmetry of information which could lead to moral hazard. Moral hazards refer to a situation where an economic agent makes profit-maximizing but socially inefficient decisions because he/she is able to avoid the full economic costs associated with their conduct. The fourth possible cause of market failure is market power. This results from insufficient degree of competition to ensure market efficiency. For instance, high start-up costs can create barriers for new competitors and produce market power. The fifth cause of market failure is externalities. Externalities occur whenever an economic activity produces benefits (positive externalities) and/or costs (negative externalities) to others which are not reflected in the prices charged for the goods and services being provided (OECD, 2007).

Among the different causes negative and positive externalities are the most common reasons of market failure in environmental economics. A graphic representation of the consequence of negative externalities is presented in Fig. I.2. The supply curve in this example represents a single-producer marginal private cost (MPC) of production, while the demand curve, D, represents the consumer demand curve (and marginal benefit) for the good Q produced by the firm. In absence of externality the optimal quantity produced would be Q_m which corresponds to the intersection of D with MPC. In this second example, however, because of the air pollution associated with the firm's production, the MPC of the firm does not reflect the true marginal social cost of producing Q. The society marginal social cost of producing Q is represented by the curve MSC which includes the private cost of production MPC plus the marginal social

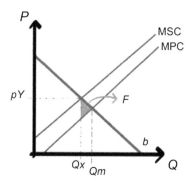

Figure I.2 Negative externalities and market failure.

damage associated with environmental pollution. The social damage associated with negative externalities in this case includes the cost of the negative health outcomes such as asthma attacks and hospital admissions caused by the firm's air pollution.

In an unregulated market the social costs associated with productions would go unaccounted and the quantity produced, Q_m, will be greater than the optimal one and the price lower ($P_m < P^*$). The vertical distance between the MPC and the MSC curves, measured over the quantity of the good purchased, represents the cost of the externalities imposed on the third parties or, in other words, the amount that those subjected to the negative externalities would be willing to pay avoid them. The deadweight loss, represented in the figure by the shaded gray area (F), represents the amount that the society loses by overproducing Q.

The presence of externalities in order to maximize the social net benefit is necessary to sum up all the private and social benefits and costs of an activity/intervention in each affected market and compare them using a single monetary metric. This is done through CBA, which allows to combine in a single framework tangible and intangible present and future consequences associated with different interventions (including no action).

CBA allows policy makers to quantify the social costs and benefits associated with environmental protection using a willingness to pay approach. For instance, it allows to quantify how much the society is willing to pay to reduce the risk of having respiratory diseases associated with health pollution. However, it is important to notice that the framework of CBA is weight equally costs and benefits without considering to whom they accrue. This is an important limitation of CBA, as based on the Kaldor—Hicks criterion the policy that produces the highest net benefit is considered welfare enhancing, because (in principle) the winners can compensate the losers and still be better off (Varian, 1992).

I.5 A brief history of cost—benefit analysis

The first practical application of CBA dates back to the 19th century when the French civil engineer and economist, Jules Dupuit, first introduced the concept of "relative utility," which nowadays correspond to "consumer surplus." The concept of externality was first introduced by the English welfare economist, Cecil Pigou, in the 1920s. Pigou argued that private and public economic products do not always coincide and cited pollution resulting from industrial production as an example. The concepts of consumer and producer surplus and externality constitute the essential foundations of CBA, as they identify how we measure social welfare accounting from previously ignored/nonmarketed elements: externalities (Boardman et al., 2018).

However, the underlying theory and the application of CBA were not consistently defined until the late the 1930s when there was a need to compare the costs and the benefits of water-related investments in the United States. After the First World War, pressure for "government efficiency" and a tool to ensure that invested public funds yielded high social benefits were sought among the available economic techniques. The US Flood Control Act (1936) mandated that all proposed projects were to be evaluated to ascertain that the benefits (whomsoever they accrued to) outweighed the associated cost (Boardman et al., 2018). The significance of the act lay in the fact that an exercise in measuring the net benefits to society invariably required the consideration of external effects and social welfare. The US Flood Act marked a turning point for CBA as it changed the objective of policy evaluation, from a simple financial appraisal using a producer perceptive to the consideration of net social benefits (Mishan and Quah, 2007). However, while it became clear what aspects ought to be included in the analysis, there was still a lack of consensus on how they could be valued, as the act did not include guidelines as to how to conduct CBA valuation. Until the 1960s, CBA has enjoyed mixed fortune mainly due to the absence of guidelines on how to carry out CBA and apply its results. It is now recognized as the most important technique to gauge the cost-effectiveness of public interventions in sectors such as infrastructure, health, and education. As suggested by Sustain (2018), the most important contribution to CBA development and its use stems from the presidents of the United States.

On December 2, 1970, President Richard Nixon established the US EPA. This new institution implemented statutory directives aimed at protecting the health, well-being and the environment from pollution. In the 15 years following its foundation, the EPA has used the tool of CBA to assess and justify its regulatory activities. After the creation of the EPA, the second most important defining moment for CBA occurred during the Reagan Presidency when he announced the Executive Order no 12291 titled, "Federal Regulation." The order imposed five requirements for the adoption of a new regulation:

1. Administrative decisions shall be based on adequate information concerning the need for consequences of proposed actions.

2. Regulatory actions shall not be undertaken unless the potential benefits outweigh the costs to society.
3. Regulatory objectives shall be chosen to maximize net benefit to society.
4. Among alternative approaches to any given regulatory objective, the alternative involving the least net cost to society should be chosen.
5. Agency shall set regulatory priorities with the aim of maximizing the aggregate net benefits to the society, taking into account the conditions of the particular industries affected by the regulations, the conditions of the national economy, and other regulatory actions contemplated in the future.

The executive order 12291 was the first to state the "Net Benefit Rule" as a criterion to evaluate and rank the cost-effectiveness of the proposed regulations (Mishan and Quah, 2007). Reagan's order also mandated the introduction of the regulatory impact analysis (RIA), which is based on three main pillars (The White House, 1981):

1. Description of the potential benefits including nonmonetary benefits and identification of the beneficiaries of the benefits.
2. Description of the potential costs including non-monetary cost and identification of those that will pay for the costs.
3. A determination of the potential net benefit accounting in the analysis for monetary and non-monetary costs and benefits.

In 1983 the EPA published its first guidelines for the Regulatory Impact Assessment (Mishan and Quah, 2007). The guidelines expanded the scope of CBA. In particular the 15 new guidelines cover a wide range of issues such as the importance of declaring the necessity and the consequences of the proposed intervention, considering alternative approaches, specific guidelines on the evaluation of the benefits, cost analysis, and how to compare the costs with the benefits. On the April 6, 1984, the US General Accounting Office published a review of EPA regulatory impact analyses entitled: "Cost–Benefit Analysis: can be useful in assessing environmental regulations, despite limitations" (US GAO, 1984). The document recommended strategies to overcome the non-legal problems and enhance the usefulness of CBA involving environmental regulations. Examples of recommendations include the need to carry out uncertainty analyses, inclusion of new sources for compliance costs of proposed regulations, and expand the range of benefits and cost, etc.

Another defining moment for CBA was the Executive Order 12866 by President Bill Clinton. Clinton's order wanted regulations to address a "compelling public need, such as material failures of private markets"; be based on an assessment of "all costs and benefits of available regulatory alternatives, including the alternative of not regulating"; and "maximize net benefits" to society unless otherwise constrained by law. The Clinton executive order also required that regulatory analysis be performed on all rules deemed to be of "significant economic impact" of $100 million or more in a given year, and that agencies submit such significant regulations for review by the Office of Information and Regulatory Affairs before publication in the Federal Register in proposed or final form (The White House, 1993).

On October 11, 1994, President Clinton issued the Executive Order no. 12898 to broaden the focus of CBA on distributional and equity issues (The White House, 1994). The second Executive Order of the Clinton presidency mandates, for the first time, to consider the environmental and human health conditions of ethical minorities and the consequences of regulation on low income populations. The main objectives of his second Executive Order were to promote non-discrimination in federal programs that substantially affect the health and the environment and to provide access to public and transparent information while enhancing public participation. A third very important Executive Order (13045) issued in 1997 during the Clinton administration discusses special issues related to children's health protection and the valuation of pediatric health outcomes for their inclusion in CBA.

During the Obama Administration there were three different Executive Orders targeting CBA: 1356361 "Improving Regulation and Regulatory Review" (January 18, 2011), Executive Order 1357962 (Regulation and Independent Regulatory Agencies) (July 11, 2011), and the latest Executive Order 1361063 "Identifying and Reducing Regulatory Burdens" (May 10, 2012) (The White House, 2011a, 2011b, 2012). The main revolutionary aspects of Obama's Administration, which explicitly embraces the Clinton's principles were to mention "human dignity" among the elements to consider in CBA and the requirement of performing retrospective analyses to review ex post the cost-effectiveness of existing regulations.

The Trump Administration's Executive Order 1377164 titled "Reducing Regulation and Controlling Regulatory Costs," (January 30, 2017) aims, as its name suggests, to reduce regulation and for the first time to limit the use of CBA (The White House, 2017). The Executive Order specifies that to limit the costs associated with regulation, at least two regulations must be eliminated for every one that is imposed. For each fiscal year, an agency recommending a new regulation must identify at least two to be repealed. Furthermore, the total incremental cost of all new regulations occurring in a fiscal year must be no more than zero (including the reduction of cost from repealed regulations), as determined by guidance issued by the Director of Office of Management and Budget. The Executive Order makes no reference to the benefits that accrue from any regulations, including those that are recommended for imposition or repeal. Logically, if only costs are those to be considered, every existing regulation should be eliminated, and no new regulations should be imposed. As suggested by a recent paper by Dillon et al. (2018) the first 6 months of the Trump administration shifted the EPA away from its original mission "to protect human and environmental health" toward a proindustry (only) mission.

I.6 Existing guidelines for cost−benefit analysis

Compared to other economic evaluation methods such as cost-utility or cost-effectiveness analysis, CBA is the most comprehensive and theoretically rigorous form of economic evaluation (Robinson, 1993). CBA has been used to guide decision making in many different areas of economic and social policy in the public sector during the last 50 years. Due to the different expertise and applications and the lack of consensus on the methodology, CBA was often carried out using similar but often noncomparable approaches. The term CBA was often substituted by Impact Regulatory Assessment or Economic Appraisal (OECD, 1993).

I.6.1 United States

In the United States, the majority of the statutory provisions require or allow some consideration of cost and benefits when setting pollution standards, but there is variation in terminology and specificity provided in each law regarding the nature and scope of the cost and benefit considerations. The most comprehensive guideline available in the US for the economic evaluation of environmental health interventions is the EPAs "Guidelines for Preparing Economic Analyses" (US EPA, 2010). The document provides the Agency with peer-reviewed guidance on how to conduct the analysis of regulatory actions to comply with E.O. 12866 and other executive orders and statutory requirements (e.g., Small Business Regulatory Enforcement Fairness Act of 1996 considerations).

EPAs guidelines describe theoretical foundation to analyse the benefits, costs, and economic impacts of regulations and policies, including assessing the distribution of costs and benefits among various segments of the population. They incorporate recent advances in theoretical and applied work in the field of environmental economics and can be freely downloaded at the following link: https://www.epa.gov/environmental-economics/guidelines-preparing-economic-analyses.

I.6.2 United Kingdom

The use of Regulatory Impact Assessment in United Kingdom dates back to the late 1980s. During the Teacher's era the objective of the Deregulation Unit was to reduce the burden of regulation on existing and emerging businesses (OECD/KDI, 2017). In 1996 the Deregulation Unit was moved to the Cabinet Office where it changed the scope of its mission: from abolishing existing burdens to assessing the impact of new regulations (OECD/KDI, 2017). In 1997 the central Deregulation Unit was transformed in a Regulatory Impact Unit and in 1998, under the Blair PM RIA was formally introduced as tool to ascertain the quality of new and existing regulations. The unit was also in charge of collaborating with EU authorities on the regulatory reform process across Europe. Between the 2003 and the 2014, the RIA process experienced major changes (OECD/KDI, 2017). Following a simplification plan in 2011, the Red Tape Challenge was launched with the specific objective to cut unnecessary regulation. This initiative was followed by a "one in one out system" shortly followed by "one in and two out" and eventually "one in and three out" systems. In 2009 a regulatory policy committee was created and in 2012 it became the sole independent advisory, nondepartmental public body in charge of overseeing the RIA in the United Kingdom (UK Department for Business, Energy & Industrial Strategy, 2012). The basic source of guidance for departments willing to conduct RIA is the Better Regulation Framework: guidance (BRFG). According to the BRFG the regulatory proposals associated with an equivalent annual net direct cost to business equal or higher than 5 million £ should require a full impact analysis and a mandatory approval of the Regulatory Policy Committee. Regulatory proposals are accompanied by an impact assessment, which assesses and estimates the likely costs and benefits, as well as presenting the associated risks, of a regulatory proposal that has an impact on business, civil society organizations, the public sector or individuals. The technical guidance on how to assess the cost and the benefits of a new or existing regulation are provided in the HM Green Book Manual. The manual was written having an ex ante analysis in mind and treating ex post or no intervention scenario as a special case. Since it was designed for different governmental bodies the guidelines provide examples on a broad range of impacts including environmental and health ones. The most updated version of the manual is accessible at the following link: https://assets.publishing.service.gov.uk/government/uploads/system/ uploads/attachment_data/file/685903/The_Green_Book.pdf.

I.6.3 European Union

In 1992 the Article 130 of the Treaty on European Union required the community to take into account the costs and benefits of new environmental regulations including the no-action option, using available scientific and technical data. In the article, however, there is no mandatory requirement for conducting and passing a CBA test. In 2003 a generic Impact Appraisal Procedure was advocated for all commission proposals associated with a significant impact on the economy, society, and environment of member states. The Appraisal Procedure was, however, not specified as well as the costs and the benefits to be included in the economic evaluation. In 2008, the first EU Guide to the Cost—Benefit Analysis of Investment Projects was published with the specific objective of providing a common and transparent methodology to conduct CBA of major Investment Projects (infrastructure projects above €50 million). An updated and expanded version has been subsequently published in 2014. According to the new Guide, "CBA—that is about measuring in 'money terms', all the benefits and costs of the project to society—should become a real management tool for national and regional authorities". The new guideline is available at the link: https://ec.europa.eu/inea/sites/inea/ files/cba_guide_cohesion_policy.pdf.

I.6.4 The World Health Organization

In 2000, the WHO published a document entitled, "Considerations in evaluating the cost effectiveness of environmental health interventions" (Hutton, 2000). The report reviewed methods are used for economic evaluations of EHIs. The document also provided recommendations on the methodology for future environmental health analyses. Compared to other guidelines such as the EU and the UK Treasury Book, the WHO document focuses specifically on the methodology to adopt when evaluating EHIs in the framework of WHO initiatives. The document provides publication reviews found in the literature search by environmental health topics and lists important aspects of each study, including authors, aims, country of study, costs and benefits included, and data sources. The interventions covered by the review are those targeting the following issues: water hygiene and sanitation, food safety, waste management, air pollution, ozone climate change and stratospheric ozone depletion. In 2003 the WHO published the official "WHO Guide to cost-effectiveness analysis". The guide complemented the existing guidelines on the use of cost-effectiveness analysis and promoted generalizability of results across different settings. In addition to the guide, software was also developed and freely available to facilitate economic evaluations; *CostIt* was designed to record cost data; a population model; *Popmod*, has been developed to automatically calculate the effectiveness of interventions for a standardized population; in terms of outcome indicators such as disability-adjusted life years (DALYs) averted and "Monte Carlo League" (*MCLeague*), a program that presents uncertainty around costs and effects to decision-makers in the form of stochastic league tables is also available. Unlike the previous document "Considerations in evaluating the cost effectiveness of environmental health interventions" that focused on EHIs, the WHO Guide to cost-effectiveness analysis targets all health interventions (including drug or medical treatments) (Hutton, 2000). Both the documents refer to cost–utility (e.g., cost per DALY) analysis. The use of CBA is rejected on the grounds that individuals are not fully informed or adequately trained on the consequences of their consumption choices when evaluating health services and interventions. The main assumption for using cost-effectiveness analysis compared to CBA is that "health contributes to social welfare separately to the consumption of non-health goods and services." This strong assumption implies that the perceptive adopted is one of a single benevolent decision-maker or provide, who seeks to maximize population health subject to the resources available. Unfortunately, it is very unlikely for EHIs to only be associated with health-related benefits and costs. As such, more than one provider is often involved in the analysis and a CBA approach should be adopted. The link to the guideline is: http://www.who.int/water_sanitation_health/economic/costeffecthutton.pdf.

I.7 Structure of the book

This book provides an in-depth, practical guide to the CBA of environmental health interventions. After defining environmental interventions, this chapter provides an overview of the foundations and the history of CBA. The following chapter illustrates how to set up a cost–benefit model with a brief overview of all the steps involved in the economic appraisal. Chapter 3, Health impact assessment: quantifying the health benefits and costs, summarizes the different environmental hazards that affect human health, describes how they are measured and the different exposure pathways. Chapter 4, Monetary analysis of health outcomes, illustrates how to quantify the health effects associated with EHIs using environmental information (e.g., change in pollutants emissions) and epidemiological and demographic data. Chapter 5, Health benefit analysis: monetization of health impacts and its use in environment and health, describes the main approaches used to assign a monetary value to the health benefits arising from EHIs. Chapter 6, Costing environmental health intervention, describes the main problems and critics associated with the issue of monetarizing health benefits. Chapter 7, Discounting benefits and costs, deals with the issue of costing associated with EHIs using a financial and, more comprehensive economic, analysis. Chapter 8, Quantifying uncertainty in environmental health models, and Chapter 9, Alternatives to cost–benefit analysis for economic evaluation, closely examine two challenging stages of CBA: discounting and accounting for uncertainty. Chapter 10, Climate change and ecological public health: an integrated framework, illustrates the main source of concerns with CBA and describes the potential alternatives to this economic evaluation approach. Chapter 12, Conclusion, provides a detailed practical case study illustrating step-by-step how to conduct a CBA of EHIs. The final chapter provides insights and examples on how to effectively communicate the results of the CBA. Supporting materials, including exercise templates and solution files, are available online at the following link: https://www.elsevier.com/books/cost-benefit-analysis-of-environmental-health-interventions/guerriero/978-0-12-812885-5.

I.8 Conclusion

This chapter provides an overview of the rational and history of the CBA with focus on the methodology available for the economic evaluation of EHIs. Compared to traditional health service interventions, EHIs deserve a specific methodological approach and different types of expertise (e.g., epidemiology, environmental engineering, economics). The objective of this book in the following chapters is to explore in depth the different steps necessary to undertake a high-quality CBA.

References

Arrow, K.J., et al., 1996. Is there a role for benefit-cost analysis in environmental, health, and safety regulation? Science 272 (5259), 221−222.

Atkinson, G., Murato, S., 2008. Environmental cost-benefit analysis. Annu. Rev. Environ. Resour. 33, 317−344.

Boardman, A.E., Greenberg, D.H., Vining, A.R., Weimer, D.L., 2018. Cost-Benefit Analysis in Practice, fourth ed. Cambridge University Press.

Dillon, L., et al., 2018. The environmental protection agency in the early trump administration: prelude to regulatory capture. Am. J. Public Health 108 (Suppl 2), S89−S942018 April. Available from: https://doi.org/10.2105/AJPH.2018.304360.

EPA, 2010. Steps in Conducting Benefits Analysis. Available from: http://www.epa.gov/ttn/ecas/econdata/Rmanual2/7.2.html.

EPA, 2011. The Benefits and Costs of the Clean Air Act from 1990 to 2020: Final Report. Office of Air and Radiation. Available from: http://www.epa.gov/air/sect812/prospective2.html.

HM Treasury, 2018. The Green Book. Appraisal and Evaluation in Central Government. < https://www.gov.uk/government/publications/the-green-book-appraisal-and-evaluation-in-central-governent > .

Hutton, G., 2000. Considerations in Evaluating the Cost-Effectiveness of Environmental Health Interventions Protection. Sustainable Development and Healthy Environments Cluster. WHO. Available from: https://extranet.who.int/iris/restricted/bitstream/10665/66744/1/WHO_SDE_WSH_00.10.pdf.

Hutton, G., 2008. Economic evaluation of environmental health interventions to support decision making. Environ. Health Insights 2, 137−155.

Mishan, E.J., Quah, E., 2007. Cost-Benefit Analysis, fifth ed. Routledge by Taylor and Francis US EPA. 2010, Guidelines for preparing economic analyses.

OECD, 1993. Glossary of Industrial Organisation Economics and Competition Law, Compiled by R. S. Khemani and D. M. Shapiro, commissioned by the Directorate for Financial, Fiscal and Enterprise Affairs. OECD, 1993. <http://www.oecd.org/regreform/sectors/2376087.pdf>.

OECD, 2006a. Economic Evaluation of Environmental Health Risks to Children. OECD Publishing, Paris.

OECD, 2006b. Cost-Benefit Analysis and the Environment: Recent Developments. OECD Publishing, Paris. Available from: https://doi.org/10.1787/9789264010055-en.

OECD, 2007. Glossary of Statistical Terms. <https://stats.oecd.org/glossary/about.asp>.

OECD, 2018. Cost-Benefit Analysis and the Environment: Further Developments and Policy Use. OECD Publishing, Paris. Available from: https://doi.org/10.1787/9789264085169-en.

OECD/KDI, 2017. Improving Regulatory Governance: Trends, Practices and the Way Forward. OECD Publishing, Paris. Available from: https://doi.org/10.1787/9789264280366-en.

Prüss-Üstün, A., Corvalán, C., 2006. Preventing disease through healthy environments. Towards an Estimate of the Environmental Burden of Disease. WHO.

Prüss-Üstün, A., Corvalán, C., 2007. How much disease burden can be prevented by environmental interventions? Epidemiology 18, 167–178.

Robinson, R., 1993. Cost-benefit analysis. BMJ (Clin. Res. Ed.) 307 (6909), 924–926.

Sustain, C.R., 2018. The Cost-Benefit Revolution. The MIT Press.

The White House, 1981. Executive order 12291: federal regulation. <https://www.archives.gov/federal-register/codification/executive-order/12291.html>.

The White House, 1993. Executive order 12866: regulatory planning and review. Available from: <http://govinfo.library.unt.edu/npr/library/direct/orders/2646.html>.

The White House, 1994. Executive order 12898—federal actions to address environmental justice in minority populations and low-income populations. <https://www.epa.gov/laws-regulations/summary-executive-order-12898-federal-actions-address-environmental-justice>.

The White House, 2011a. Executive order 13563: improving regulation and regulatory review. <https://obamawhitehouse.archives.gov/the-press-office/2011/01/18/executive-order-13563-improving-regulation-and-regulatory-review>.

The White House, 2011b. Executive order 13579: regulation and independent regulatory agencies. <https://obamawhitehouse.archives.gov/the-press-office/2011/07/11/executive-order-13579-regulation-and-independent-regulatory-agencies>.

The White House, 2012. Executive order 1361063: identifying and reducing regulatory burdens. <https://obamawhitehouse.archives.gov/the-press-office/2012/05/10/executive-order-identifying-and-reducing-regulatory-burdens>.

The White House, 2017. Executive order 1377164: presidential executive order on reducing regulation and controlling regulatory costs. <https://www.whitehouse.gov/presidential-actions/presidential-executive-order-reducing-regulation-controlling-regulatory-costs/>.

UK Department for Business, Energy & Industrial Strategy, 2012. Better Regulation Framework

US GAO, 1984. Cost-Benefit Analysis Can Be Useful in Assessing Environmental Regulations, Despite Limitations RCED-84-62. <https://www.gao.gov/products/RCED-84-62>. Publicly Released: Apr 6, 1984

Varian, H.R., 1992. Microeconomic Analysis, third ed. Norton & Co.

Watkiss, P., Pye, S., Holland, M., 2005. CAFE CBA: Baseline Analysis 2000 to 2020. European Commission, Brussels, http://ec.europa.eu/environment/archives/cafe/activities/pdf/cba_baseline_results2000_2020.pdf.

Further reading

Adamowicz, W., et al., 2013. Household Decision-Making and Valuation of Environmental Health Risks to Parents and their Children. US EPA Environmental Series, 2013

Alberini, A., Scansy, M., 2011. Context and the VSL: evidence from a stated preference study in Italy and the Czech Republic. Environ. Resour. Econ. Manage. 48 (4), 511–538.

Alberini, A., et al., 2007. Paying for permanence: public preferences for contaminated site clean-up. J. Risk Uncertainty 34 (2), 155–178.

Alberini, A., et al., (Eds.), 2010. Valuation of Environment-Related Health Risks for Children. OECD.

Bateman, I.J., Munro, A., 2009. Household versus individual valuation: what's the difference? Environ. Resour. Econ. 43 (1), 119–135.

Bloomquist, G.C., Dickie, M., O'Conor, R.M., 2010. Willingness to pay for improving fatality risks and asthma symptoms: values for children and adults of all age. Resour. Energy Econ. 33 (2), 410−425.

Browning, M., Chiappori, P., Lechene, V., 2010. Distributional effects in household models: separate spheres and income pooling. Econ. J. 120 (545), 786−799.

Cairns, J., 1994. Valuing future benefits. Health Econ. 3 (4), 221−229.

Cairns, J., Van der Pol, M., 1998. Constant and decreasing timing aversion for saving lives. Soc. Sci. Med. 45 (11), 1653−1659.

Cairns, J., Van der Pol, M., 1999. Do people value their own future health differently from others' future health? Med. Decis. Making 19 (4), 466−472.

Chiappori, P., Donni, O., 2011. Non-unitary models of household behaviour: a survey of the literature 2009. In: Molina, A. (Ed.), Household Economic Behaviors. Springer, Berlin, pp. 1−40.

Dickie, M., 2005. Parental behaviour and the value of children's health: a health production approach. South Econ. 71, 855−872.

Dickie, M., Gerking, S., 2007. Altruism and environmental health risks to health of parents and their children. Environ. Resour. Econ. Manage. 53, 323−341.

Dickie, M., Messman, V.L., 2004. Parental altruism and the value of avoiding acute illness: are kids worth more than parents. J. Environ. Resour. Manage. 48, 1146−1174.

Dolk, H., et al., 1998. Risk of congenital anomalies near hazardous-waste landfill sites in Europe: the EUROHAZCON study. Lancet 352 (9126), 423−427.

EPA, 2003. Handbook of Valuing Children's Health. EPA.

Geschwind, S.A., et al., 1992. Risk of congenital malformations associated with proximity to hazardous waste sites. Am. J. Epidemiol. 135 (11), 1197−1207.

Hammitt, J.K., Haninger, K., 2010. Valuing fatal risks to children and adults: effects of disease, latency, and risk aversion. J. Risk Uncertainty 40, 57−83.

Harbaugh, T.W., 1999. Valuing children's health and life: what does economic theory say about including parental and societal willingness to pay. In: University of Oregon Economics Working Paper

The White House, 1997. Executive order 13045: protection of children from environmental health risks and safety risks. <https://www.epa.gov/children/executive-order-13045-protection-children-environmental-health-risks-and-safety-risks>.

Viscusi, W.K., Magat, W.A., Huber, J., 1987. An investigation of the rationality of consumer valuations of multiple health risks. RAND J. Econ. 18 (4), 465−479.

Wigle, D.T., et al., 2007. Environmental hazards: evidence for effects on child health. J. Toxicol. Environ. Health, B: Crit. Rev. 10, 3−39.

CHAPTER 1

The key steps in cost—benefit analysis of environmental health interventions

Carla Guerriero
Department of Economics and Statistics, University of Naples Federico II, Naples, Italy; Centre for Studies in Economics and Finance (CSEF), Naples, Italy

Contents

1.1 Introduction

The main principle behind cost—benefit analysis (CBA) is simple: if the total costs are outweighed by the total benefits, the intervention can be implemented. Nevertheless, CBA may appear complex and intimidating given the many types of possible interventions. A common problem in CBA of Environmental Health Intervention (EHI) is its timing: policy makers require fast responses, their power is limited to their political mandate, and during emergencies a CBA approach is considered time consuming. This chapter helps making the process of conducting a CBA more manageable by dividing the analysis into seven main consecutive steps: (1) specifying the decision problem, (2) quantifying the benefits, (3) assigning monetary values to each benefit, (4) quantifying the costs of the

Cost-Benefit Analysis of Environmental Health Interventions
DOI: https://doi.org/10.1016/B978-0-12-812885-5.00001-9

Figure 1.1 The key steps in cost–benefits analysis of EHIs.

intervention, (5) including considerations of the life span for costs and benefits and reexpressing these as present values, (6) comparing the estimated costs with the benefits, and (7) performing uncertainty analysis to assess the robustness of the study results (OECD, 2006a, 2006b). The remaining part of this chapter will focus on a brief overview of each step with special focus on Step 1 which is not covered in the remaining chapters of this book (Fig. 1.1).

1.2 Step 1: Identifying the decision problem to be addressed and the alternatives to include

The first step in CBA requires the analyst to make key decisions about the objective and the main components of the economic evaluation. The most important decision is to identify the question(s) being answered and more specifically: (1) specifying the problem and (2) the policy alternatives, including nonaction, considered in the analysis. Answer to these questions requires an assessment of the pollutants/hazards that are causing the problem and (3) the medium (e.g., air, soil, water) through which the exposure is taking place.

Once the environmental data have been gathered and assessed, it is possible to select the range of alternatives. The selection of the policy (ies) or intervention(s) included in the economic evaluation depends on their availability and feasibility but is also based on political factors (OECD, 2006a). The rationale for choosing the alternatives (and excluding others) should be clearly provided in the analysis. All alternatives included should be described in sufficient detail to assess the relevance of the analysis. In general, it is advisable not to include more than six possible alternatives. It has been shown that the advantages of a larger set would be offset by the cognitive and analytical burden of considering a larger number of options.

The form of evaluation (CBA) should be clearly stated with a clear justification of the chosen evaluation approach in relation to the question being addressed.

Another important preliminary decision for the first stage of CBA is the selection of the relevant viewpoint (OECD, 2016; HM Treasury, 2018). According to the selected perspective, different costs/benefits (e.g., health service, societal, employer) may or may not be considered in the analysis. For example, if the Minister of Health perspective is adopted, the benefits in terms of visibility improvements associated with air pollution interventions will go unaccounted. According to Hutton (2008), given the broad range of possible benefits, the best approach is to estimate the costs and benefits for all relevant perspectives and to present them separately in the results to leave the most relevant perspective decision to politicians. However, this approach is both challenging and time consuming, and in practice, the perspective is likely to change according to the type of selected intervention. A societal perspective, for instance, is useful if the intervention has a wide range of benefits/stakeholders (OECD, 2016). Alternatively, a narrower perspective (e.g., employer) is commonly adopted where the application of the intervention is sector-specific, such as improving ventilation and thermal control in an office building.

In general, three are the possible perspectives to adopt when conducting a CBA: private/business, institutional, and societal perspective.

These perspectives correspond to three types of CBA:

1. **Financial:** This type of CBA meets the criteria of private assessment regardless of the subject involved. The objective is to chime with the maximization of profit according to the criteria of financial efficiency.

2. **Economic:** This CBA meets public evaluation criteria that vary according to the nature of the subject involved (e.g., Minister of Health or Education or Transport). In this case the objective is the maximization of the social well-being according to the criteria of economic efficiency. This CBA considers all possible determinant effects of the intervention beyond "market prices."

3. **Societal:** This CBA meets public evaluation criteria but also takes into account the effects of the investments on equity and income distribution. The reference parameters for this analysis are social prices, that is, those established on the basis of the references of public decision makers with the aim of improving temporal and spatial distributions of income. This is the most comprehensive but also the most challenging type of CBA.

The first stage of CBA should also set out which benefits and costs will be included in the analysis. This issue "standing" will be discussed later and in further detail in Sections 1.3 and 1.5 of this chapter and in Chapter 5, Health benefit analysis: monetization of health impacts and its use in environment and health, and Chapter 7, Discounting benefits and costs.

Once the perspective for the analysis has been selected, it is essential to identify the target population, namely, the population affected by the range of interventions. The final beneficiaries of EHIs may include specific subgroups of individuals, for example, motorways users, a population located in a geographical area, for example, individuals living close to an industrial site, or an entire nation, for example, a new regulation on national air quality standards.

The health effects on the target population change according to the types of pollutants and media of exposure, but they are also affected by individual characteristics such as age in which exposure is taking place (e.g., low birth weight due to air pollution exposure during pregnancy) and the gender of the exposed individual (e.g., the risk of dying from cancer in proximity to toxic waste disposals may differ between females and males).

Thus, it is essential, especially for large CBA analysis, to gather information on the age distribution and gender composition of individuals affected by the policy. In addition to the demographic characteristics, economic indicators may also be relevant for the analysis. Equity and efficiency cannot be separated, especially when the objective of the policy is to reduce health inequalities of disadvantaged groups. The issue of weighing the monetary values in CBA to account for distributional concerns will be discussed in Chapter 12, Conclusion.

Finally, in the first stage of CBA, the analyst should determine how long the impacts of the proposed interventions should last. According to the HM Treasury (2018), 10 years is suitable as a base case scenario for many interventions. Similarly, the EU Guidelines for CBA recommend a long-term outlook ranging from 10 up to a maximum of 30 or more years.

The relevant time period depends on the characteristics of the intervention as there are no predefined rules. For infrastructures such as roads and ports, the typical time span ranges between 30 and 50 years [European Commission (EC), 2014]. In the case of polluted sites, excavation eliminates the hazards forever, but capping the contaminated land has a shorter life span (Environmental Protection Agency, 2014a, 2014b). Importantly, if the project is expected to last many years, it is important to consider elements that change over time such as the demographic dynamics, the expected GDP growth, the labor market conditions, and the unemployment trend. For large interventions (e.g., new air pollution regulations), these elements likely play a significant role in the valuation of intervention consequences. Table 1.1 presents a useful checklist of the actions required in Step 1.

1.3 Step 2: Benefits analysis

There are many types of benefits besides the health outcomes when undertaking a CBA of EHIs. The total benefits can be divided into three categories: (1) human health improvements (mortality and morbidity risk reductions); (2) ecological improvements such as improvements to market products (e.g., harvest of food), recreational activities (e.g., wildlife viewing), valued ecosystem functions (e.g., biodiversity), nonuse values (e.g., ecosystems communities etc.); and (3) finally "other benefits" such as visibility improvements or reduced damage to monuments (OECD, 2006a, 2006b; HM Treasury, 2018). As suggested by the EPA Guidelines for CBA, this list is not exhaustive, but its broad categories can easily

Table 1.1 Checklist for step 1 appraisal.

Issue	Question
General	1. Is the type of analysis adopted clearly stated? 2. Has an incremental approach been adopted? 3. Is the counterfactual credible? 4. Are all the possible interventions considered? 5. Is a clear justification for the intervention(s) included in the analysis provided?
Presentation of the context	1. Is the social, institutional, and economic context clearly described? 2. Has the impact area been identified? 3. Have all the most important socioeconomic effects of the intervention(s) being considered in the region, country, or sector concerned? 4. Are these effects actually attainable given the context? 5. Are there any major potential constraints to intervention(s) implementation?
Definition of objectives	1. Does the intervention constitute a clearly identified self-sufficient unit of analysis? 2. Have the final beneficiaries of the intervention(s) been identified? 3. Whose costs and benefits are going to be considered in the economic welfare calculation? 4. Are all the potentially affected parties considered?

Source: Adapted from European Commission (EC), 2014. Guidelines to cost–benefit analysis of investment projects. Economic appraisal tool for cohesion policy 2014–2020. <https://ec.europa.eu/inea/sites/inea/files/cba_guide_cohesion_policy.pdf>.

accommodate any benefits [Environmental Protection Agency (EPA), 2010a, 2010b, 2010c].

Principal among all direct benefits arising from EHIs are those to the human health. In most CBAs the baseline number of health outcomes attributable to pollution exposure is determined using a dose–response function. This function is "an estimate of risk per unit of exposure to pollutant." The dose–response functions can have different shapes. They can be linear, meaning that any change in the pollutant concentration produces a corresponding change in the health outcome, or they can be nonlinear, meaning that health outcomes increase proportionately to pollutant concentrations, but then level off, and/or they can present a threshold dose, meaning that there is a level of pollution at which health outcomes become apparent [Environmental Protection Agency (EPA),

2010a, 2010b, 2010c]. Where the health outcomes attributable to pollution exposure result from a single pollutant (e.g., asbestos), the population attributable proportion (PAP) or, in other words, the number of cases that would have not occurred in the absence of pollutant can be estimated using the following formula (Hurley et al., 2002):

$$PAP = (p - (RR - 1))/(1 + p * (RR - 1))$$

where RR is the relative risk of developing the health outcome given the pollutant concentration and p is the proportion of the population exposed (e.g., workers only).

In most cases, identifying the individual pollutants responsible for the health effects in the exposed population is problematic. As in the case of landfills or illegal waste disposals, impacts are likely to result from different compounds discharged in the same site. Thus the PAP is estimated using primary epidemiological data according to the following formula:

$$PAP = \text{Observed number} - \text{Observed number}/SHR$$

where SHR is standardized mortality/hospitalization ratios (SMR, SHR), which are estimated by dividing the observed cases (e.g., individuals with lung cancer) by the expected cases. SHR and SMR are adjusted for population characteristics such as socioeconomic class and other risk factors (e.g., prevalence of smokers). This step will be described in further detail in Chapter 4, Monetary analysis of health outcomes.

The ecological improvements associated with EHIs can be classified into four main subgroups: market products, recreational activities and esthetics, valued ecosystem functions, and nonuse values. Market products are easier to quantify and price as traded in the market. In the last decades, there has been an increased number of studies including other ecosystem services. Markandya (2015) documents an exponentially increasing number of published articles on ecosystem services. As for the human health benefits, once the pollutant(s) and their corresponding dose–response function are identified, it is possible to quantify the potential improvements using the same formula of health outcomes. Further details on this step are reported in Chapter 4, Monetary analysis of health outcomes.

1.4 Step 3: Assigning a monetary value to (nonmonetary) benefits

The human capital and the willingness-to-pay (WTP) approach are the two main methods for placing a monetary value on changes in health

(Bateman et al., 2002). The human capital approach assumes that an individual's life can be valued in terms of future production potential. As its name suggests, the WTP approach measures how much individuals are willing to pay to reduce the likelihood of an adverse event.

Within human capital approach, the cost of illness (COI) method is a measure of the monetary loss due to a negative health outcome (e.g., case of an asthma exacerbation) (Bateman et al., 2002). COI has several advantages over WTP. COI is straightforward. It is an objective measure of direct monetary costs of a given health outcome. In other words, it does not depend on personal preferences. However, COI also tends to underestimate the true value of a health outcome and does not consider the intangible aspects associated with illness such as stress, pain, and suffering. Moreover, given that COI values can be estimated only a posteriori, it is impossible to elicit the values that individuals assign to future environmental health risk reductions.

As a result, the most popular approach adopted in CBAs is the WTP approach. The WTP method can be divided into two main categories: revealed and stated preferences. The revealed preference method derives values from the observed actions of individuals (Bateman et al., 2002). The stated preference method elicits valuations by asking individuals how much they are willing to pay to reduce the risk of a given health outcome (Atkinson and Mourato, 2008).

It has been suggested that revealed preference techniques provide the most reliable indicator of preferences because estimates are based on actual decisions than on individual choices under hypothetical scenarios. In many cases, however, WTP information cannot be inferred from the market. Sometimes markets do not yet exist for the effect or cost being evaluated. Or, where EHIs target children and the elderly, the subjects are outside the workforce (OECD, 2006a, 2006b; OECD, 2018).

Another limitation of the revealed preferences method is that it does not consider the risk context (OECD, 2006a, 2006b). The revealed preferences approach does not allow valuations of different types of risk (mortality risk) and may lead to biased WTP estimates (OECD, 2006a, 2006b). Several studies report that individual WTP for averting cases of immediate death (road traffic accident) is lower than for chronic degenerative disease, given the fear and pain associated with long-term illness (Alberini and Scansy, 2011; Sunstein, 1997). For example, empirical studies have found that the WTP for avoiding cancer is higher than other diseases provided the dread and pain effects associated with this particular pathology (Alberini et al., 2009a, 2009b; Van Houtven et al., 2008). To account for the "cancer premium," the European Commission recommends that cases of cancer should be inflated by 50% (DG Environment, 2002). Finally, revealed preference techniques assign a monetary value to immediate risk reductions or that will occur quite soon. Especially in the context of environmental-related health effects, the risk reduction (e.g., cancer risk) is observed years after the implementation of the policy.

For these reasons, stated preference methods provide a more flexible tool with which to elicit individual WTP. Under this method, individuals are directly asked how much they would be willing to pay for an improvement in their health status or their willingness-to-accept values for an increased risk. Compared with the COI, stated preference approach has the advantage of taking into account the intangible consequences like premature death and the suffering from an illness. In addition, stated preferences methods can also be used to elicit WTP estimates from individuals who are not in the labor force and can easily account for different types of risk context.

There are two stated preference techniques for estimating WTP for environmental health risk reductions: contingent valuation (CV) and discrete choice experiments (DCEs). The CV approach asks respondents to make a monetary evaluation of the change in health risk. Among the many methodologies for eliciting WTP/Willingness to Accept (WTA) values from CV studies the most common methods are dichotomous choice and open-ended and payment card format (Bateman et al., 2002). All the elicitation formats have certain advantages and disadvantages. For example, compared with dichotomous choice and payment card format, the open-ended format has several major advantages, which include avoiding starting point bias, range bias, and anchoring bias (Bateman et al., 2002). However, this method is rarely used given its wider cognitive demands, which often produce nonresponse or a high proportion of protest and zero answers (Bateman et al., 2002). The payment card elicitation method presents respondents with a series of ordered amounts (from the smallest to the largest) and usually asks respondents to indicate the maximum bid they would likely pay for the health risk reduction (Bateman et al., 2002). But the payment card is also subject to bias because it requires the analyst to make assumptions about the range and the number of price bids. Another disadvantage of the payment card approach is that it cannot readily be used in telephone interviews. Compared with open-ended and payment card formats, the single and double-bounded elicitation methods are less cognitively demanding. However, both these approaches also have weaknesses. Close-ended formats leave less freedom to the respondents to select the exact amount they are willing to pay (Ryan, 2009). However, approaches are subject to anchoring bias (Bateman et al., 2002).

Unlike CV studies that directly ask respondents the amount they are willing to pay for a specific change (e.g., in health risk), DCEs present respondents with a number of choice sets in which alternatives, described as a set of attributes, are mutually exclusive. The alternatives presented in each choice set vary in one or more attribute levels. The selected combination of attributes is used to infer indirect information on individual preferences about the parameters considered. Compared with the CV technique, DCEs are able to describe a choice situation with a range of attributes that reflect the different characteristics of the particular good being valued, and when the cost factor is included, they allow WTP estimates to be made for changes in different attributes (Ryan, 2009). The methodologies and issues related to this step will be discussed in greater details in Chapters 5 and 6.

1.5 Step 4: Cost analysis

To evaluate a priori the cost of EHIs is as difficult as evaluating its benefits. An additional difference in the cost valuation is that there is no uniform approach to costing environmental health interventions.

According to OECD (2006a, 2006b), for instance, there are three major cost components to consider in CBA of environmental interventions: the compliance, the regulatory, and the damage cost. The compliance costs include the resources necessary for policy implementation such as the cost of remediating a polluted site, including both the capital and the operating cost. Given the information asymmetries between the intervention provider (e.g., government) and supplier (e.g., contractors in charge of the remediation activities), initial compliance costs estimated a priori may be overestimated or underestimated compared with the final cost incurred to implement the policy [OECD, 2006a, 2006b; European Commission (EC), 2014; Environmental Protection Agency (EPA), 2010a, 2010b, 2010c]. Estimating ex ante the compliance cost is even more difficult when the intervention is new and/or, as in the case of large projects or regulatory interventions there are significant spillovers in different economic sectors (HM Treasury, 2018).

The second cost component to consider is the regulatory costs, which are the costs to the government of implementing the policy. Regulatory costs are often substantial, particularly where the project involves a large area (e.g., European regulation) or a large number of industries (OECD, 2016). The transaction costs associated with new regulations involve the cost of gathering, implementing, and monitoring the new regulation [Environmental Protection Agency (EPA), 2010a, 2010b, 2010c]. Sometimes the new regulation may even require the creation of property rights for previously nonmarketed goods (e.g., emission trading in California) and an establishment of institutions to control the newly created markets [Environmental Protection Agency (EPA), 2010a, 2010b, 2010c]. Finally, additional regulatory costs may be incurred as a result of changes to the institutional and legal system to create the new policy [Environmental Protection Agency (EPA), 2010a, 2010b, 2010c]. The third cost to consider is the damage cost or environmental loss arising from the intervention. The monetary value of environmental loss is quantified using the different approaches described in the benefits section. Once this cost is quantified, it must be subtracted from the total economic value attached to the intervention.

There are no specific guidelines for costing EHIs in CBA, and the different guidance developed for CBA recommends different approaches to costing. Regulatory, compliance, and damage costs are briefly discussed in this section, but depending on the type of intervention, the perspective adopted in the analysis, and the number of markets affected, there are potentially more types of costs that need to be considered. For further details on this costing approach see Chapter 8, Quantifying uncertainty in environmental health models.

1.6 Step 5: Time adjustment for cost and benefits

The cost and benefit of EHIs may materialize over lengthy periods. Thus discounting plays a crucial role in estimating the value of future costs and benefits (HM Treasury, 2018). Where different types of interventions are compared, discounting future costs and benefits to present values renders them more easily comparable. Discounting implies that the further in the future the benefits and the costs occur, the lower the weight that should be attached to them.

The general formula of discounting is the following:

$$W_t = 1/(1+s)^t$$

where W_t is the discount factor for time t and s is the discount rate.

Thus the conversion of future benefits to a present value can be estimated with the following formula (OECD, 2006a, 2006b):

$$\text{Present Value} = \Sigma \, \text{Future Value}_t \times W_t$$

where economists use discounting to adjust the value of costs and benefits occurring in the future, the standard approach is to assume a constant discount rate common to both costs and benefits (OECD, 2016). For example, since 1992 the US discount rate suggested as the base case for CBAs was fixed at 7% for both cost and benefit estimates [Environmental Protection Agency (EPA), 2010a, 2010b, 2010c]. A 3% discount rate was also suggested for sensitivity analysis [Environmental Protection Agency (EPA), 2010a, 2010b, 2010c]. The European Commission recommends the use of a discount rate of 4% for environmental CBAs and a lower discount rate of 2% for sensitivity analyses (DG Environment, 2002). However, there has been extensive discussion of whether the discount rate for health benefits should be lower than that applied to monetary costs. Also, where the effects under consideration are long-lived, a case has been made for discount rates declining over time (OECD, 2006a, 2006b). There is also an ongoing debate whether the normative discount rate should account for the discount rate estimated directly from individuals in stated choice studies (positive discount rate). Previous studies suggest that individuals' discount rate is not fixed but varies over time (Cairns and Van der Pol, 1999). Economists are paying increasing attention to hyperbolic models that reflect time inconsistent models of discounting. According to Cairns, hyperbolic models present two major advantages over traditional exponential models: they seem to reflect real individual time prefaces and, compared with a constant discount rate, do not attach very low weight to benefits occurring in the distant future. For example, Viscusi and Huber (2006) found that the discount rate shown for improvements in environmental quality do not follow the standard discount utility model; rather its pattern is consistent with the hyperbolic model. Also, Alberini et al. (2009a, 2009b) found that discounting rates for saving lives in the hazardous waste context are not constant over time. For time spans longer than 10 years, in particular, they found that the discount rate was decreasing. For policy that displays health benefits occurring in a distant future, there is a strong incentive to consider intergenerational equity. Indeed, using a constant discount factor would highly depreciate benefits occurring in the distant future. Given the uncertainty surrounding the future discount rate, and also the necessity to ensure intergenerational equity, UK government departments introduced new guidelines recommending the use of time-varying discount rate (HM Treasury, 2018).

Time lags between the policy and its related benefits are also an important issue (HM Treasury, 2018). When a policy is implemented, there may not be immediate reductions in the number of health outcomes (e.g., cancer cases). Following this "cessation lag," there will be a gradual (proportional/nonproportional) decline in the effects of reduced emissions on health up to the point where the number of health outcomes is the same as observed in the general population.

The following formula can be used to account for both the discounting and the latency of benefits (Guerriero and Cairns, 2009):

$$\text{Present value of benefits} = \lambda * X_a * 1/(1 + d)\mathbf{l} * \left(1 - 1/(1 + d)t\right)/d$$

where X_a is the number of health endpoints averted by the intervention, t is the number of years over which the benefits accrue, and d is the discount rate. λ is the WTP for the health outcome an and latency period l, which is the time occurring between the reduction of the exposure and the improvement in population health.

1.7 Step 6: Cost–benefit analysis evaluation

The objective of CBA is to provide transparent evidence on the net benefit associated with an environmental intervention versus the do nothing scenario. If more than one intervention is available, CBA allows to compare the net benefit of competing options. Summary measures of net benefits are the outcomes of CBA. They should include the net present value (NPV) of benefit, the benefit–cost ratio, and the results of sensitivity analyses.

The main condition for the adoption of EHIs is that the present value of the benefit (PVB) exceeds the present value of the cost (PVC), or that the NPV > 0 (OECD, 2006a, 2006b). The NPV rule is usually adopted to decide whether to accept or reject an option, to rank different projects, and to choose between mutually exclusive projects. An equivalent feasibility test is the benefit–cost ratio test:

$$\text{PVB/PVC} > 1.$$

Table 1.2 Generic appraisal summary template.

	Do nothing scenario	Option 1	Option 2	Option 3
Present value of benefits				
Present value of costs				
Net present value				
Benefit−cost ratio				
Switching values				
Time horizon and reason				
Significant unmonetized Costs/Benefits				

However, there are differences between the two tests. The first evaluates the excess in benefits and is a more direct way of measuring the social benefits of the intervention. The second evaluates the benefits per dollar of cost incurred. For example, a cost ratio of 2.2 means that for each dollar invested, $2.20 of social benefit is realized. There is general agreement that benefit−cost ratio can be misleading when used outside the rationing context (when only one project should be evaluated).

A modified version of the Appraisal Summary Table as recommended by the UK Green Book is shown in Table 1.2. The table provides a comprehensive summary of the main outputs of CBA. Each column of the table is associated with an intervention appraisal including the do nothing alternative which should be presented in absolute terms. The first four rows report key CBA measures such as the PVC, PVB, the NPV, and the benefit−cost ratio. One-way sensitivity analysis results (switch values) can be reported only for the preferred option.

The table also allows to summarize the key assumptions of the analysis, including time horizon used and the unquantified values of the analysis. Whenever possible, the table should be completed by graphical representations of the uncertainty around the CBA estimates [e.g., cost−benefit acceptability curves (CBACs) and tornado diagrams].

1.8 Step 7: Risk and uncertainty

As with economic evaluations of healthcare interventions in cost-utility and cost-effectiveness analyses, extensive sensitivity analyses address the lack of certainty and also allow an assessment of the robustness of economic evaluations and their comparability (OECD, 2006a, 2006b). As mentioned above, costs and benefits are difficult to ascertain a priori. As a consequence, they are associated with high degrees of risk and uncertainty. Risk denotes the possibility of attaching a probability to costs or benefits that are not known with certainty. Uncertainty denotes a case in which the probability distribution is not available, but in which crude end points, like the minimum and maximum values, are known. Despite the importance of addressing risk and uncertainty in CBA, there is still a lack of core methodologies for conducting uncertainty analysis to facilitate the comparison between CBA results (Drummond, 1993).

If the objective of sensitivity analysis is to assess the degree of uncertainty associated with single-model parameters, deterministic sensitivity analysis and one-way or multiway sensitivity analyses can be used (Drummond, 1993).

One-way deterministic analysis tests the sensibility of the expected NPV to changes of a single variable in the model (Drummond, 1993). Alternatively, multiway sensitivity analyses test the effect of changes to two or more variables on the expected NPV of the EHIs.

The main advantage of deterministic sensitivity analysis is its easy computational abilities. It allows assessments of which specific parameter value the expected NPV changes. The main disadvantage, however, is that deterministic sensitivity analysis does not account for cases where variables change simultaneously. Monte Carlo analysis is a computational method that uses statistical sampling and probability distributions to show how parameter uncertainty affects model results. In CBA of EHIs, Monte Carlo simulation can be used to model the effects of key variables such as policy associated health risk reduction on the NPV of a given proposal (Doubilet et al., 1985). Compared with crude deterministic methodologies that generate a single point estimate, Monte Carlo method can be used to account for parameter variability and uncertainty. Monte Carlo simulation is carried out in two consecutive steps: first, it requires the analyst to select and assign a probability distribution to the variables used for the NPV calculation; second, it requires the simulation of a large number of draws, usually between 1000 and 10,000 simulations from the distributions selected. The most difficult task in performing Monte Carlo simulation is the selection of the appropriate probability distribution, which depends on the characteristics of the variable (e.g., bounds of the variable and symmetry of the distribution) and also on information available about the variable. According to Briggs et al. (2008), the choice of the appropriate distribution for the model parameter depends on the parameter characteristics, and also on the information available about the parameter.

For example, the authors suggest the adoption of a beta distribution for binomial data, such as proportion and probabilities, as these are naturally bounded between 0 and 1. The gamma probability constrained between 0 and positive infinite is the perfect candidate for simulating uncertainty in the cost parameter for cost parameters (Briggs et al., 2008).

Once the Monte Carlo simulation results have been obtained, they can be presented using CBAC. CBACs are a modified version of the cost-effectiveness acceptability curves used in healthcare decision-making that have been employed to represent uncertainty within economic evaluation of healthcare technologies (Fenvick et al., 2006). In pure healthcare decision-making, CEACs indicate the probability that an intervention is cost-effective compared with the alternative(s), given a range of λ WTP values (e.g., for an additional quality of life year gained). In the case of CBA of EHIs, both cost and benefits are reported in monetary values. Thus the condition for the pollution control policy to be implemented is the following (Lothgen and Zehraeus, 2000):

$$NPB = PVB - PVC > 0$$

where NPB is the net present benefit and PVB and PVC are the present values of benefits and costs associated with the intervention.

An application of the CBAC to describe uncertainty in CBA results has been provided in Chapter 12.

1.9 Conclusion

This chapter provides a brief description of the main steps involved in estimating the costs and benefits associated with EHIs. In particular the chapter describes the main steps for assessing the health benefits and costs associated with EHIs. The first step in conducting CBA consists of identifying the decision problem and specifically determining the perspective and time span for the analysis along with the relevant types of benefits and costs. The second step of CBA quantifies the benefits arising from the intervention using different sources of data including environmental, demographic, and epidemiological statistics. Once these benefits have been quantified, the following steps consist of assigning a monetary value to the quantified nonmarketed benefits. Monetization of the health benefits is probably one of the most challenging step in CBA. The most commonly used method for assigning monetary value to environmental health benefits is the stated preferences technique. However, WTP estimates elicited using this approach are associated with a high degree of uncertainty, because they are calculated on the basis of respondent answers to hypothetical scenarios rather than real decision-making. The fifth step of CBA is to assess the cost of the intervention. Depending on the type and size of the intervention, its potential for cost can vary significantly. For this reason, ascertaining a priori costs can be difficult. Further, establishing costs and benefits arising from EHIs require analysts to fix a period of time in which these are expected to occur. And if the relevant time horizon is longer than 1 year, discounting can play a crucial role in the CBA as it allows translating both future costs and benefits to their present value. Once the costs and the benefits have been reported to their present value, the sixth step of CBA compares the total cost with the total benefits and ranks the assessed alternatives from the most to the least cost-effective. Given the uncertainty associated with estimates of benefits and costs, the last step of CBA requires the conduct of deterministic and/or probabilistic sensitivity analyses.

References

Alberini, A., Scansy, M., 2011. Context and the VSL: evidence from a stated preference study in Italy and the Czech Republic. Environ. Res. Econ. Manage. 48 (4), 511—538. 2011.

Alberini, A., Tonin, S., Turvani, M., 2009a. Rates of time preferences for saving lives in the hazardous waste site context. In: Working Paper 09.03, 2009. FEEM

Alberini, A., Tonin, S., Turvani, M., 2009b. The Value of Reducing Cancer Risks at Contaminated Sites: Are More Heavily Exposed People Willing to Pay More? Fondazione Eni Enrico Mattei, p. 2009

Atkinson, G., Mourato, S., 2008. Environmental cost-benefit analysis. Annu. Rev. Environ. Resour. 33, 317—344.

Bateman, I.J., et al., 2002. In: Department for Transport (Ed.), Economic Evaluation with Stated Preference Techniques: A Manual. Edward Elgar Publishing.

Briggs, A., Claxton, K., Sculpher, M., 2008. Decision Modelling for Health Economic Evaluation Oxford Handbook in Economic Evaluation. O.U. Press, 2008.

Cairns, J., Van der Pol, M., 1999. Do people value their own future health differently from others' future health? Med. Decis. Making 19 (4), 466—472. 1999.

DG Environment, 2002. Recommended Interim Values for the Value of Preventing a Fatality in DG Environment Cost Benefit Analysis

Doubilet, R., et al., 1985. Probabilistic sensitivity analysis using Monte Carlo simulation. Med. Decis. Making 5 (2), 157—177. 1985.

Drummond, M., 1993. Standardizing methodologies for economic evaluation of health care. Practice problems and potential. Int. J. Technol. Assess Health Care 9 (1), 26—36. Winter.

Environmental Protection Agency, 2014a. Step 2—dose-response assessment. <http://www.epa.gov/risk_assessment/dose-response.htm>.

Environmental Protection Agency, 2014b. Superfund green remediation strategy. <http://www.epa.gov/oswer/greenercleanups/strategy.html>.

Environmental Protection Agency (EPA), 2010a. Steps in conducting benefits analysis. <http://www.epa.gov/ttn/ecas/econdata/Rmanual2/7.2.html>.

Environmental Protection Agency (EPA), 2010b. Regulatory impact analysis. <http://www.epa.gov/ttnecas1/ria.html>.

Environmental Protection Agency (EPA), 2010c. Regulatory impact analysis. <http://www.epa.gov/ttnecas1/ria.html>.

European Commission (EC), 2014. Guidelines to Cost–Benefit Analysis of Investment Projects. Economic appraisal tool for cohesion policy 2014–2020. <https://ec.europa.eu/inea/sites/inea/files/cba_guide_cohesion_policy.pdf>.

Fenvick, E., et al., 2006. Using and interpreting cost-effectiveness acceptability curves: an example using data from a trial of management strategies for atrial fibrillation. BMC Health Serv. Res. 6 (52), 1–8. 2006.

Guerriero, C., Cairns, J., 2009. The potential monetary benefits of reclaiming hazardous waste sites in the Campania region: an economic evaluation. Environ. Health 8, 28. 2009.

HM Treasury, 2018. The Green Book. Appraisal and Evaluation in Central Government. <https://www.gov.uk/government/publications/the-green-book-appraisal-and-evaluation-in-central-governent>.

Hurley, F., et al., 2002. Methodology for the cost-benefit analysis of the CAFE programme. Volume 2: Health impact assessment, 2002. Louvriere J, Flynn T, and Carson N, 2010. Discrete choice experiments are not conjoint analysis. J. Choice Modell. 3 (3), 57–72. 2010.

Hutton, G., 2008. Economic evaluation of environmental health interventions to support decision making. Environ. Health Insights 2, 137–155. 2008.

Lothgen, M., Zehraeus, N., 2000. Definition, interpretation and calculation of cost-effectiveness acceptability curves. Health Econ. 9, 623–630. 2000.

Markandya, A., 2015. The Economic Feedbacks of Loss of Biodiversity and Ecosystems Services OECD Environment Working Papers, No. 93. OECD Publishing, Paris. <https://doi.org/10.1787/5jrqgv610fg6-en>.

OECD 2006a. In: Pearce, D., Atkinson, G., Mourato, S. (Eds.), Cost-Benefit Analysis and the Environment. OECD, Geneva

OECD, 2006b. Economic Evaluation of Environmental Health Risks to Children. OECD, Paris

OECD, (2018). Cost-Benefit Analysis and the Environment: Further Developments and Policy Use. OECD Publishing, Paris. <https://doi.org/10.1787/9789264085169-en>.

Ryan, M., 2009. A comparison of stated preference methods for estimating monetary values. Health Econ. 13 (3), 291–296. 2009.

Sunstein, C.R., 1997. Bad deaths. J. Risk Uncertainty 14, 259–282.

Van Houtven, G., Sullivan, M.B., Dockins, C., 2008. Cancer premiums and latency effects: a risk trade-off approach for valuing reductions in fatal cancer risks. J. Risk Uncertainty 36, 179–199. 2008.

Viscusi, W.K., Huber J., 2006. Hyperbolic Discounting of Public Goods. Centre for Law, Economics and Business Discussion Paper Series. Paper 543

Further reading

Barbier, E.B., Markandya, A., 2013. A New Blueprint for a Green Economy. Routledge, p. 2013.

Boardman, A.E., et al., 2006. Cost Benefit Analysis: Concepts and Practice. Prentice Hall, 2006.

Cairns, J., 1994. Valuing future benefits. Health Econ. 3 (4), 221—229. 1994.

Cairns, J., Van der Pol, M., 1998. Constant and decreasing timing aversion for saving lives. Soc. Sci. Med. 45 (11), 1653—1659. 1998.

Campbell, H.F., Brown, P.C., 2003. Benefit-cost analysis. Financial and Economic Appraisal Using Spreadsheets. Cambridge University Press, p. 2003.

Depuit, A.J., 1952. On The Measurement of the Utility of Public Works International Economic Papers 2. 1844

Drummond, M., et al., 1997. Methods for the Economic Evaluation of Health Care Programmes. Oxford University Press, p. 1997.

Enhealth, 2003. Enhealth-Guidelines for Economic Evaluation of Environmental Health Planning and Assessment, Volume 1

Environmental Protection Agency (EPA), 1993. Policy for use of Probabilistic Analysis in Risk Assessment. <http://www.epa.gov/spc/2probana.htm>.

European Commission (EC) 2001. Recommended Interim Values for the Value of Preventing a Fatality in DG Environment Cost Benefit Analysis. <ec.europa.eu/environment/enveco/others/pdf/recommended_interim_values.pdf>.

Hammitt, J.K., Liu, J.T., 2004. Effects of disease type and latency on the value of mortality risk. J. Risk Uncertainty 28, 73—95. 2004.

Hutton, G., 2000. Considerations in Evaluating the Cost-Effectiveness of Environmental Health Interventions Protection. WHO. <https://extranet.who.int/iris/restricted/bitstream/10665/66744/1/WHO_SDE_WSH_00.10.pdf>.

Pruss-Ustun, A., Corvalan, A., 2006. Preventing Disease through Healthy Environments: Towards an Estimate of the Environmental Burden of Disease. WHO

Stæhr, K., 2006. Risk and Uncertainty in Cost-Benefit Analysis. Toolbox Paper 2006. Environmental Assessment Institute

Tonin, S., 2014. Assessing the impact of the remedial actions taken at a contaminated Italian site: an ex-post valuation analysis. Rev. Environ. Sci. Biotechnol. 13, 121. Available from: https://doi.org/10.1007/s11157-014-9332-8.

CHAPTER 2

Environmental health interventions for the treatment of waters, solids, and soils

Stefano Papirio and Francesco Pirozzi

Department of Civil, Architectural and Environmental Engineering, University of Napoli Federico II, Napoli, Italy

Contents

2.1 Production of drinking water and treatment of wastewater

Water is fundamental for the physiological functions of human cells and life in all the natural ecosystems. Is it of extreme importance that humans can benefit of high-quality water for their primary needs and uses. Although water covers most of the Earth's surface, approximately 97% of water is saline and 2% lies in icecaps. Hence, below 1% of the worldwide water is easily usable for potable water purposes, but this amount is diminishing due to the increasing phenomena of environmental pollution and

Cost-Benefit Analysis of Environmental Health Interventions
DOI: https://doi.org/10.1016/B978-0-12-812885-5.00002-0

21

the more and more frequent water-scarcity periods (Barlow and Clarke, 2017).

In order to supply safe drinking water, proper sanitation interventions have to be arranged for the production of potable water and an adequate treatment of human excretions and sewage. Indeed, the contamination of drinking water sources can be due to the transmission of pathogenic microorganisms and waterborne diseases through the fecal-oral route, occurring in the absence of well-functioning drinking water and wastewater treatment plants (WWTPs) (Fig. 2.1).

Therefore on the basis of European Commission directives, all the countries in Europe have adopted national legislations that impose the

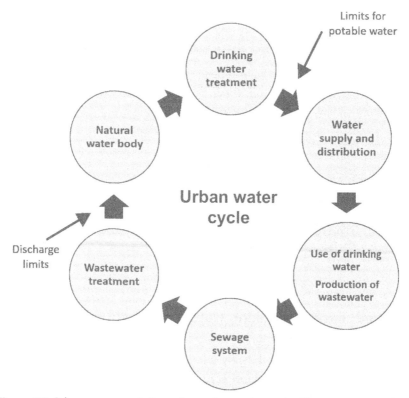

Figure 2.1 Scheme representation of an urban water cycle. Water source can be a surface body or an aquifer, from which drinking water is produced in a proper treatment plant. Then, water is distributed and used, altering its physical and chemical characteristics. Prior to being safely released to the natural ecosystem, wastewater passes through a treatment plant where its characteristics need to become compatible with the imposed discharge limits.

limits for specific compounds in potable water and in the WWTP effluents. In drinking water—production plants, the aim is to obtain a potable water having requirements of palatability and safety for public health and infrastructures. In regard to wastewaters, quality parameters have to be met in order to safely discharge them in natural water bodies without negatively affecting the hydrosphere and biosphere.

2.1.1 Characteristics of surface and ground water to be used for drinking water production

Water supply is most of the times performed from surface water bodies (i.e., rivers and lakes) and groundwater. Surface waters derive from the runoff of rainwater on the ground until ending-up in a river or a lake. While running off, rainwater results in soil erosion and transports high amounts of particulate matter, which increases the concentration of the suspended solid fraction. This induces the presence of mainly physical process units (i.e., coarse screening, sieving, sedimentation, and filtration) in drinking water—treatment plants. On top of that, surface waters are characterized by a high total bacterial count, requiring the use of a more intensive disinfection process prior to water distribution to the citizens.

If rainwater infiltrates through the soil, the suspended solid concentration decreases in spite of an increase of the dissolved solid fraction, due to the leaching of minerals. Hence, water from aquifers are rich in dissolved species (e.g., Ca^{2+}, Mg^{2+}, Na^{+}, HCO_3^{-}, SO_4^{2-}, and Cl^{-}) and poor in suspended solids and microorganisms (Barlow and Clarke, 2017). Chemical process units (e.g., chemical precipitation) are essential constituents of the treatment scheme, with disinfection being the last treatment phase also in this case.

In the absence of different water sources, water from seas and oceans can also be used for drinking water production. In this case, the treatment requires the use of advanced process units due to the high salinity levels, thus leading to higher energy consumption and operating costs (Karagiannis and Soldatos, 2008). Processes such as ion exchange and membrane filtration are commonly employed and coupled to disinfection.

2.1.2 Main treatment processes for drinking water production

The main process units in a drinking water—treatment plant depends on the physical—chemical characteristics of the influent water (see Section 2.1.1) and are meant for the removal of suspended and dissolved solids and the destruction of disease-bearing microorganisms. Thus, no or low amounts of biodegradable organic solids are present, implying the use of simply physical and chemical processes, as described in the following subsections.

2.1.2.1 Coarse screening and microscreening

In a drinking water—treatment plant, the first unit operation encountered is generally a coarse screening when water is derived from a surface water body. Screening consists of bar screens that are devices with openings of uniform size, which allow to retain solids with a higher size than 1 cm. For water pumped from lakes, which are natural settling basins, containing suspended solids with lower dimensions (approximately 10 μm), micro-screening (or microsieving) is used. This involves low-speed (1—3 rpm) rotating drum screens with a dense filtering stainless steel fabric on the drum periphery.

2.1.2.2 Sedimentation

The objective of sedimentation is to remove most of readily settleable solids and, if present, floating material simply by the means of gravity. This unit is typically present in plants aimed at the treatment of water derived from rivers, which contain a higher concentration of suspended solids than lakes due to the flow turbulence. Another sedimentation unit is a part of the coagulation—flocculation process (see Section 2.1.2.3) to remove those heavy flocs incorporating colloidal particles.

2.1.2.3 Coagulation—flocculation process

Coagulation—flocculation is a chemical process, since chemicals are used to develop specific reactions and remove particular suspended solids from water, namely colloids. In natural waters, derived both from lakes and rivers, colloids are essentially clay particles. Thus, the particle size is approximately 1 μm (or lower), with the particles being generally negatively charged. Given the high surface area and the electrical charge, the body forces (repelling and attractive) between colloids prevail over the gravity force, resulting in a chaotic Brownian motion that prevents colloids to settle down.

The supplementation of coagulants, mainly iron (Fe) and aluminum (Al) salts, results in the destabilization of the colloidal movement and particle aggregation. Moreover, the same salts react with bicarbonate in water and form insoluble iron and aluminum hydroxides, known as flocs, which incorporate the colloidal aggregates during flocculation. A proper stirring velocity of the solid suspension has to be maintained in order to facilitate the contact between flocs and colloids. Finally, the "floc—colloid complexes" have high settleability properties and, thus, are removed in a sedimentation unit.

2.1.2.4 Chemical precipitation

In this case the addition of chemicals is aimed to alter the physical state of dissolved solids and transform them into suspended solids, facilitating their removal by sedimentation. Chemical precipitation is mostly performed for spring water and groundwater, typically having higher dissolved solid concentrations than surface water. Softening (i.e., decrease of water hardness), due to the presence of calcium (Ca) and magnesium (Mg) ions, and removal of iron and manganese (Mn) compounds are common applications of chemical precipitation in potable water.

2.1.2.5 Filtration

Filtration of particulate materials can be operated by using a thick filter bed, comprising a granular medium (e.g., sand), or a thin septum (e.g., a membrane) by mechanical sieving. In the former case, the process is known as depth filtration, while in the latter case, it is a surface filtration. During the treatment of potable water, the filtration unit is typically located after coagulation/flocculation to achieve a supplemental removal of suspended solids, prior to the disinfection as final stage of the drinking water treatment plant.

2.1.2.6 Ion exchange and adsorption

When natural water, being treated in a drinking water—treatment plant, contains high amounts of dissolved compounds, an advanced treatment technology needs to be used. Ion exchange consists of a process unit in which ions of a given species are retained by an insoluble exchange material, while a different ionic species is released in solution. Water softening is a typical ion-exchange application. Calcium and/or magnesium ions are retained, with sodium (Na) ions, which are not responsible for hardness and not hazardous for public health, being released. Polymeric resins are the most used ion-exchange materials. The elevated treatment efficiency justifies the high costs for resin purchase and regeneration.

Adsorption in a mass-transfer process in which a soluble compound (in both dissociated and nondissociated form) in the liquid phase is transferred to a solid phase. Activated carbon is the most common adsorbent used for water treatment. It is obtained by preliminary incinerating a carbon-based material at approximately 400°C–500°C and then activating it at 800° C–900°C in the presence of steam or CO_2. This two-step process results in the formation of a highly porous material, with an extremely high surface area to entrap soluble compounds onto it.

2.1.2.7 Disinfection

Disinfection is the final unit in a drinking water treatment plant and is aimed at the destruction of pathogens, that is the disease-causing microorganisms having severe consequences on water hygiene and public health. Disinfection is most commonly accomplished by the use of chlorine compounds throughout the world, as these guarantee the protection from microbial presence in the water-distribution networks. However, some health concerns were raised in the past years related to the use of chlorine disinfectants (Chowdhury et al., 2009). Indeed, it has been demonstrated that chlorine reacts with organic constituents to produce disinfection by-products (DBP), especially trihalomethanes (THM), known to be carcinogenic and mutagenic. Nonetheless, the low levels of organics in potable water significantly reduce the risk to obtain higher THM concentrations than the limits imposed by legislation.

Alternatively, physical disinfection methods can be used such as ultraviolet radiation at a wavelength between 100 and 400 nm. The use of UV light does not result in the production of hazardous by-products, but necessarily require the use of chlorine as secondary disinfectant for the protection of drinking water in distribution systems.

2.1.3 Wastewater engineering

2.1.3.1 Wastewater characteristics and environmental pollution

The characteristics of a wastewater are intimately correlated to its origin. Municipal wastewaters are commonly a mixture of domestic wastewaters and rainwater, with the first being polluted by suspended solids, putrescible organic matter and nutrients (nitrogen and phosphorus), and the second mostly containing grit and traces of hydrocarbons collected while running off on the street surface. For industrial wastewaters, it is not possible to know "a priori" the physical–chemical water composition, since it depends on the specific industrial process.

In regard to the origin of wastewater and the main pollutants contained, different phenomena of environmental pollution can occur in the receiving water bodies when the wastewater is not adequately treated:

- Oxygen consumption or anoxia. It is mainly related to the improper discharge of organic compounds or reduced inorganic compounds (e.g., NH_4^+ or hydrogen sulfide—H_2S). These compounds are oxidized by indigenous microorganisms at the expense of free oxygen within the natural ecosystem, negatively affecting the survival conditions of living micro- and macrofauna.
- Eutrophication due to nitrogenous and phosphorous compounds, contained in municipal and livestock wastewaters as well as fertilizers. Eutrophication is associated with an initial uncontrolled growth of microalgal and algal species and their consequent degradation after death. Degradation of dead algal biomass is performed by bacteria, which require high concentrations of free oxygen and lead the water body to anoxia.
- Release of toxic and persistent compounds, mainly due to the dispersal of industrial wastewaters containing compounds such as heavy metals, hydrocarbons, and solvents. These substances inhibit the activity of the microorganisms living in the receiving aquatic ecosystem and reduce its natural attenuation potential, persisting in the environmental matrixes for many years.

On the basis of the Directive 2000/60 issued by the European Commission, the national legislation of each EU country reports the limits for the following compounds in municipal wastewaters:

- Biochemical oxygen demand (BOD_5) and chemical oxygen demand (COD), which are two indicators of the presence of organic matter;
- Total suspended solids (TSS);
- Nutrients, that is total nitrogen (N) and phosphorus (P).

In particular, Table 2.1 reports the limits for the discharge of the above listed compounds imposed by the Italian legislation.

It is noteworthy to report that it is urgent to update the current environmental legislation, as new compounds, namely, emerging pollutants, are more and more frequently detected in both drinking water and wastewaters (Deblonde et al., 2011). These molecules are mainly pharmaceuticals, medicinal metabolites from human excretions, drugs, endocrine disrupting chemicals, and DBP. The existing plants are not equipped with process units capable for the degradation or removal of such compounds, also because they are usually present at $\mu g/L$ or ng/L concentrations.

Table 2.1 Main compounds to be removed from urban wastewater and discharge limits imposed by the Italian legislation on the basis of the EU Directive 2000/60.

Compound	Discharge limit (mg/L)
BOD_5	25
COD	125
TSS	35
Total N	10 or 15[a]
Total P	1 or 2[a]

BOD_5, Biochemical oxygen demand; COD, chemical oxygen demand; TSS, total suspended solids.

[a]The limits for total nitrogen and phosphorus depend on the number of inhabitants served by the wastewater treatment plant.

Thus besides a regulatory upgrading, the adoption of more efficient technologies is strongly encouraged.

2.1.3.2 Wastewater treatment plants

A WWTP is a sequence of process units aimed at the treatment of a given wastewater (Tchobanoglous et al., 2003). Specifically to municipal wastewaters, a typical scheme of treatment is shown in Fig. 2.2.

In addition to the physical unit processes (i.e., coarse screening, sedimentation, and filtration) described for drinking water—treatment plants, a phase of grit removal is present in municipal WWTPs when treating also part of the stormwater. Grit mainly consists of sand, gravel, and other heavy solid materials having a density higher than that of the organic putrescible solids. Grit removal is performed with grit chambers or by the centrifugation-separation of solids.

The core of a municipal WWTP is the secondary treatment, consisting of biological phases as well as a sedimentation. The final treatment is a disinfection.

2.1.3.3 Biological removal of organic and nitrogenous compounds from wastewaters

Organic content, ammonium (NH_4^+), and nitrate (NO_3^-) are removed from wastewaters through the use of biological processes, in which the bacteria originally present in water catalyze the oxidation/reduction reactions with the aim to reduce the concentrations of biodegradable substances below (or very close to) the discharge limits imposed. The main advantage of using bioprocesses is their cost-effectiveness, as they spontaneously occur in natural ecosystems. The task of WWTP designers and

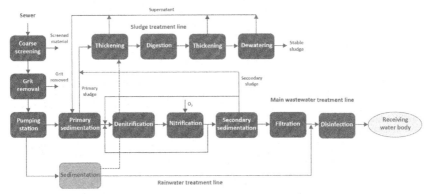

Figure 2.2 A typical block scheme of a municipal WWTP aimed at removal of suspended solids, and organics and nitrogenous compounds from wastewater. WWTP consists of pretreatments, primary, secondary, and tertiary treatments as well as disinfection. The sludge generated from the two sedimentation phases is treated in a dedicated line. Rainwater is treated in a third line of the WWTP and undergoes a simple sedimentation prior to be disinfected and discharged in the receiving water body. *WWTP*, Wastewater treatment plant.

operators is to optimize and control the microbial activity in order to achieve high removal efficiencies and reduce the retention times as much as possible.

When the receiving water body is sensitive to eutrophication, the WWTP scheme consists of two biological phases, with denitrification preceding nitrification (Fig. 2.2). Denitrification is the anoxic process that is aimed at the reduction of nitrate to dinitrogen gas (N_2), which is naturally released to the atmosphere. Heterotrophic microorganisms break down the molecule of NO_3^- while degrading organic matter in the absence of oxygen. The lack of O_2 supplementation results in a further saving of operating costs. In the nitrification basin, the oxidation of organic molecules continue in the presence of oxygen. Aerobic conditions are needed in this phase as the activity of autotrophic nitrifying bacteria requires concentrations of oxygen to be typically higher than 2 mg/L. During nitrification, NH_4^+ is oxidized to NO_3^-, implying the need of having a recirculation stream to report NO_3^- to denitrification.

The most common bioreactor configurations used in municipal WWTPs are activated sludge systems and biotrickling filters, operated with suspended cells and attached cells, respectively. In the first configuration, microorganisms grow in suspension, settle down during secondary sedimentation, and recirculate back to the biological phases (Fig. 2.2) in order to maintain constant their concentration. In biotrickling filters, bacteria form a different aggregate, namely, biofilm, and are not washed out by the wastewater stream as they adhere to inert supporting materials. Both technologies have advantages and shortcomings and require high volumes. Hence, as today the objective is to reduce the footprint of WWTPs, the use of innovative systems requiring lower reaction volumes is increasing.

2.1.3.4 Innovative bioprocesses

Membrane biological reactors (MBRs), moving bed biofilm reactors (MBBRs), fluidized-bed reactors (FBRs), up-flow anaerobic sludge blanket, packed-bed reactors (PBRs), and biological aerated filters (BAFs) are among the innovative bioreactor configurations used for the removal of biodegradable compounds from wastewater having different origins.

Most of them combine the advantages of traditional suspended and attached cell systems, resulting in higher treatment efficiencies and a lower footprint. For instance, MBBRs consist of biofilms grown on moving carriers, which are continuously maintained in suspension by means of mixers (Ødegaard, 2006). This enhances the contact between substrates (molecules to be degraded) and biomass (microorganisms) and, thus, the biodegradation kinetics. MBRs couple the biodegradation to the membrane filtration allowing to achieve high-quality water, which has the requisites to be reused in agriculture. MBRs and FBRs allow to retain high biomass concentrations, speeding up the removal of organic and nitrogenous pollutants (Papirio et al., 2013).

However, many operational challenges still have to be faced, such as the quick occurrence of membrane fouling in MBRs (Le-Clech et al., 2006) or clogging in BAFs and PBRs. Also, capital and operating costs are to date rather high, which partly limit their widespread application.

2.1.3.5 Treatment of sewage sludge from wastewater treatment plants

Sludge treatment and disposal in WWTPs generally amount to 50% of the total expense of the WWTP operation (Spinosa and Vesilind, 2001). Thickening is essential, as it allows to economically remove the first fraction of water (simply by gravity) and significantly reduce the moisture content of the slurry. In this way, a lower amount of sludge is treated in digestion and dewatering, which are the most costly process units.

Digestion is aimed at sludge stabilization. The putrescible organic matter and living microorganisms are maintained inside closed-vessel anaerobic digesters and biologically transformed into biogas $(CH_4 + CO_2)$. Although having high retention times, the anaerobic digestion of sludge results in the production of a biofuel, which can be burnt and used to cover the WWTP energy needs. Alternatively, aerobic digestion can be performed. In this case the biological reactions occur more quickly and the bioreactor size is lower, but oxygen has to be provided and no high-energy products (i.e., biogas) are produced.

Finally, dewatering is aimed at decreasing the content of bound water, consisting of interstitial, vicinal, and hydration water, which are the most difficult fractions to separate from solids (Pontoni et al., 2018). This induces high treatment costs because of the considerable energy consumption. However, high dewatering efficiencies lead to low amounts of final sludge to be disposed, permitting to decrease the disposal costs.

2.2 Technologies for solid-waste management

When persons decide that an object is no longer useful in its current form and discard it, that is the moment when a waste is generated. This operation is often done without thinking much about the fate of that waste or who will be taking care of it.

Nowadays, with the increased availability of single-use disposals and the reduced spaces for landfill building and operation, it has become a problem to get rid of all this waste that, in many cases, inevitably ends up in natural ecosystems and remains there for years or centuries (see the invasion of oceans by plastics and microplastics).

As waste management issues gain public awareness, the appropriateness of various disposal methods is often debated. Today, modern societies are moving in the direction of reduction, reuse, and recovery. Solid waste professionals and public authorities encourage citizens, public offices, and companies to produce less waste (reduction) and use items for longer prior to discard them (reuse). Moreover, recapturing as much energy and materials as possible from discarded items (recovery) is an excellent strategy to extract economic value from wastes and limit their final disposal.

With all the aspects above, also depending on the composition of waste produced and the attitude of people, each community has to develop its own "integrated solid waste management cycle." All the phases and processes (Fig. 2.3) are of major importance in order to pursue

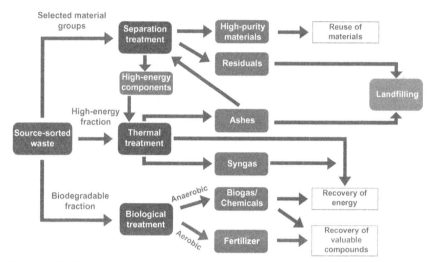

Figure 2.3 Scheme representation of an integrated cycle for solid-waste management starting from a source-sorted waste and aiming at the maximization of the production of energy and materials.

the objectives of reduction, reuse, and recovery and dispose the lowest possible amount of waste in landfills, which are anyway necessary for a correct management.

2.2.1 Recycling of materials: waste sorting plants

Waste sorting—treatment plants industrially process waste flows, either obtained from a nonsource sorted or a source-sorted collection system, in order to reform them into new or similar products. In particular, the objective of a recycling system, also known as mechanical biological treatment, can be the following:

- The production of high-quality secondary materials, especially when the original waste derives from a source-sorted collection system. This mainly allows the recovery of plastics, glass, metals, aluminum, and cardboard.
- Separation of the biodegradable organic fraction to be used in a biological process for composting or anaerobic digestion.
- Separation of the materials with a high heat of combustion, aiming to produce refuse-derived fuel (RdF) to be used in thermal plants. RdF can be pelletized in order to obtain a higher combustion efficiency.

Several technologies are available for the separation of single materials or groups from mixed waste flows:

- Manual sorting, consisting of workers who manually separate specific materials from other ones moving on conveyors. This technique results in high separation efficiencies and high-purity secondary materials, but many studies have reported occupational health problems of the employees (Malmros et al., 1992; Nadal et al., 2009).
- Sieving or dimensional sorting, aiming at the removal of the finest particles, such as inert material and soil.
- Magnetic, electromagnetic, and induction sorting, having a high efficiency for the separation of metals (mostly iron and aluminum) and highly conductive materials (e.g., the organic fraction of municipal solid waste—OFMSW—with a high water content).
- Air classifiers, which separate the materials on the basis of their density and aerodynamic resistance.

2.2.2 Biological processes

In addition to water reclamation, microbes can also be used for the treatment of solid wastes. Microorganisms are only capable to decompose the biodegradable matter, such as OFMSW, which is mainly composed of kitchen and green waste. However, many other organic wastes, for example, animal manure, agro-industrial waste (lignocelluloses or food production residues) and energy crops, are nowadays more and more often biologically degraded, in order to reduce their amount to be landfilled. Composting and anaerobic digestion are the most common biological processes operated for organic waste treatment, depending on whether the process is performed in the presence or absence of oxygen, respectively.

2.2.2.1 Composting

Composting is a traditional decomposition process of OFMSW aimed at the production of a solid product, namely, compost, to be used in agriculture for soil amendment. Microbes lead to the mineralization (i.e., production of stable inorganic compounds) and partial humification of OFMSW under aerobic conditions.

The process is developed in two main phases:

- Composting active time, consisting of a first subphase performed under mesophilic conditions (temperature increasing from ambient up to approximately 45°C−50°C) and a second subphase operated under thermophilic conditions ($T > 55°C$ for at least 3 days). In this period, bacteria hold the principal responsibility of the biological transformation. The waste becomes more stable, and pathogens are abated due to the high temperatures achieved. The duration of the active time can be only 1 week in closed-vessel biocontainers or up to 2 months in open systems.

- Curing phase, in which temperature is gradually decreased until returning to ambient values and humic acids are produced, also due to the activity of fungi and helminthes. This phase can take from 2 to 4 months.

2.2.2.2 Anaerobic digestion

In the absence of oxidative species (i.e., O_2, NO_3^- or SO_4^{2-}), the decomposition of OFMSW leads to a mixture of methane (CH_4) and carbon dioxide (CO_2), as a result of the biochemical activity of microorganisms under anaerobic conditions. This natural process is known as anaerobic digestion, with CH_4 and CO_2 being the main constituents of biogas. Both CH_4 and CO_2 are greenhouse gases, contributing to global warming when released to the atmosphere. In particular, CH_4 shows approximately 35-times stronger greenhouse effect than CO_2 (Vieitez et al., 2000).

However, when the biogas stream is collected, it can be burnt in a cogeneration plant for the production of heat and electricity. Thus anaerobic digestion is a promising biotechnology having both economic and environmental benefits. On one hand, the recovery of energy represents an economic profit of the process. On the other, the production of biogas is one of the technological solutions that promote the energy transition from fossil resources toward sustainable, renewable, and clean-energy sources, which is urgently needed in the modern society.

The decomposed solid and liquid fractions, namely, digestate, obtained during anaerobic digestion can be further treated with the aim to recover important resources such as nitrogen (N) and phosphorus (P). As N and P are essential nutrients for plant growth, digestate can be accordingly "manipulated" for the production of biofertilizers to be used in agriculture. Considering that most of chemical fertilizers are from industrial synthesis and this represents another source of greenhouse gas emissions (Brentrup, 2009), the development of biofertilizer economy would result in a lower environmental impact.

2.2.2.3 Biorefinery applications

Global energy and resource consumption is exponentially rising in the last years, in spite of a considerable decrease of primary sources of energy and materials and increasing negative effects on human health. Besides obtaining biogas from anaerobic digestion, further scientific, economic, and political efforts have lately been made to promote and encourage sustainable biotechnologies toward the production of biofuels and high-value biobased materials from organic waste (Mohan et al., 2016). Indeed, the European Commission has adopted the "Circular Economy Action Plan," which aims to close the loop between waste production and resource/energy recovery.

Biorefinery is a concept that includes a group of anaerobic bioprocesses aiming at "extracting value from waste" in a sustainable way. Among those, it is noteworthy to list:

- dark fermentation, addressed at the production of mainly hydrogen (H_2), organic acids and alcohols (e.g., bioethanol and biobutanol);
- photo fermentation, having the same end-products of dark fermentation with a more pronounced formation of organic acids, which can be subsequently transformed in biopolymers as main constituents of bioplastics;
- microalgae biorefinery, which allows the simultaneous removal of N and P (for instance, from anaerobic digestate) and production of biofuels (e.g., biodiesel and bioethanol) and biobased chemicals (e.g., pharmaceutical and nutritional compounds).

2.2.3 Thermal processes

Increasing the operating temperature up to values higher than 500°C, solid wastes are broken down into more simple gaseous molecules as well as fixed and flying ashes. The advantages of performing a thermal process over other types of treatment are as follows:

- The total amount of ashes is below 20% of the original mass of influent solid waste, indicating a significant decrease of waste to be eventually landfilled.
- A Lower plant footprint is required at constant influent flow-rates of solid waste.
- Thermal plants are versatile to simultaneously treat different categories of solid wastes (e.g., municipal, industrial, and clinical) as well as sludge from wastewater treatment plants.
- It is possible to recover and reuse the energy deriving from the combustion (or thermal destruction) of solid wastes and transform it into heat or electricity.

On the other side, the main drawback of a thermal treatment is the production of flue gases. These contain CO_2 (as the major greenhouse gas

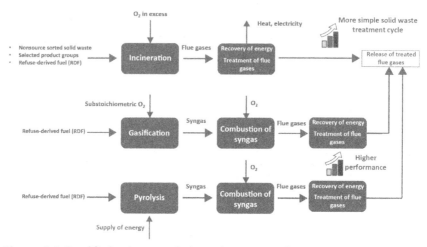

Figure 2.4 Simplified schemes of thermal processes for solid waste treatment. Incineration can be flexibly operated with wastes having different origin and influent characteristics, inducing a more simple integrated solid waste management. In contrast, to exploit the advantages of gasification and pyrolysis plants, the use of refuse-derived fuel is strongly encouraged in order to achieve higher performances in terms of energy recovery and flue gas treatment.

worldwide), other gaseous substances (such as NO_x, SO_2, HCl, and HF), and particulate matter often present as nanoparticles, which require the use of efficient gas treatment systems. However, the modern techniques still have a low efficiency for the abatement of nanoparticles (Walser et al., 2012), which are particularly hazardous as the adsorption of harmful and carcinogenic molecules (e.g., heavy metals) occurs on their high surface area. An optimal control of flue gas emissions from thermal plants treating solid wastes is, thus, of major importance, in order to contain the negative impact on public health.

Based on the amount of oxygen used to maintain the thermal process, it is possible to distinguish (Fig. 2.4):
- incineration, when oxygen is supplemented in excess to the stoichiometric conditions;
- gasification, when oxygen is present at substoichiometric conditions;
- pyrolysis, in the complete absence of oxygen supplemented.

2.2.3.1 Incineration

Incineration is a combustion of solid matrixes at working temperatures ranging around 1000°C. During incineration the solid waste is oxidized to mainly CO_2 and H_2O, but also sulfur and nitrogen oxides, depending on the amount of S and N in the original waste mixture and the type of waste supplemented. Nonetheless, the use of high temperatures and oxygen concentrations does not result in the production of undesirable compounds, such as carbon monoxide (CO) as well as dioxins and furans.

Waste incineration is commonly performed in moving grate combustion chambers, in which the waste is mixed with oxygen due to the turbulence guaranteed by the grate that allows the waste to move from the initial to the final section of the chamber. The ashes fall down through the elements or at the end of the grate. A higher turbulence can be obtained in rotary kiln or fluidized-bed incinerators, resulting in a higher combustion efficiency, a more controlled flue gas composition and a better recovery of energy. However, the fraction of nanoparticles in the flue gases increase in the last two incineration configurations.

2.2.3.2 Pyrolysis

When the aim is to produce a new fuel starting from the thermal decomposition of a solid waste, oxygen supplementation has to be drastically reduced or completely absent in order to transform the waste into a gaseous mixture known as "syngas," and a solid carbon residue, namely, "char."

Pyrolysis, also known as "thermal cracking," is performed with no oxygen feeding and requires the use of external energy as it occurs under endothermic conditions. Depending on the retention time used in the pyrolysis chamber (from a few seconds to approximately 30 minutes) and temperature ($350°C-600°C$), the composition of the end products (i.e., syngas, char, and pyrolysis oil) changes as well as the concentration of the syngas constituents (i.e., CO, CH_4, and H_2) (Li et al., 1999). For instance, at decreasing retention times and increasing temperatures, the main end product is syngas with a higher percentage of hydrogen, which increases the heat of combustion of syngas.

Transforming the waste into syngas allows the combustion of a gaseous fuel (and not directly a solid waste as occurring in conventional incineration), leading to the following benefits:
- a better control on the combustion process
- a better recovery of the energy released
- a more stable flue gas composition

However, in order to gain the above-cited benefits, the use of RdF is required. Therefore, a separation plant is needed prior to the thermal process within an integrated solid-waste management cycle (Fig. 2.3).

2.2.3.3 Gasification

Gasification is "at halfway" between conventional incineration and pyrolysis (Arena, 2012). Indeed, gasification is operated by supplying oxygen, but the oxygen amount is maintained below the stoichiometric level to obtain nonoxidized compounds (i.e., CO, CH_4, and H_2), which are the main constituents of syngas. Some of the reactions occurring in a gasification system are:

$$C + O_2 \rightarrow CO_2$$

$$C + H_2O \rightarrow CO + H_2$$

$$C + CO_2 \rightarrow 2CO$$

$$C + 2H_2 \rightarrow CH_4$$

$$CO + H_2O \rightarrow CO_2 + H_2$$

with all being endothermic, except the first being exothermic. The overall energy balance is $\Delta H > 0$, which means that the process is exothermic and is self-sustained while producing compounds with high heat of combustion.

During gasification, oxygen can be supplied as pure O_2 or in an air stream. The first option results in higher operating costs, as pure O_2 requires additional energy to be produced but allows a syngas with a higher energy content. Alternatively, the use of air as a source of oxygen is a more cost-effective solution, but N_2 dilutes the percentage of CO, H_2, and CH_4 in syngas and reduces its heat of combustion.

2.2.4 Landfilling

"Controlled" landfilling is the final step of the entire solid waste management cycle, consisting of a containment of compacted waste into cells, which are daily covered with low-quality soil or stabilized organic fraction. Over the years, cells are placed one on top of another forming several layers until the completion of the landfill volume.

Although landfilling is the most cost-effective technique for solid waste management, landfills should contain only the residuals of all the above-described processes, that is, the nonrecyclable, nonbiodegradable, and nontransformable into energy waste fractions. This virtuous waste management would allow maintaining the landfill volume as small as possible or allowing a longer duration of landfill operation.

The major environmental concern related to the operation of a landfill is the production of leachate and biogas. A landfill is not a "perfectly confined" container of solid waste but is a "high-volume reactor" where biogeochemical reactions occur. Rainwater passes through the amount of waste and allows the leaching of soluble compounds as well as the microbial degradation of the biodegradable organic fraction, mostly under anaerobic conditions.

Depending on the chemical characteristics of the landfilled waste, low- or high-strength leachates are formed, which need to be collected, pumped out, and properly treated. In order to avoid the uncontrolled release of leachate, landfills are commonly insulated at the bottom and on the sides with a layer of clay and polymeric membrane sheets. In the case of an inadequate design, and construction or maintenance of the insulation layer, the leakage of leachate would result in a high risk for groundwater pollution (Bjerg et al., 2003).

In regard to the biological degradation of the organic fraction, a system of pipes can be used to drain the biogas produced, which is potentially used to cover the energy needs of the landfill operation. When biogas is not collected, landfills contribute to greenhouse gas emissions or dispersal of gases in the underground soil (Hoornweg and Bhada-Tata, 2012).

2.3 Remediation of contaminated sites

The remediation of contaminated sites and soils is today one of the most appealing environmental restoration subjects (Panagos et al., 2013). Approximately 40 years ago, the attention of public authorities, citizens, and scientific community was attracted by the occurrence of local major events reported by mass media. Nowadays, land contamination is considered as a global infrastructural and environmental concern (Ferguson, 1999).

It is widely recognized that it is not technically and economically feasible to remediate all the contaminated sites to the background concentrations. Therefore, European and worldwide policies have developed a decision support system, specifying that the aim of site remediation is the "fitness for use," depending on the land use (e.g., industrial, recreational, and residential) planned for each specific site.

2.3.1 Legislative approach: risk-assessment analysis

Prior to the adoption of the above-mentioned approach, the "quality of a soil" depended on the criterion of the maximum tolerable concentration. A site was defined contaminated when the actual concentration of the detected contaminant was higher than the highest imposed by the legislation. Although being quickly applicable, this method presented several limitations as not related to the peculiarity of the site. In particular, the method did not account for

- the chemical, geological, geotechnical, and hydraulic characteristics of the site;
- the distribution of the contaminant in the different matrixes (air, water, and soil);
- the targets of the exposure (e.g., natural ecosystems or human beings) and the land use after the remediation.

Thus, a "simple comparison" between the revealed concentrations in the soil and the legislation limits would not give a complete picture of the risk associated with a specific contamination. Therefore the latest approach adopted by the European Union, and earlier by the United States of America, is based on the assessment of the sanitary (for public health) and environmental (for the environment) risk. A site is defined as "contaminated" if the environmental risk associated with the presence of a specific contaminant (or a group of contaminants) is higher than the maximum value tolerated.

The risk assessment analysis is mainly aimed at the achievement of two objectives:

- Determine whether the contaminated area represents a serious risk for humans and environmental matrixes.
- In the case of verified risk, evaluate the best technology for the remediation or the containment of the polluted area.

Moreover, in regard to the steps for the evaluation and management of the risk, the risk assessment analysis is a multiphase procedure consisting of the following phases:

1. Site assessment, addressed at (1) identifying the potential sources of contamination (e.g., deposits of waste, mine tailings, damaged pipes and reservoirs, drainage from wells), (2) preparing a plan of on-site and underground investigations and sampling, and (3) analyzing the samples collected.

2. Preparation of the conceptual model of the site based on the data collected in the previous site-assessment phase. The contamination

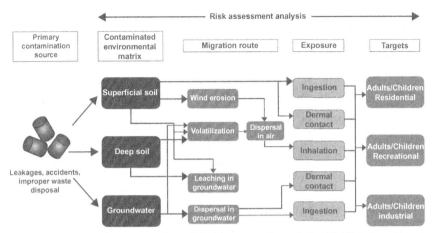

Figure 2.5 A typical conceptual model of a contaminated site highlighting the primary source of contamination, the contaminated environmental matrixes, the migration pathways and exposure routes, and the targets affected by contamination.

sources, the polluting markers to be monitored, the migration and exposure routes of the contaminants, and the final targets are included in the model (Fig. 2.5).

3. Evaluation of the "point of exposure (POE)" concentration, that is the value of concentration in the point where the final target is located. The information concerning the fate and transport of the contaminants, acquired when building the conceptual site model, is useful to calculate the POE concentration, which can be significantly lower than that revealed in the contaminated area due to the presence of natural attenuation factors across the migration route.

4. Mathematical calculation of the sanitary-environmental risk as

$$R = \mathrm{CDI} \cdot T$$

where CDI is the chronic daily intake, calculated based on the POE concentration and the flow rate of contaminant during the time of exposure, and T is the toxicity of the contaminant, depending on whether it has carcinogenic effects or not. The value of T is generally adopted based on epidemiological studies.

5. Risk management, when finally comparing the risk obtained in the previous phase with the maximum value tolerable for that specific contaminant (carcinogenic or not) and target. When the contamination results in a higher risk than the threshold value, the best

remediation technology is identified, and it is possible to proceed with the remediation activities. Otherwise, the site is periodically monitored in order to evaluate any possible increase of the risk.

2.3.2 Categories of pollutants

A first classification of the main pollutants in contaminated soils can be done on the basis of their chemical characteristics:

- Inorganic contaminants, with heavy metals being the most common for their bioaccumulation properties in vegetal and animal tissues till entering the food chain;
- Organic contaminants, mainly derived from oil extraction and refinery, industrial activities, or combustion plants

Regarding the behavior of the molecules in the environmental matrixes, the contaminants are as follows:

- "Nonreactive," when their amount does not change over time due to biological or chemical reactions, but they are only transferred from one phase to another. Nonreactive compounds are defined as persistent pollutants.
- "Reactive," when biological or chemical reactions decrease their total amount, besides being transferred from one phase to another due to mass-transportation phenomena.

Finally, depending on their physical—chemical properties (Table 2.2), the contaminants can do the following:

- Be adsorbed to a solid matrix, which can be the inorganic (i.e., minerals and ores) or organic (e.g., peat and humic acids) fraction of a soil. The interaction of the contaminant with soil fractions can be intimately strong, indicating a higher resistance to remediation but, at the same time, a lower sanitary-environmental risk.
- Dissolve in nondissociated or dissociated forms in groundwater. Depending on the soil permeability, the contaminant can be more or less mobile and, thus, hazardous.
- Remain on the surface of ground water as immiscible substance (e.g., hydrocarbons in the saturated zone of soils). The migration route and velocity depend on the movement of the groundwater and the piezometric head variations.
- Volatilize in the gaseous phase of the pores between soil particles. Also in this case, the contaminant can be transported rather easily and result in a high risk for the targets.

Table 2.2 Classification and physical–chemical properties of the most common families of pollutants detectable in a contaminated site.

Family of contaminant		Anthropogenic sources	Exposure pathways for human beings	Physical–chemical properties		
				Solubility	Volatility	Biodegradability
Inorganic contaminants	Heavy metals	Mining, industry, exhausted batteries	Ingestion from water, dermal contact, bioaccumulation in living organisms	✓[a]	X[a]	X
	Acids and cyanide	Mining and chemical industry	Ingestion from water	✓	X	X
	Asbestos	Construction waste	Inhalation, dermal contact	X	✓[b]	X
	Radioactive compounds	Nuclear power plants	Ingestion from water, inhalation	✓	✓	X
	Anions (e.g., NO_3^-, NH_4^+, and SO_4^{2-})	Agriculture and industry	Ingestion from water	✓	X	✓
Organic contaminants	Hydrocarbons	Oil refinery and extraction	Ingestion from soil, dermal contact	X[c]	X[c]	X
	Hydrocarbon derivatives	Oil refinery and extraction	Ingestion from water and soil, dermal contact	✓[c]	X	X
	Polycyclic aromatic hydrocarbons	Combustion plants, vehicular transportation	Inhalation, dermal contact, bioaccumulation in living organisms	X	X	X

(Continued)

Table 2.2 (Continued)

Family of contaminant	Anthropogenic sources	Exposure pathways for human beings	Physical–chemical properties		
			Solubility	Volatility	Biodegradability
Nonchlorinated solvents (BTEX)	Oil refinery and extraction (e.g., benzene, toluene, and xylene)	Ingestion from water, inhalation	✓	✓	✓
Chlorinated solvents	Chemical, food, and pharmaceutical industry	Inhalation	X[d]	✓	X[d]
Polychlorinated biphenyls	Paint, dye, and insulating materials production	Dermal contact, bioaccumulation in living organisms	X	X	X
Dioxins and furans	Waste improper burning	Inhalation, dermal contact, bioaccumulation in living organisms	X	X[e]	X
Pesticides and fertilizers	Agriculture and chemical industry		✓	X	X

[a]Heavy metals are soluble especially under acidic conditions or in the presence of chelating substances. Mercury (Hg) is the only volatile metal at ambient conditions.
[b]Asbestos is not a volatile compound but the risk associated with asbestos is due to the formation of flying ashes and fibers.
[c]The soluble or volatile nature depends on the number of C atoms.
[d]Less soluble and biodegradable than nonchlorinated solvents
[e]Not volatile at ambient temperature

In Table 2.2, an in-depth list of the potential soil contaminants is reported.

2.3.3 Soil remediation technologies

The common technologies used for the remediation of contaminated sites (Hamby, 1996) can be classified depending on

- the actual degradation of the pollutant,
- the place where the remediation activities take place,
- the mechanism used to degrade or remove the pollutants from the soil.

When the overall amount of the polluting substance (or substances) decreases after the treatment, the technique allows the transformation of the pollutant into some metabolic products due to chemically or biologically catalyzed reactions. When no decrease of the overall amount of the compound occurs, but the contaminant concentration decreases in the solid matrix, the technique is "simply" based on a solid—liquid or solid—gas mass transfer. The pollutant is not transformed into "more simple" molecules but transferred to a liquid or gas phase, which subsequently requires to be properly treated.

Depending on the mechanism used for the removal of the contaminants, the soil remediation techniques can be

- biological, when aimed at the stimulation of living indigenous or enriched microorganisms, capable to directly or indirectly catalyze the degradation kinetics of the contaminant;
- physical—chemical, when the substance is extracted from soil with a liquid or gaseous agent or chemically oxidized into less hazardous products across the formation of reaction intermediates;
- thermal, when the use of high temperatures ($>150°C$) leads to the vapor extraction or even the thermal destruction of the contaminant molecules.

Generally, moving from biological toward thermal processes allows the removal of a wider range of contaminants in spite of increasing operating costs.

Finally, based on the place where the remediation is performed, the technique is defined as "in situ" or "ex situ," that is, in the place of the contamination or in a location different from where the contamination exists, respectively. The in situ and ex situ technologies are in-depth analyzed in the next two subsections (Sections 2.3.3.1 and 2.3.3.2).

2.3.3.1 "In situ" techniques

Compared to the ex situ interventions, the in situ techniques result in the following operating advantages:

- lower operating costs, as the intervention takes place directly in the site of the past or ongoing contamination, and do not require the soil excavation and transportation to a treatment plant;
- more suitable for a widespread and deep contamination;
- applicable without necessarily interrupting ongoing activities at the ground level.

However, the performance of the process is considerably influenced by the permeability of the soil indicating that, in case the fractions of silt and clay are rather high, the remediation times are significantly extended. Moreover, if the lithology of the underground soil or the hydraulic flow of the groundwater are not well known, the polluted area or eluates might not be intercepted with a high risk of contamination of the surrounding areas.

2.3.3.1.1 Phytoremediation

This a technique suitable for the treatment of contaminated soils, sediments, and groundwater, especially when the contamination is extremely wide but only a few meters deep. Indeed, the plant species commonly adopted have a root apparatus only reaching the first layers of soil. In case the contamination is deeper, phytoremediation can be used as an ex situ intervention.

Phytoremediation occurs through different physical mechanisms, such as rhizodegradation, phytoextraction, phytostabilization, and phytodegradation, and has been reported to be effective for a wide range of contaminants, including both organic and inorganic compounds (Kamath et al., 2003; Pulford and Watson, 2004).

2.3.3.1.2 Bioventing and biosparging

Bioventing and biosparging are "twin technologies" aimed at the remediation of a contaminated site from biodegradable organic compounds through the ventilation of an air stream in the unsaturated and saturated zones (Fig. 2.6), respectively. The idea behind these techniques is that the supplementation of air stimulates the activity of microorganisms, previously inactive or not performing well. In order to further enhance the biological kinetics, preheated air can be used and water, nutrients, and supplements for the microbial metabolism can be added.

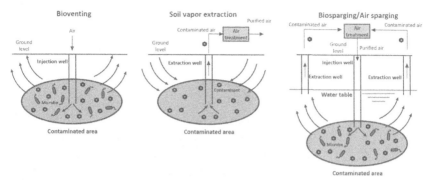

Figure 2.6 Differences in the operation of bioventing, soil vapor extraction, biosparging, and air sparging for the in situ treatment of soils contaminated by biodegradable and volatile compounds.

2.3.3.1.3 Soil vapor extraction and air sparging

Similarly to bioventing and bioventing, soil vapor extraction and air sparging also consist of an air-supplementation system that provides air to the contaminated area. In this case, the removal mechanism is purely physical, and a solid—gas mass transfer of the contaminant occurs due to the volatility of the polluting molecules. Hence, air cannot be supplemented into the contaminated area but has to be aspirated by means of a vacuum pumping system and extraction wells (Fig. 2.6). Finally, the pollutant-containing air stream is collected and properly treated at the ground level prior to being released in the atmosphere.

2.3.3.1.4 Soil flushing

Soil flushing is a technique that allows the mass transfer of the contaminants from the solid matrix to a liquid phase through mechanisms of desorption and solubilization. In order to do so, liquid extracting agents or aqueous solutions are used, having a high affinity with the specific contaminant. For instance, metals can be removed from soils using acidic solutions or chelating agents. Organic contaminants are scarcely soluble in water and, thus, organic solvents can be used as extracting solutions.

Fig. 2.7 shows a schematic representation of a soil flushing installation. The liquid extracting agent is pumped into the soil through an injection well, filtrates in the contaminated area desorbing the contaminant, and, finally, is extracted by means of extraction wells. At the ground level the contaminated solution is treated and possibly recirculated in the injection wells. The contaminant is finally disposed.

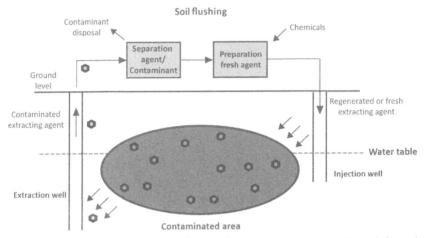

Figure 2.7 Soil flushing treatment scheme. The extracting agent is injected through the contaminated area and results in the desorption/solubilization of the contaminant. Then, the agent is extracted and pumped back to the ground level in order to separate the contaminant and regenerate the solution.

2.3.3.1.5 Electrokinetic remediation

Two electrodes are installed in the soil for the generation of an electric field, which promotes the migration of contaminating ions toward the anode or the cathode. This technology is highly efficient for the removal of anions and cations deriving from fertilizers, cyanide, heavy metals, and polar hydrocarbon derivatives. The application of such technique is mainly performed in the saturated zone of soils, as the presence of water enhances the electric conductivity and, thus, removal performance.

2.3.3.1.6 Chemical oxidation

Polluting molecules are completely mineralized or transformed in less hazardous compounds via chemical degradation kinetics, which are stimulated by the injection of strong oxidative agents in the soil. Compounds such as sodium and potassium permanganate ($KMnO_4$ and $NaMnO_4$), hydrogen peroxide (H_2O_2), and ozone (O_3) result in the production of hydroxyl radicals (HO), which are capable to quickly react with persistent pollutants and break down their molecules. High efficiencies can be achieved for the removal of nonchlorinated and chlorinated organic solvents, polycyclic aromatic hydrocarbons, and polychlorinated biphenyls.

2.3.3.1.7 Thermal desorption and destruction

Increasing the treatment temperatures initially results in the desorption of most molecules (T ranging between 150°C and 600°C) and, then, the thermal breakage of the chemical bonds ($T > 600$°C). The range of removable contaminants and the treatment efficiencies increases at higher operating temperatures, as well as the operating costs.

2.3.3.2 "Ex situ" techniques

When the excavation and transportation of the soil (or the pumping of the contaminated groundwater) are performed prior to treating the soil in a specific treatment plant, an ex situ technique is used. In spite of the higher operating and treatment costs when compared to in situ interventions, the ex situ techniques allow:

- higher removal efficiencies;
- a lower risk associated with the loss of part of the contaminants or chemical agents in the environment.

Indeed, remediating a soil under "ex situ" conditions means that its treatment occurs in a controlled and engineered reactor where (1) a better contact is maintained between the reagent (e.g., air, chemicals, or washing solutions) and the pollutant, (2) the degradation reactions are more predictable and result in expected by-products, and (3) the soil characteristics (e.g., permeability) and native environmental factors have no influence on the remediation process. Moreover, all these features result in lower treatment times allowing to build reactors with a lower working volume and significantly decreasing the capital costs.

2.3.3.2.1 Landfarming

The biological remediation of contaminated soils can be performed by using landfarming. The soil is initially spread out over a surface and periodical turned to promote its aeration. Oxygen enhances the biodegradation kinetics and the removal of organic and inorganic contaminants by direct metabolism or cometabolism. Enriched bacteria, water, and nutrients can be also added to obtain a faster process. Operating costs are relatively low.

2.3.3.2.2 Soil washing

When soil flushing is performed in an engineered system, the treatment is known as soil washing, but the mechanisms of removal/transfer of the contaminants are substantially the same of those of soil flushing. The process is optimized, with a lower probability of hazardous emissions as the uncontrolled dispersal of the extracting agent and contaminant cannot occur.

2.3.3.2.3 Engineered reactors

Biological and chemical transformation of pollutants can be performed in controlled (bio)reactors. Enhanced hydraulic and working conditions allow to obtain a higher removal efficiency, due to a continuous monitoring and control of the main operational parameters.

2.3.3.2.4 Thermal desorption, destruction, and incineration

Desorption and breaking down of the polluting molecules from a soil can be also achieved in ex situ installations. To this aim, existing incinerators for solid waste treatment can be properly used.

References

Arena, U., 2012. Process and technological aspects of municipal solid waste gasification: a review. Waste Manage. 32, 625−639.

Barlow, M., Clarke, T., 2017. Blue Gold: The Battle Against Corporate Theft of the World's Water. Routledge, London, UK.

Bjerg, P.L., Albrechtsen, H.-J., Kjeldsen, P., Christensen, T.H., 2003. The groundwater geochemistry of waste disposal facilities. Treatise Geochem. 9, 579−612.

Brentrup, F., 2009. The impact of mineral fertilizers on the carbon footprint of crop production. In: Proceedings of the XVI International Plant Nutrition Colloquium, Sacramento, CA.

Chowdhury, S., Champagne, P., McLellan, P.J., 2009. Models for predicting disinfection byproduct (DBP) formation in drinking waters: a chronological review. Sci. Total Environ. 407, 4189−4206.

Deblonde, T., Cossu-Leguille, C., Hartemann, P., 2011. Emerging pollutants in wastewater: a review of the literature. Int. J. Hyg. Environ. Health 214, 442−448.

Ferguson, C.C., 1999. Assessing risks from contaminated sites: policy and practice in 16 European countries. Land Contam. Reclam. 7, 33−54.

Hamby, D.M., 1996. Site remediation techniques supporting environmental restoration activities − a review. Sci. Total Environ. 191, 203−224.

Hoornweg, D., Bhada-Tata, P., 2012. What a waste. A global review of solid waste management. In: Unit, U.D.L.G. (Ed.), Urban Development Series. World Bank, USA, Washington, DC.

Kamath, R., Rentz, J.A., Schnoor, J.L., Alvarez, P.J.J., 2003. Phytoremediation of hydrocarbon-contaminated soils: principles and applications. In: Vazquez-Duhalt, R., Quintero-Ramirez, R. (Eds.), Studies i Surface a Catalysis. Elsevier, The Netherlands.

Karagiannis, I.C., Soldatos, P., 2008. Water desalination cost literature: review and assessment. Desalination 223, 448−456.

Le-Clech P., Chen V., Fane T.A.G. (2006). Fouling in membrane bioreactors used in wastewater treatment.

Li, A.M., Li, X.D., Li, A.Q., Ren, Y., Chi, Y., Yan, J.H., et al., 1999. Pyrolysis of solid waste in a rotary kiln: influence of final pyrolysis temperature on the pyrolysis products. J. Anal. Appl. Pyrolysis 50, 149–162.

Malmros, P., Sigsgaard, T., Bacj, B., 1992. Occupational health problems due to garbage sorting. Waste Manage. Res. 10, 227–234.

Mohan, V.M., Nikhil, G.N., Chiranjeevi, P., Nagendranatha Reddy, C., Rohit, M.V., Kumar, A.N., et al., 2016. Waste biorefinery models towards sustainable circular bioeconomy: critical review and future perspectives. Bioresour. Technol. 215, 2–12.

Nadal, M., Inza, I., Schuhmacher, M., Figueras, M.J., Domingo, J.L., 2009. Health risks of the occupational exposure to microbiological and chemical pollutants in a municipal waste organic fraction treatment plant. Int. J. Hyg. Environ. Health 212, 661–669.

Ødegaard, H., 2006. Innovations in wastewater treatment: the moving bed biofilm process. Water Sci. Technol. 53, 17–33. Papir.

Panagos, P., Van Liedekerke, M., Yigini, Y., Montanarella, L., 2013. Contaminated sites in Europe: review of the current situation based on data collected through a European network. J. Environ. Public Health 2013, 158764.

Papirio, S., Villa-Gomez, D.K., Esposito, G., Pirozzi, F., Lens, P.N.L., 2013. Acid mine drainage treatment in fluidized-bed bioreactors by sulfate-reducing bacteria: a critical review. Crit. Rev. Environ. Sci. Technol. 43, 2545–2580.

Pontoni, L., Papirio, S., D'Alessandro, G., Caniani, D., Gori, R., Mannina, G., et al., 2018. Dewaterability of CAS and MBR sludge: effect of biological stability and EPS composition. J. Environ. Eng. 144, 04017088.

Pulford, I.D., Watson, C., 2004. Phytoremediation of heavy metal-contaminated land by trees – a review. Environ. Int. 29, 529–540.

Spinosa, L., Vesilind, P.A., 2001. Sludge Into Biosolids: Processing, Disposal and Utilization. IWA Publishing, London, UK.

Tchobanoglous, G., Burton, F.L., Stensel, H.D., Metcalf & Eddy, Inc., 2003. Wastewater Engineering: Treatment and Reuse, [th] ed. McGraw Hill, New York.

Vieitez, E.R., Mosquera, J., Ghosh, S., 2000. Kinetics of accelerated solid-state fermentation of organic-rich municipal solid waste. Water Sci. Technol. 41, 231–238.

Walser, T., Limbach, L.K., Biogioli, R., et al., 2012. Persistence of engineered nanoparticles in a municipal solid-waste incineration plant. Nat. 7, 520–524.

CHAPTER 3

Health impact assessment: quantifying the health benefits and costs

Andrea Ranzi
Centre for Environmental Health and Prevention, Regional Agency for Prevention, Environment and
Energy of Emilia-Romagna, Modena, Italy

Contents

3.1 Introduction

A health hazard is a source of risk to human health or wellbeing. A health risk assessment scientifically evaluates potential adverse health effects resulting from human exposure to an hazard. Traditional methods of risk assessment have provided good service in support of policy, mainly in relation to standard settings and regulations of hazardous chemicals or practices.

The work undertaken in two large EU-funded projects (INTARESE and HEIMTSA) provided information on the range of approaches to applicable assessment. A comprehensive review of these methods analyzed and proposed a framework for integrated environmental health impact assessments (IEHIA) (both as a basis for bringing together and choosing between different methods of assessment, and extending these to more

Cost-Benefit Analysis of Environmental Health Interventions
DOI: https://doi.org/10.1016/B978-0-12-812885-5.00003-2

complex problems) and discussed the challenges involved in conducting integrated assessments to support policy (Briggs, 2008).

Other relevant documents were developed regarding methods for health risk assessments of air pollution, such as the WHO report "Health risk assessment of air pollution. General principles" (World Health Organization Regional Office for Europe, 2016). European project Aphekom (Pascal et al., 2013) performed calculations of burden of disease (BoD) related to air pollution in different European cities, providing principles and guidelines on how to perform a health impact assessment (HIA).

HIA is defined in different ways; the consensus definition is that of the 1999 Gothenburg consensus paper by the WHO Regional Office for Europe: "... a combination of procedures or methods by which a policy, program or project may be judged as to the effects it may have on the health of a population."

HIA is a systematic process to assess the actual or potential effects on the health of individuals, groups, or communities arising from environmental conditions or hazards arising from policies, objectives, programs, plans, or activities. It looks at both potential health benefits and health impacts from an activity or situation.

In this framework an IEHIA can be viewed as a tool for appraising health risk and/or benefits deriving from exposures to environmental stressors.

The present chapter reviewed these concepts by presenting general definitions and principles of this approach, discussing how an IEHIA can help policy makers and decision processes, and providing a step-by-step general guide on how to perform an IEHIA.

This approach is presented as preliminary step to the calculations of the economic impacts and the theme of cost benefit analysis.

We refer to air pollution as an environmental hazard, but general principles are extendible to other environmental risk factors. The urban environment is the main scenario for these approaches, but focuses on industrial settlements, contaminated sites, and situations related to authorization procedures are also considered.

3.2 Epidemiological study and health impact assessment

The question about the more suitable tool to assess the health effects of pollution is an open debate in international research, especially when related to the choice between epidemiological studies and HIA.

This debate has been fueled by a recent commentary, dedicated to the opportunity to carry out new research in situations characterized by environmental pollution (Savitz, 2016). The question posed is the choice of the most appropriate approach if a population "discovers" that they have been exposed to a dangerous pollutant, and there is a justified public request to obtain an appropriate response from authorities.

The authors discuss the role of public health in ensuring actions for pollution reduction and in providing health care to affected population. The need of an epidemiological study, often required in these situations, is discussed and highlights how it is rarely considered a direct advantage to those affected, given the possibility for involuntary damage. The epidemiological study may not give definite indications, increase uncertainty due to inconclusive results, limited power, or other methodological weaknesses, or, in an extreme way, can be viewed as an instrument to hold over actions that would have direct benefits.

It is therefore suggested that, rather than conducting an epidemiological study (sometimes of long duration and of limited quality), a HIA is more appropriate, considering this as applied research of better value in such circumstances.

It is certainly useful and necessary to examine the risks and benefits of undertaking an epidemiological study to communicate from the start what can be expected from the study and its usefulness.

Several scientific findings point to a causal relationship between exposure to air pollution and health. They also show that current levels of air pollutants observed in European cities are associated with health risks. The impact of the effects at the individual level may appear low compared to other risk factors. However, since the whole population is exposed to air pollution, this impact results in a nonnegligible public-health burden.

The Global Burden of Diseases, Injuries, and Risk Factors Study provides an up-to-date synthesis of the evidence for risk factor exposure and the attributable BoD (GBD 2015 Risk Factors Collaborators, 2016). An interesting comparative scheme shows that a ambient particulate matter is the first environmental leading risk, at a global level, since 2005. Any reduction in air pollution would therefore benefit a large number of people and large health gains.

Together with the quantification of damage attributable to environmental risk factors, research is still necessary. We need to increase and update knowledge about the relationship between exposure to known pollutants and the effects on health and study the effects of emerging pollutants. Numerous etiological studies recently offered relevant results for public health decisions and better HIA procedures as a demonstration of the importance of consolidating and expanding epidemiological knowledge, both on the scientific and public health level.

In October 2017 the Lancet Commission on pollution and health published (Landrigan et al., 2018) a paper on the BoD due to pollution, declared as the world's largest cause of disease and premature deaths. Authors estimated 9 million deaths due to global pollution; air pollution resulted in a greater health burden than water, soil, or occupational exposures. Ambient and household air pollution were considered responsible for 6.5 million deaths per year (very similar to the estimation of 7 million due to tobacco smoke); authors claimed a robust "call to arms" against pollution, stark in its warnings, but brimming with optimism, considering that the needed urgent actions are known.

Legally mandated regulation is considered an essential step to attain the goal of reduction of exposure to pollution, together with the need to continuously research new evidences on the effects of air pollution. Authors explain how the current assessment of attributable deaths represent a kind of tip of the iceberg of diseases caused by pollution. They introduce the concept of *pollutome*, defined as the totality of all pollution that potentially harm human health. The pollutome can be viewed as a fully contained (nested) subset of the *exposome*, including pollutant exposures during the whole life (gestation, infancy, childhood, adolescence, adult, and old age). Scientific knowledge about the health effects of pollution varies by pollution type; for this reason, actual estimation is possible related only to the zone above the "sea level" (i.e., the level of scientific knowledge), while the numbers of deaths attributable to the forms of pollution also include the zones under the sea level where effects are still unknown or not adequately quantified (Fig. 3.1).

The capacity for the evaluation ex ante and of the whole route of substances released into the environment should be improved, and our expertise in developing integrated environmental impact and health methodologies must be strengthened.

In this assessment, time and uncertainty help decide if and when the epidemiological study should be carried out for the growth of scientific knowledge and public health purposes.

The chapter discusses the theories, methods, and tools for the application of IEHIA procedures. It is useful to remember that they have

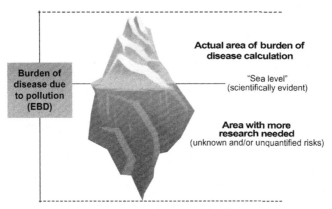

Figure 3.1 Burden of disease due to environmental pollution.

different methodological protocols from epidemiological studies, respond to different objectives, and differentiate in uses.

IEHIA is a procedure that integrates the best knowledge derived from toxicological and epidemiological studies and transfers them in a participatory manner to public health decisions. IEHIA is both a research and public health activity that assesses ex ante different scenarios due to harmful interventions or positive improvements.

When considering the comparison between actual (reference) and counterfactual (alternative) scenario, different aspects can modify, and each of these can potentially affect differences in impacts. The main aspect is related to the difference in the concentration values and population exposure.

Generally, assessment procedures only consider this difference, putting the other factors as unmodified during time between the two scenarios. This procedure certainly introduces some distortions/uncertainties, linked to possible modifications of the other parameters, that is, the potential onset of new hazards, the population distribution and characteristics, the updates in the concentration−response functions, and the health effects recognized as associated to environmental risks in the study.

An IEHIA mainly answers policy questions about the likely health impacts of planned policies or modifications of air quality. Identified questions range from the quantification of the public health burden associated with current levels of pollution to the potential health benefits associated with changing an air quality policy (intervention or application of more stringent air quality standard) (WHO Regional Office for Europe, 2014).

Input data are required on a ranging of factors from the levels of air pollution, the exposed population, the health outcome affected (concentration—response functions). The selection of the most suitable methods may depend on data availability or determine the data requirements.

3.3 Steps in performing integrated environmental health impact assessment

Performing an IEHIA requires different steps. Different input data are required (the level of air pollution, the exposed population, the health status of people under investigation); several assumptions and choice have to be made by the health impact assessors (as the study area to be investigated, the health outcome considered, the concentration—response functions). All these steps and decisions are potentially affected by uncertainties.

Fig. 3.2 shows the connection between different steps in performing an IEHIA. Following suggestions from literature, some general steps can be identified.

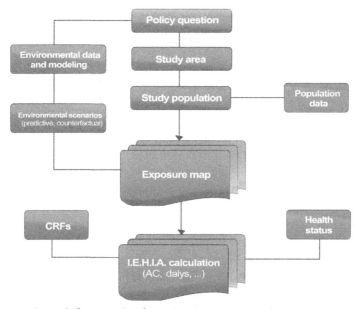

Figure 3.2 General framework of IEHIA. *IEHIA*, Integrated environmental health impact assessment.

3.3.1 Study area and population

The definition of the study area is a key step in the IEHIA process. In the case of an assessment applied to a city (or region), where general pollution is under examination, an important aspect is to consider a study area where the average of pollutant levels measured at fixed monitors or modeled in the area can represent a good estimate of the average population exposure.

In the case of a single-point source (i.e., industrial site), dispersion models and other considerations reported in the environmental impact assessment report must drive the definition of the study area.

Policy aspects drive the choice of a study area (i.e., boundaries of a city), which is useful to demographic and health data that must be available and homogeneous on a geographical scale consistent with the study area.

The study area influences the number of the exposed population and the calculation of the background incidence of the pathologies; they represent determining factors that influence the calculation of attributable cases.

Health data availability is relevant to the definition of the baseline BoDs in the study population. A good quality of these information in terms of standardized rates provided for the same period, the same area, and the same age groups is related to an adequate health baseline scenario.

3.3.2 Study period and scenarios

The study period is defined according to the availability of environmental and health data, and on the question we are raising. For example, if the request is related to an impact assessment of a new plant, the study period must cover the period before and after an activation of the plant.

Whenever possible, environmental and health data should be collected for the same period. The objective is to obtain data representative of the usual situations observed in the study area. A period of some consecutive years is therefore advisable to smooth year-to-year variations in pollutant concentrations and health outcomes, avoiding known anomalous years both from a weather-climatic point of view and unusual health events.

Several approaches can be used for assessing the health impact of air pollution (Künzli et al., 2008): the purpose of the assessment can influence the study setting and in particular the concept of alternative scenario.

In a predictive approach, we are interested in understanding the health of the population in a given time frame if we change pollutants levels. This approach assesses the difference in health outcomes between what will be observed in the future if pollutant levels remain the same and what will be observed if pollutant levels decrease (e.g., as the result of a given emission-control scenario) or increase (by adding an environmental pressure factor, such as a new industrial plant). Within this approach, we can include designs aimed to assess the future health impact of a given policy, which is the classical definition of a HIA (Mindell et al., 2003). On the other hand, this approach requires several assumptions between the two scenarios, as usually the time period is quite long, and this implies possible changes in several factors involved in the assessment, such as trends in population and health events, the time required to achieve the decrease of pollutant levels, the lag between the decrease in pollutant levels, and the occurrence of health benefits (Miller and Hurley, 2003). To consider these aspects, ad hoc tools are available, such as the IOMLIFET tool developed by the Institute of Occupational Health (Miller, 2008) or the AIRQ software developed for WHO.

A related but different approach is a classical counterfactual scenario where the aim is to assess the difference in health outcomes between what is currently observed and what could have been observed if air-pollutant concentrations had been lower and the benefits for health effects had been achieved for the different age groups. This approach gives an idea of the current burden of air pollution on health with the assumption that policies targeting reductions in pollutant levels could lead to a reduction in the assessed health burden. The approach is based on the epidemiological concept of the attributable fraction (AF), defined at the population level as the proportion of disease cases that can be attributed to a given exposure level (Steenland and Armstrong, 2006). This was the approach used in different projects (Medina et al., 2009) and is the theoretical basis of all in the global BoD projects managed by WHO (Cohen et al., 2017).

3.3.3 Exposure assessment

Exposure is defined as "an event that occurs when there is a contact at a boundary between a human and the environment at a specific contaminant concentration for a specified period of time" (National Research Council, 1991).

Thus it occurs when a person and an agent (contaminant) are in the same (micro)environment at the same time. The quantification of exposure includes the concentration of the contaminant and the duration of the contact.

Exposure processes range between ingestion of contaminants (in groundwater, surface water, soil, and food), inhalation of contaminants in air (dust, vapor, gases), dermal contact with contaminants in water, soil, air, food, and other media, external exposure to radiation. Exposure by inhalation is often the main route of exposure considered in health studies and risk assessment processes.

Exposure assessment is a process that investigates how, how much, and for how long a substance comes in contact with the individuals of a population.

Data on population exposure to air pollutants generally come from monitoring local or national institutions. This approach is often limited in capturing spatial heterogeneity of pollutant distribution.

Generally speaking, two approaches assess exposure to air pollutants: direct and indirect methods. Direct methods cover personal monitoring and biological markers; though precise, they generally apply to limited populations. Indirect methods are less precise but suitable for exposure assessment of large populations. Indirect methods range from questionnaire and diaries to environmental monitoring and modeling.

The application of modeling techniques for exposure assessment has long been suggested with the involvement of different types of expertise, including environmental modeling, monitoring, Geographic Information System (GIS), and statistics (World Health Organization, 2003).

A wide range of models have been applied in epidemiological studies to assess exposure at different spatial scale (Table 3.1).

Recent progress in combining these different models (satellite remote sensing, global chemical transport modeling, land use regression models, and high-resolution local dispersion models) together with existing ground-based monitoring has made information on key air pollutant indicators increasingly available. The Outdoor Air Pollution Expert Working Group of the Global Burden of Disease Project has provided useful indications on exposure assessment approaches for estimation of the global BoD attributable to outdoor air pollution. The authors reviewed recent developments in availability of environmental data and modeling approaches and how to use these information and determine the models necessary to calculate global population exposure to outdoor PM2.5 and O3 that represent the most interesting pollutants associated with health outcomes in GbD/HIA approaches.

At a more local level, the same philosophy is used with different and more accurate data, models, and methodologies. Approaches commonly used at a local level are dispersion models and land use regression models.

Table 3.1 Air pollution modeling approaches.

Type of model	Description	Application
Proximity models	Measurement of the distance between receptors (population) and the source of pollution	Used with any type of source, when a direct relationship is supposed
Spatial interpolation	Geostatistical models (i.e., inverse distance weighting, kriging) to reconstruct pollution values in areas not covered by measurements	Required an adequate number of distributed measurements
Land use regression	Statistical models on the relationship between the land use and characteristics and the pollutants concentrations in a specific point	Useful for differences within urban areas, they require ad hoc measurements campaigns
Dispersion models	Mathematical models that simulate processes of pollutant diffusion into the environment	Require detailed input information; reconstruct the spatiotemporal variation of pollutant due to specific sources
Remote sensing	Analyses of satellite images to estimate atmospheric pollution at ground level	Require a calibration with measured data. Information both on spatial and temporal level
Source apportionment	Statistical models to disentangle the contribution of each considered emission source to total pollution	Required detailed pollution measures and chemical profiles of each considered emission source

Dispersion models are deterministic models that simulate emission, transport, dispersion, and deposition of airborne pollutants while also considering their chemical reactions. They can be of different degrees of complexity depending on the sources they include, characteristics of the territory, source types, and meteorological conditions. They are usually used for point-sources of pollution, such as industries, incinerators.

In general, they require quantities of emitted pollutants, plant characteristics, structure of relevant meteorological parameters, characteristics of the territory.

Land-use regression models are statistical models aimed to predict pollutant concentrations in different spatial location by taking advantage of the spatial relationship between observations and land use characteristics (Briggs and Collins, 1997). They become a widely used methodology in air pollution epidemiology in the last decades. Land Use Regression (LUR) models can be at different levels of complexity and reliability depending on the data they include: road/traffic networks, population density, land cover, orography. In general, they need observed measurements of the modeled pollutant as inputs derived from two or three monitoring campaigns and geographic data on land use characteristics. LUR models have mainly been applied to pollution mapping and exposure assessment for modeling longer term average concentrations in urban areas (Hoek et al., 2008; Beelen et al., 2009).

Models represent an effective approach when the interest is aimed at grasping the spatial heterogeneity in the concentrations of the pollutants and therefore in the consequent different levels of exposure of the population. These approaches are used in the epidemiological literature to evaluate chronic effects related to long-term exposures.

In the event that you are interested in assessing the health impacts of short-term exposure (in the order of hours or days), the heterogeneity of pollutant concentrations is linked to temporal variations, that is, to the daily or hourly differences. In this case the historical series of the fixed measuring networks are usually used.

Another key aspect in defining the most appropriate environmental indicator is the availability of population data. In the case of overall population data over a municipal area, the availability of spatially resolved pollution concentration data within the urban area, as described before through the use of models, becomes of little use. In this case a single-exposure indicator is sufficient for the entire urban population, and this must be representative of the population's average exposure to air pollution. Therefore an appropriate knowledge of the measuring network in the city is crucial in the selection of the relevant monitoring stations.

Regarding the use of time-series from fixed monitoring sites, the indicator should be as close as possible to the one used in the epidemiological studies from which the exposure–response functions (ERFs) are derived. Since the objective is to obtain an indicator of the mean exposure to air pollution, the recommendation is to consider monitoring stations that represent background pollution (urban background monitors for PM10 and PM2.5, urban and suburban background monitors for ozone). Traffic and industrial monitors are not appropriate choices.

The exposure indicators are calculated by averaging the data measured by the different monitoring stations. The indicators should be calculated as close as possible to the indicators in the epidemiological studies from which the ERFs are derived. The main consideration is the comparability of the measurement techniques.

Measurement technique can be an issue for PM, as most epidemiological studies calculate the ERFs using concentrations measured with the gravimetric method. In case of another method, a correction is suggested.

Regarding temporal scale of these indicators, epidemiological evidence on particulate matter are available at daily scale, while for ozone, the daily maximum 8-hour average is solely used, as indicated in the WHO air quality guidelines (World Health Organization Regional Office for Europe, 2006).

3.3.4 Exposure–response functions

ERFs may be defined as the slope of a regression line with the health response as the dependent variable and the stressor as the independent variable.

The HIA relies on the assumption that the chosen ERF is linear at the population level and lies in the range of concentrations observed in the original studies.

The choice of a suitable ERF is a key point in the process of a HIA and directly affects the results of the assessment. Since several studies provide estimates of ERFs in the literature, the recommendation is to perform sensibility analyses to report how HIA findings vary when applying different ERFs.

ERFs should be chosen favoring meta-analyses of multicenter studies when available for their higher reliability. Alternative options are to develop an ad hoc systematic review and/or meta-analysis, or to query to a panel of experts.

Within the Global Burden of Disease Study an integrated exposure response (IER) function is used (Burnett et al., 2014). The IER combines the epidemiological evidence for outdoor air pollution, second-hand smoke, household air pollution, and active smoking to estimate the level of disease risk (e.g. stroke) at different levels of PM2.5 concentrations. The same mathematical relationship is used to estimate the risk of a specific disease from particulate matter originating from outdoor air pollution as that of second-hand smoke or household air pollution.

When the assessment is related to scenario comparison, the concentration—response functions applied the estimation of current exposure and the counterfactual (cut-off) values below which the health impact is not predicted, using linear or log-linear functions relating pollutants to natural (all causes of death excluding violent deaths and suicides) and cause-specific mortality or diseases.

In 2011 WHO enrolled a group of experts to review the evidence on the effects of air pollution on human health. The result of the work was a report updating knowledge and guidelines on the use of ERFs in HIA studies of exposure to atmospheric pollution.

The document "Health risks of air pollution in Europe — HRAPIE project recommendations for ERFs for cost—benefit analysis of particulate matter, ozone and nitrogen dioxide" (World Health Organization Regional Office for Europe, 2013) presents detailed tables with ERFs to be used, organized on the considered pollutant, the type of assessment (short-term and long-term effects), and the type of health outcome, specifying which age group the evidence of literature refers to and classifying the different ERFs according to the robustness of the assessment.

Most of the published studies used in the review of the scientific evidence on health effects from ambient air pollution comes mainly from studies conducted in urban areas located in Western Europe and North America. As a result, the applicability of these ERFs for assessments carried outside of these regions can be associated with additional uncertainties and should be considered with caution and involves expert judgment.

The question becomes more relevant when the focus of assessment is on a specific source, such as an industry or a new settlement, where the characteristics and composition of the released pollutants are probably different from urban air pollution.

If the study area has already been investigated with epidemiological studies, specific estimates of the exposure—response relation exist for that specific place. They present the advantages of specific estimates and the weakness of the power of the evidence, related to a single study.

In these situations a recommended solution could be the calculation of a weighted mean of the local value and the pooled estimate derived from literature (shrunken estimate). In this Bayesian approach, you use information of the pooled estimate and the local estimate, with a predefined set of weights applied to initial values (Le Tertre et al., 2005).

In the case of study on contaminated sites, as industrial or waste management settlements, it could be useful to define more appropriate ERF, related to study on the similar contexts.

In this sense the available literature or evidence is weaker, and HIA process has to underline this potential introduction of large uncertainties in the assessment.

Different reviews attempt to provide information in this sense. For example the SENTIERI project aimed at describing the health profile of populations living in national priority contaminated sites in Italy (Pirastu et al., 2010). The authors identified and classified contaminated sites within the whole country. The classification can be based on the sources of contamination documented in each contaminated site. A matrix of epidemiological a priori evidence about the strength of the causal association between each health outcome and source of environmental contamination was defined on the basis of literature review. This selection has to be accompanied by a choice of the best ERF that connects that type of exposure to that particular disease. Another Italian experiment focused attention on providing guidelines and methods for HIA of population exposed to pollution due to waste management plants (SESPIR Project— Epidemiological Surveillance of Health Status of Resident Population Around the Waste Treatment Plants) (Ranzi et al., 2014), assessing the impact on health of residents near incinerators, landfills, and mechanical biological treatment plants in five Italian regions. The assessment procedure took into account the available knowledge on health effects of waste disposal facilities. Within the project, suitable ERF to be used for exposure of population resident in proximity of different plants were provided.

3.3.5 The attributable cases

Different formulation of attributable cases calculation are available, with very slight differences.

A commonly used formula, applied also by WHO software for HIA (AIRQ +), is

$$AC = \gamma - \gamma_0 = \gamma - \gamma / e^{\beta * (x - V)}$$

where AC is the attributable cases, y is the annual observed deaths, β is the effect estimate $= \ln(RR)$, where RR is the relative risk for the given health outcome, y_0 is the baseline annual number of deaths (the expected number of events we would observe for $x = V$), x is the exposure, and V is the counterfactual (exposure threshold).

The effect of air pollution is assumed to be linear without any threshold on a logarithmic scale. We counted the events attributable to exposure levels (x) exceeding a given threshold (V).

Confidence interval of this calculated estimation take into account the uncertainty in the estimate β in the original study or meta-analysis. A comprehensive consideration of uncertainties should take into account other sources of uncertainty (exposure assessment, transfer from the context of the original study to the context of the city where the HIA is performed, etc.).

When assessing short-term impacts of air pollutants, baseline health-outcome data should be calculated using the same years as for air-pollution data. When assessing long-term impacts of air pollutants, baseline health outcome data can be estimated using all available years, implicitly considering that the estimated chronic exposure from the available years is representative of the cumulative average population exposure.

A valuable work on calculation of environmental BoD (EBD) (Hänninen et al., 2014) had the objective of developing a harmonized EBD methodology for different environmental stressors in several European countries. Three different methods were used to estimate the EBD, depending on the type of ERF estimate available for each exposure—outcome pair, either a relative risk (RR) based on environmental epidemiology, or a unit risk (UR) based on toxicological or occupational data (Box 3.1).

3.3.6 The metrics

Different health outcomes are considered in a complete IEHIA with varying degrees of severity. Usually, the more severe the disease, the less the proportion of population affected by the health outcome. The count of the different attributable cases would not allow a direct comparison of the numbers for the purposes of an overall assessment of the BoD of different scenarios.

For this reason, suitable metrics have been introduced to aggregate these different types of health impacts in a unique quantitative indicator,

> **BOX 3.1 Risk assessment approach**
> **Risk assessment approach**
> When considering polluted sites, in particular when the assessment procedure within authorization procedures, classical risk assessment approach has a relevance, related to the acceptability of estimation provided.
>
> The following formula are related to the risk assessment calculation for carcinogenic and noncarcinogenic substances.
>
> **Risk assessment for carcinogenic substances**
>
> $$R = C_{air} \times UR$$
>
> where UR is the additional risk of cancer throughout the lifespan (75 years) of a hypothetical population whose components are exposed continuously throughout life to a concentration of $1\ \mu g/m^3$ of the substance; C_{air} is the atmospheric concentration of the contaminant to which the population is exposed.
>
> **Risk assessment for noncarcinogenic substances**
>
> $$HQ = ADD/RfD_{inal}$$
>
> HQ is the hazard quotient expressing how much exposure to the substance exceeds the reference dose; ADD is the average daily dose in mg/kg/day; and RfD_{inal} is the inhalation reference dose that estimates the maximum amount of substance inhaled daily and throughout life without causing any appreciable risk to health.

with a view to guaranteeing the appropriate "weighing" of the various diseases (Box 3.2).

These estimated impacts can be used for further estimation of the monetary costs and benefits in a health benefits analysis.

3.4 Uncertainties

A risk assessment procedure aims to specify the potential consequences of a particular event or situation, calculate the probability of these occurring, and aggregate the consequences and probabilities into a single metric.

The intrinsic probabilistic nature of this approach involves a load of uncertainty, the nature, and distribution of which is often difficult to evaluate. The uncertainty of an assessment is related to a lack of knowledge about one or more components of the assessment.

BOX 3.2 Different metrics for IEHIA

Number of attributable cases (AC): The calculation of the number of deaths or cases of a specific disease expressed as a difference in the number of cases between the incidence/rate at the exposure measured over a specific period and that at baseline exposure, for example, difference between the studied situation compared to the reference scenario (zero exposure or a predefined threshold value).

Years of life lost (YLL). It measures the years of life lost as a result of premature death. Related to attributable cases (of death), YLL multiplies AC by the standard life expectancy at the age at which death occurs. More sophisticated versions of YLL take into account disability weights, time discounting, and age weights, which assign different values to the time lived at different ages (WHO Regional Office for Europe, 2014).

Years lost due to disability (YLD). It is a measure that reflects the number of years lost due to disability. It is calculated by multiplying the number of incident cases of a specific health outcome in a defined period by the average duration of the case until remission or death (years); this value is then weighted by a coefficient that reflects the severity of the disease [0 (health) to 1 (dead)].

Disability-adjusted life years (DALYs). This measure takes into account both YLL and YLD and sum them. It is useful when considering a burden of disease of a specific population exposed to a risk factor that involves both deaths and different diseases. One DALY represents one lost year of healthy life. The sum of DALYs across a population represents a measurement of the gap between actual health status and an hypothetical scenario in which the whole population lives to an advanced age in a status of perfect health.

Study protocols should include methods to assess the distribution of error in exposure estimates with respect to the study hypothesis and objectives, usually through validity, reliability, or calibration substudies.

Components of uncertainties are related to structural uncertainty (uncertainty on model assumptions, exposure assessment, definition of health outcomes), uncertainty related to parameters (precision of effects estimates), and another part related to intrinsic variability (population variability, individual variability). Uncertainty in HIA is usually quantified by probabilistic methods.

Experts cannot always express the uncertainty on their results in statistical terms; when it is only possible for them to identify that scientific knowledge is limited in a given area, the potential for surprise is therefore large, and it is related to the severity of the uncertainty from the viewpoint of the decision maker.

References

Beelen, R., et al., 2009. Mapping of background air pollution at a fine spatial scale across the Eur. Union. Sci. Total Environ. 407, 1852–1867.

Briggs, D.J., 2008. A framework for integrated environmental health impact assessment of systemic risks. Environ. Health 7, 61.

Briggs, D., Collins, S., 1997. Mapping urban air pollution using GIS: a regression-based approach. Int. J. Geogr. Inf. Sci. 11, 699–718.

Burnett, R.T., et al., 2014. An integrated risk function for estimating the global burden of disease attributable to ambient fine particulate matter exposure. Environ. Health Perspect. 122 (4), 397–403.

Cohen, A.J., et al., 2017. Estimates and 25-year trends of the global burden of disease attributable to ambient air pollution: an analysis of data from the Global Burden of Diseases Study 2015. Lancet 389 (10082), 1907–1918.

GBD 2015 Risk Factors Collaborators, 2015. Global, regional, and national comparative risk assessment of 79 behavioral, environmental and occupational, and metabolic risks or clusters of risks, 1990–2015: a systematic analysis for the Global Burden of Disease Study 2015. Lancet 388 (10053), 1659–1724. Oct 8.

Hänninen, O., et al., 2014. Environmental burden of disease in Europe: assessing nine risk factors in six countries. Environ. Health Perspect. 122 (5), 439–446.

Hoek, G., et al., 2008. A review of land-use regression models to assess spatial variation of outdoor air pollution. Atmos. Environ. 42, 7561–7578.

Künzli, N., Perez, L., 2008. Health risk assessment. In: Baker, D., Nieuwenhuijsen, M.J. (Eds.), Environmental epidemiology. Study methods and applications. Oxford University Press, Oxford, pp. 319–348.

Landrigan, P.J., et al., 2018. The Lancet Commission on pollution and health. Lancet 391 (10119), 462–512. Feb 3.

Le Tertre, A., et al., 2005. Empirical Bayes and adjusted estimates approach to estimating the relation of mortality to exposure of PM(10). Risk Anal. 25 (3), 711–718.

Medina, S., et al., 2009. The Apheis project: air pollution and health—a European information system. Air Qual. Atmos Health 2 (4), 185–198. Dec.

Miller, B., 2008. IOMLIFET version 2008. Spreadsheets for Life-Table Calculations. Institute of Occupational Medicine, Edinburgh.

Miller, B.G., Hurley, J.F., 2003. Life table methods for quantitative impact assessments in chronic mortality. J. Epidemiol. Community Health 57, 200–206.

Mindell, J., et al., 2003. A glossary for health impact assessment. J. Epidemiol. Community Health 2003 (57), 647–651.

National Research Council, 1991. Human exposure assessment for airborne pollutants. Advances and Opportunities. National Academy Press, Washington, DC.

Pascal, M., et al., 2013. Assessing the public health impact of urban air pollution in 25 European cities: results of the Aphekom project. Sci. Total Environ. 449, 390–400.

Pirastu, R., et al., 2010. SENTIERI Project Mortality study of residents in Italian polluted sites: evaluation of the epidemiological evidence. Epidemiol. Prev. 34 (5–6), suppl. 3 [Italian].

Ranzi, A., et al., 2014. Health impact assessment of policies for municipal solid waste management: findings of the SESPIR Project. Epidemiol. Prev. 38 (5), 313–322 [Italian].

Savitz, D.A., 2016. Response to environmental pollution: more research may not be needed. Epidemiology 27 (6), 919–920.

Steenland, K., Armstrong, B., 2006. An overview of methods for calculating the burden of disease due to specific risk factors. Epidemiology 17 (5), 512–519. Sep.

WHO Regional Office for Europe, 2014. WHO Expert Meeting. Methods and Tools for Assessing the Health Risks of Air Pollution at Local, National and International Level.

Copenhagen   <http://www.euro.who.int/__data/assets/pdf_file/0010/263629/WHO-Expert-Meeting-Methods-andtools-for-assessing-the-health-risks-of-air-pollution-at-local-national-and-international-level.pdf?ua = 1>.

World Health Organization Regional Office for Europe, 2016. Health Risk Assessment of Air Pollution. General Principles <http://www.euro.who.int/en/publications/abstracts/health-risk-assessment-of-air-pollution.-general-principles-2016>.

World Health Organization, 2003. Exposure assessment in studies on chronic effects of log-term exposure to air pollution. In: Report on a WHO/HEI Workshop, Bonn Germany, 4−5 February 2002. <https://apps.who.int/iris/bitstream/handle/10665/107472/E78992.pdf?sequence = 1&isAllowed = y>.

World Health Organization Regional Office for Europe, 2006. Air Quality Guidelines. Global Update 2005. Particulate Matter, Ozone, Nitrogen Dioxide and Sulfur Dioxide. Copenhagen. <http://www.euro.who.int/Document/E90038.pdf>.

World Health Organization Regional Office for Europe, 2013. Health Risks of Air Pollution in Europe − HRAPIE Project: Recommendations for Concentration − Response Functions for Cost-Benefit Analysis of Particulate Matter, Ozone and Nitrogen Dioxide.

Further reading

Ballester, F., et al., 2008. Reducing ambient levels of fine particulates could substantially improve health: a mortality impact assessment for 26 European cities. J. Epidemiol. Community Health 62 (2), 98−105. Feb.

Hoek, G., et al., 2018. A review of exposure assessment methods for epidemiological studies of health effects related to industrially contaminated sites. Epidemiol. Prev. 42 (5−6S1), 21−36. Sep-Dec.

Mindell, J., Joffe, M., 2003. Health impact assessment in relation to other forms of impact assessment. J. Public Health Med. 25 (2), 107−112. 2003 Jun.

World Health Organization Regional Office for Europe, 2012. Contaminated Sites and Health Report of Two WHO Workshops: Syracuse, Italy, 18 November 2011 Catania, Italy, 21−22 June 2012. <https://apps.who.int/iris/handle/10665/108623>.

CHAPTER 4

Monetary analysis of health outcomes

Verity Watson[1], Stéphane Luchini[2], Dean Regier[3] and Rainer Schulz[4]
[1]Health Economics Research Unit, University of Aberdeen, Aberdeen, United Kingdom
[2]Aix-Marseille Univ., CNRS, EHESS, Centrale Marseille, AMSE, Marseille, France
[3]Cancer Control Research, BC Cancer and School of Population and Public Health, University of British Columbia, Vancouver, Canada
[4]University of Aberdeen Business School, University of Aberdeen, Aberdeen, United Kingdom

Contents

4.1 Introduction

Environmental health interventions aim to improve people's health by reducing the amount of pollution to which people are exposed. People exposed to pollution face an increased risk of illness (morbidity) or death (mortality). In this chapter, we present an intuitive overview of the different methods that can be used to place a monetary value on the health impacts of environmental health interventions. Researchers can combine the different approaches to obtain a comprehensive value for the full range of health impacts that arise from a policy.

Cost-Benefit Analysis of Environmental Health Interventions
DOI: https://doi.org/10.1016/B978-0-12-812885-5.00004-4

73

In Section 4.2, we first explain the concepts from welfare economics that allow us to assign a monetary value to changes in individual utility. This section provides the background necessary to understand what researchers aim to value in cost—benefit analyses of environmental health interventions. We then describe how health impacts are measured in valuation studies. We categorize the valuation methods that researchers use into *stated preference methods*, which ask people their values for health impacts directly (Section 4.3) and *revealed preference methods*, which infer people's values from the choices they make in observable markets (Section 4.4). We summarize the steps of a typical study and discuss the strengths and weaknesses of both methods. In Section 4.5, we discuss the cost of illness method, which is widely applied to value health impacts, but is neither a stated nor a revealed preference method. The chapter ends with a range of methodological issues that apply to both stated and revealed preference methods.

4.2 Assigning a monetary value to a health change

When an environmental policy is introduced, individuals face a new situation in which some people will benefit, while others will lose out. For example, consider a congestion charge that is introduced to reduce city center air pollution. After the charge is introduced, there will be fewer vehicles in the city center, and the pollution caused by combustion engines will be reduced. This reduced pollution means that the health of people who live or work in the city center will be improved. However, the congestion charge will increase the transport costs for some people who drive in the city center and will incur administration costs for the authorities. Cost—benefit analysis aims to find out which situation (or state of the world) is better. By applying cost—benefit analysis to the previous example, we want to know whether society is better off in the original situation with higher air pollution and lower transportation costs or in the new situation with lower air pollution and higher transportation costs.

Cost—benefit analysis is based on the Kaldor—Hicks compensation test, which states that a policy should be introduced if those who benefit from the policy could, in principle, compensate those who lose out *and* still be better off than before (see, e.g., Boadway and Bruce, 1984). The Kaldor—Hicks compensation test requires information about two things: the amount of money the losers need to receive to leave them indifferent between the situations before and after the policy and the maximum amount of money the gainers can pay and still be indifferent between the two situations. It is important to note that in the Kaldor—Hicks compensation test the compensation is hypothetical and does not need to be paid.

The two commonly used money-metric measures are *compensating variation* and *equivalent variation*. Bockstael and McConnell (2007) present a comprehensive discussion of the economics of welfare measurement in Chapter 2 of their book. Compensating and equivalent variation measure the effect of price changes on individuals' utility. However, many environmental policies change the quantity or quality of an environmental good, for instance, air quality. In this case, *compensating surplus* and *equivalent surplus* are the appropriate money-metric measures (Freeman et al., 2014). Compensating surplus measures *the change in expenditure that would make the individual indifferent between the situation before the policy and the situation after the policy.* Equivalent surplus measures *the change in expenditure that would have an effect on individual's utility that is equivalent to the effect of the policy.* Compensating and equivalent surplus can be linked to individual's willingness to pay (WTP) for improvements or willingness to accept (WTA) compensation for deteriorations in the welfare that they face.

There are two types of health impacts that occur when environmental policies are introduced. Lower pollution levels may reduce the number of deaths (*mortality*). Lower pollution levels may also reduce the number of days or episodes of ill-health (*morbidity*). The methods used to value reduced mortality and reduced morbidity differ. The most common way in which reduced mortality is valued is through the value of a statistical life (VSL). This approach does not value reduced deaths. VSL aims to place a monetary value on small changes in mortality risk. The value placed on a small change in mortality risk is then scaled up to value a *statistical* life. Suppose we consider a reduction in the risk of death over the next year of 1 in 100,000 people. If we estimate that an individual is willing to pay €70 for this risk reduction, then the individual's value of a statistical life is €7 m (€70—€1/100,000).

While VSL values changes in mortality, often additional measures are needed to value morbidity. This is challenging because pollution can cause many different illnesses that can vary in severity and can occur at different time points after exposure to the pollution (Cameron, 2014). Morbidity caused by pollution can be either *acute*, meaning the sudden onset of mild or serious symptoms, or *chronic*, meaning a long-term health problem that requires ongoing medical care or self-management. For instance, air pollution can cause chronic conditions, such as asthma, and air pollution can trigger acute symptoms, such as asthma attacks. Similarly, water pollution can cause both acute, short-term gastrointestinal problems, and long-term health problems, such as cancer. Researchers value morbidity either by valuing a case of ill-health (usually short-term, acute illness, e.g., acute bronchitis or an asthma attack) or by valuing the reduction in the risk of a long-term chronic condition. Harrington and Portney (1987) and Alberini and Krupnick (2000) present a structural model of individuals' WTP for the health impacts of lower pollution. The model incorporates four ways in which pollution impacts on an individual's health: lost earnings due to health problems, medical costs of treating health problems, costs of avoiding pollution, and discomfort due to health problems.

4.3 Stated preference methods

Stated preference methods can be used to value the health impacts of environmental health interventions. Stated preference methods ask individuals to complete surveys that contain questions that ask about how much money an individual would be willing to pay for a health improvement. There are three main parts in a stated preference survey. The first part is an introduction that sets the scene, explains clearly the current situation and new policy, and motivates the valuation questions. The second part contains a set of valuation questions. The third part asks survey respondents about their sociodemographic characteristics. For an in-depth discussion of stated preference methods, see Champ et al. (2017) and Kanninen (2007), and for best-practice recommendations, see Johnston et al. (2017).

The data obtained from a stated preference survey is then used to estimate either the mean or median WTP (or WTA) of the sample. Researchers might also use the information collected in the third part of the survey to explore how WTP is affected by respondents' sociodemographic characteristics or other relevant characteristics, such as attitudes toward the environment or knowledge about air pollution.

The introduction of the survey describes the good being valued, in this case health impacts due to reduced pollution. This description must provide enough detail to enable respondents to understand what they are being asked to value and how this is different from the current situation. The description may include what causes the pollution, how the pollution affects health, how the pollution impacts on the environment, and how the pollution could be reduced. It is important that all respondents understand what the health impacts would mean for their daily life, so that, as far as possible, all respondents are valuing the same good. For instance, Alberini and Krupnick (2000) value an episode of acute respiratory illness for residents of Taiwan. In the survey, they ask respondents questions about their last episode of respiratory illness. These questions help respondents to imagine respiratory illness accurately in terms of symptoms, duration, severity, and use of health-care and medication. Afterward, Alberini and Krupnick (2000) ask respondents how much they are willing to pay to avoid a recurrence of this illness in the coming days.

Before respondents are asked the valuation questions, they should receive information about who will provide the good being valued, how it will be financed (*payment vehicle*), and how the survey responses can be used to make a decision about the policy (*the provision rule*). This information must be credible (Vossler and Watson, 2013). Several payment vehicles have been used in the literature and these include increased prices or utility bills in exchange for lower pollution, increased taxes on pollution, or a payment to a special charitable fund to reduce pollution. Usually the provision rule is the benefit cost criterion, that is, that the policy will be implemented if the value of the policy is larger than the cost. It is important that researchers *test* the acceptability of their provision rule before they undertake the main survey. Such tests can be done using qualitative methods, such as interviews or focus groups, verbal protocol analysis, or debriefing questions. There are two main stated preference methods that are used to value the health impacts of environmental health policies: *contingent valuation* (CV) and *choice experiments* (CEs). We will discuss each of these in turn in the following section.

4.3.1 Contingent valuation

The basic idea of a CV survey is to ask respondents how much they are willing to pay for a defined policy (Mitchell and Carson, 1989). However, respondents can find it difficult to answer questions about their WTP because they are never asked this in the real world. Researchers try to make CV surveys as easy as possible for respondents to answer. Typically, researchers ask respondents if they are willing to pay a specific monetary amount, or *bid*, $X, for the policy. This question format is referred to as *dichotomous choice contingent valuation* or *referendum* format. This format easier for respondents to answer, but it provides researchers with less information about respondents' WTP. Therefore to collect more information about WTP, researchers ask different respondents across the sample about different bids.

This referendum format has the advantage that respondents have the incentive to answer the question truthfully (Kling et al., 2012; Carson et al., 2014). For instance, consider a respondent who values the policy at $12.50 per year. In a CV survey, if this respondent is asked whether they are willing to pay $10 then the respondent should answer "yes." If the respondent lies and answers "no" it is possible that the policy is not be implemented even though the respondent would benefit from it. Similarly, if this respondent is asked if they are willing to pay $15 then the respondent should answer "no," otherwise the respondent risks that the policy is implemented even though the respondent will be asked to pay more than they are willing to. The referendum format leads to information about whether an individuals' WTP is higher or lower the bid presented in the survey. Hanemann (1984) details how such data can be analyzed and used to calculate the mean or median WTP for the sample. See Haab and McConnell (2002) for a thorough discussion of the analysis of CV data.

In a CV survey, respondents are asked their WTP for a defined policy. For instance, consider a policy that reduces air pollution. This can have several positive impacts on health and the environment. These impacts may include reduced risk of asthma or death from cancer, and the slow-down of global warming. But this policy may have a cost to people such as higher household electricity bills. In a CV survey in this situation, respondents could be asked how much they are willing to pay through higher electricity bills for the specified policy that could be described as a percentage point reduction in the risk of asthma and cancer and a speci-fied slowdown in global warming. A weakness of the CV survey is that it is not be possible to calculate respondents' WTP for each of the different outcomes of the policy separately. Policymakers might be interested to learn how the different outcomes are valued, because this information would allow them to design the optimal policy. If it were of interest to know the value of each outcome separately, a CV survey would need to ask one WTP question for each outcome.

4.3.2 Choice experiments

A CE survey allows the researcher to compare respondents' valuations of several possible policies simultaneously. CEs are based on the idea that people value the features of a good or service. In a CE the policy change and new situation are described by a set of features (or attributes) and costs of provision. This means that researchers do not ask respondents about their WTP directly, instead researchers ask respondents to choose the policy they prefer from a set of two or more policies available, each with slightly different features and costs. Respondents' choices are then used to infer WTP for each feature based on the trade-offs respondents make between the features and the cost (Small and Rosen, 1981).

In a CE survey, respondents are asked to make several choices between different sets of policies. The policy's features and the possible levels that these features can take will determine the total number of different policies that can be described. For most applied studies the number of policies that can be described is larger than the number that can reasonably be included in one survey. Researchers use statistical (or experimental) design theory to select a subset of policies in a way that allows the researcher to estimate a model of respondents' choices. For a detailed discussion of experimental design for CEs, see Johnson et al. (2013).

The researcher observes respondent choosing one policy in each choice that is included in the survey. These choices are analyzed using choice modeling methods within a random utility theory framework (McFadden, 1974; Manski, 1977). This assumes that, in each choice, respondents choose the policy that would provide them with the highest utility. Respondents know the utility of each policy, but not all factors that influence respondents' choices can be observed by the researcher. Thus the utility u that respondent i receives from policy j in a choice comprises a systematic component, v, which is observable because it is based on the CE features, and a random component, ε, which is unobservable. The assumptions that the researcher makes about ε lead to different choice models (Train, 2003; Hess and Daly, 2014). For instance, if a CE includes four features: risks of asthma and cancer, slowdown of global and cost, then V_j is the systematic component of utility for policy j:

$$V_j = \beta_{asthma} x_{asthma,j} + \beta_{cancer} x_{cancer,j} + \beta_{slow} x_{slow,j} + \beta_{cost} x_{cost,j} \qquad (4.1)$$

In CEs the systematic component is a linear additive function of the features. A choice model would be used to estimate the effect of a unit change of each health feature on respondents' utility, these are represented by β_{asthma}, β_{cancer}, β_{slow}, and β_{cost}, respectively. The researcher would use (4.1) to calculate the utility of policy j replacing $x_{asthma,j}$ with the percentage point reduction in the risk of asthma due to policy j and so on for each feature.

WTP can be calculated for different policies that can be described by these four features. If we assume that the current situation is described by V_0 and a new policy is described by V_1, then utilities of V_0 and V_1 can be calculated using (4.1). The WTP for this policy can be calculated as:

$$\text{WTP} = \frac{V_1 - V_0}{-\beta_{cost}} \qquad (4.2)$$

This calculates the WTP for a policy in which some, or all, of the features are different from the current situation. Researchers can also calculate the marginal rate of substitution between two features. This represents how much of one feature respondents are willing to give up to obtain more of another feature while holding the respondents' utility constant. When the marginal rate of substitution between one feature and the cost of provision is calculated this can be interpreted as respondents' *marginal* WTP for the feature. For instance, β_{asthma} represents the change in utility due to a 1 percentage point (pp) increase in risk of asthma. The marginal WTP (MWTP) for a 1 pp increase in risk of asthma is calculated as:

$$\text{marginal WTP} = \frac{\beta_{asthma}}{-\beta_{cost}} \qquad (4.3)$$

4.3.3 Strengths and weaknesses of stated preference methods

Stated preference methods are flexible and can be used to value health impacts that cannot be directly linked to individuals' behavior and therefore cannot be valued by revealed preference methods. Furthermore, stated preference methods can be used to value the nonhealth and nonuse benefits of reduced pollution (Krutilla, 1967; Arrow and Fisher, 1974).

However, stated preference methods also come with methodological challenges. Stated preference surveys ask *hypothetical* questions and may not measure respondents' WTP accurately and this would lead to *hypothetical bias* in the estimated WTP. Studies find that WTP estimated using stated preference methods differs from WTP estimated using observed behavior (List and Gallet, 2001; Little and Berrens, 2004; Murphy et al., 2005). Kochi et al. (2006) find that CV surveys produce lower estimates of VSL than those that are based on revealed preference hedonic methods using wage data. Murphy et al. (2005) and Kling et al. (2012) show that the magnitude of hypothetical bias depends on the survey design and the good being valued.

Studies also find that WTP elicited in stated preference studies is insensitive to the magnitude of the health impact being valued. The *scope effect* occurs when the WTP estimated for different health risk reduction is not proportional to the magnitude of the risk reduction. The *embedding effect* occurs when respondents' WTP is the same for a large set of health impacts and for a subset of these health impacts. One explanation for why a scope effect is found in WTP for health risk reductions is that respondents do not understand the risk reductions presented to them in the stated preference survey (Baron, 1997; Hammitt and Graham, 1999). The risk communication literature suggests that visual aids can improve respondents' understanding (Lipkus, 2007; Visschers et al., 2009). Corso et al. (2001) find risk is better understood and respondents' WTP is more sensitive to the magnitude of the risk change when risk is presented as a visual representation.

4.4 Revealed preference methods

4.4.1 Hedonic methods

While stated preference methods infer people's WTP for health impacts using survey questions, revealed preference methods infer WTP indirectly by using observations from situations in which people are exposed to different health impacts or risks through their jobs or the location they live. For instance, workers in some occupations (such as offshore oil workers) face higher health risks than others and we would expect that workers in these jobs "trade off wealth or income against the risk of death or injury" (Jones-Lee, 1994, p. 306). All else equal, workers who face a higher risk should be compensated for this and earn higher wages. If we observe wages for jobs with different risk profiles and we can control for other factors that might impact on wages, then it might be possible to extract the WTA for risk exposure from wage data. Similarly, prices of houses next to a polluting road or hazardous waste site should be, all else equal, lower than similar houses located beside a quiet lake. If we observe house prices and all other characteristics that might affect house prices, then we might be able to estimate the compensation that households require if exposed to sources of hazard. If a source of hazard can be converted into units of mortality risk, then such estimates could also be used to compute the VSL.

While intuitively appealing, it is necessary that we know whether wage premia (house price discounts) are linked with worker's (household's) preferences. The seminal paper of Rosen (1974) provides the theory that explains how heterogeneous goods such as jobs or houses are priced in competitive equilibrium. In the labor market, for instance, firms offer jobs with different characteristics x and workers match themselves to these jobs. This leads, in equilibrium, to a hedonic price function $p(x)$ that gives the wage (price of labor) that must be paid to attract a worker to the job. Given two jobs that differ in the risk of a fatal accident, but are otherwise equal, we expect that the riskier job must pay workers a higher wage to keep them indifferent between the jobs. Rosen's paper is important, because it clarifies the link between $p(x)$ and preferences. Applied to the job example, the paper shows that $\partial p(x)/\partial x_{risk}$ corresponds to the marginal WTA higher wages for a marginal increase of risk on the job by the worker holding it. Rosen's paper thus "outlines a method for estimating [. . .] individuals' willingness to pay for goods and services for which there are not explicit markets" (Greenstone, 2017, p. 1891). Since then, further research has shown that the link is clear, but that empirical applications must deal with several potential problems. We present two simple examples and use them to discuss some of these problems.

Let us assume that we observe a cross-sectional random sample of annual wages w_n of $n = 1 \ldots N$ workers. For each worker, we observe the exposure to risk, measured as the risk r_n of death on the job per 10,000 workers. For instance, the risk could be exposure to radiation and some workers in our sample could work in nuclear power plants or in radiology departments of hospitals. It is important that the risk variable varies for workers in our sample and we assume that some hold safer jobs than others. In this situation, we expect that workers will trade off higher risk for higher pay. To be specific, we observe for each job a set of characteristics collected in the column vector x_n. We also assume that the equilibrium hedonic price function is log linear:

$$\ln w_n = \alpha + \theta r_n + x_n \beta \qquad (4.4)$$

The coefficients θ and β are called the *implicit* characteristics prices. The coefficients α, θ and the coefficients in the vector β are unknown and need to be estimated. To do so, we use our data and add the error term ϵ_n to the right-hand side of (4.4). The error term considers unsystematic effects that may impact on the wage that is paid in a job. On average, we expect that the wage of a job is explained by the hedonic price function. The regression specification can be estimated with ordinary least squares. Our main interest lies in θ, which gives the marginal compensation a worker will require if the risk of the job increases by a small unit. As this coefficient translates a unit of risk into a monetary term, we will call this the implicit price *risk premium*. We obtain the average marginal WTA extra risk overall jobs (workers) in our sample from (4.4) as:

$$\frac{1}{N}\sum\nolimits_{n=1}^{N} \frac{\partial w_n}{\partial r_n} = \frac{1}{N}\sum\nolimits_{n=1}^{N} \frac{\partial \ln w_n}{\partial r_n} w_n = \theta \overline{w} \qquad (4.5)$$

Assume that the estimate of the risk premium θ from the regression is 0.02 and that the average yearly wage $\overline{w}$ is £30,000. The risk measure is expressed in deaths per 10,000 people, so that we estimate

$$\text{VSL} = 0.02 \times £30,000 \times 10,000 = £6,000,000 \qquad (4.6)$$

Given estimates of the standard error of our estimator for θ, we can also construct an interval estimator for the VSL that takes estimation uncertainty into account. This uncertainty results from the unsystematic effects on the wage and is represented by the noise term in the regression equation, see Wooldridge (2013, Chapter 4) for a detailed discussion.

Instead of wages and jobs, house prices can also be used to estimate the marginal WTA. Assume a locality close to a nuclear power plant or a nuclear waste facility. All else equal, we would expect that prices of houses in the locality are lower than in localities further away from a source of radiation risk. Given data on house transactions, which include the transaction price, house characteristics and the risk variable r_n for each transacted house n, we assume a function hedonic function like (4.4). The house price replaces the wage rate and $\mathbf{x}_n$ collects characteristics of the house, such as its size, age, and location. All these variables that are likely to have an impact on the price. Assume that we estimate a risk premium θ of 0.003 and that the average house price in the sample is £250,000, then we estimate

$$\text{VSL} = 0.003 \times £250,000 \times 10,000 = £7,500,000 \qquad (4.7)$$

This estimate of VSL differs from the one we have obtained in (4.6) from the wage regressions. Two comments are in order. First, while the point estimates differ, there might be no significant difference once we take estimation uncertainty into account. Such a test will be straightforward whenever the observations are not related but will become more complicated once houses come from the same area where most of the workers live that are in our wage sample. Second, the expected time horizon of exposure to the risk of radiation might be different. A worker will be no longer exposed to the risk once she retires from the job, whereas a home owner in an affected area will be exposed even after retirement. The duration of exposure would then also influence the risk premium estimate.

While it appears that the hedonic approach is based on hard (revealed) evidence on the WTA health risks, there are several aspects that must be considered. First, the hedonic function and its interpretation only hold if there is perfect competition and transaction costs can be ignored. In the absence of these conditions the interpretation of estimated coefficients as implicit prices is limited. For instance, if it is costly for households to move between areas, then estimated implicit prices are no longer truly marginal. Second, if workers base their risk premium on the *perceived* risk of a job and this differs from the actual risk r_n, then this introduces measurement error into the regression and the estimator for the risk premium θ will be biased. Third, even if a market works under conditions for the coefficients to be interpreted as implicit prices, it is possible that the econometrician specifies the function incorrectly. For instance, assume the true hedonic function is the one from (4.4), but the econometrician regresses the wage instead of the log wage on a linear function of characteristics. The estimator for the risk premium will then be biased. Bias will also pose a problem if the econometrician uses the correct function in principle, but some relevant variables are omitted from the model, either because the econometrician was not aware of their importance or because observations were not available (Cropper et al., 1988; Kuminoff et al., 2010). Fourth, workers might have sorted themselves into the riskier jobs, because they are less risk averse. This does not imply that their average MWTP will be estimated incorrectly if no variables are omitted and the hedonic price function is specified correctly. It will be, however, only the MWTP of a subset of the population.

4.4.1.1 Example of an empirical application

Davis (2004) estimates the MWTP for an increase in the risk for a type of pediatric cancer from house price data. Davis exploits that the incidence for this type of cancer increased in a county in Nevada over several years to a level far above what one should expect. An unaffected neighboring county is used as a nontreated control group. In one regression specification, Davis uses only repeat sales of a set of houses. This controls for unobserved house characteristics (the unobserved characteristics of the same houses will remain unchanged). As the increase in cancer incidence was not anticipated, "there is no reason to expect sorting of households according to preferences prior to the increase" (Davis, 2004, p. 1693). Davis computes a VSL for this type of cancer of about $5 m, one "of the first market-based estimates of the value of health for children" (p. 1703). This is important, as wage-based regressions cannot be used to value mortality risk reductions for nonworking age individuals, see discussion in Section 4.8.

4.4.2 Averting behavior

When faced with environmental pollution, people can change their behavior to avoid exposure or reduce their exposure. This *averting behavior* allows individuals to minimize the health impacts of exposure. Examples of averting behavior include staying indoors or using air purifiers to reduce air pollution exposure and changing drinking water sources, buying bottled water or installing a filtration system to avoid water pollution exposure. Averting behavior may incur costs for individuals and a rational individual should only take averting behavior when the benefits of doing so exceed the costs. The costs to individuals of their averting behavior can be used as their WTP to avoid health impacts (Dickie, 2017).

Three factors complicate the use of averting behavior to estimate WTP to avoid health impacts, however. First, the cost of averting behavior can be difficult to observe accurately. For instance, it is difficult to observe the time people spend on taking averting behavior. It is also difficult to assess the exact time value for everyone in a population. Second, averting behavior may produce additional effects that can either positively or negatively affect individuals' utility. For instance, if someone chooses to go to the cinema while staying indoors to avoid air pollution, they not only incur the cost of the cinema but also experience the positive effect of an enjoyable film. Conversely, if a nature lover goes to the gym to exercise instead of running in the park, they incur the cost of gym entry and the additional cost of not being in nature. If the additional effect is negative, then averting behavior estimates do not include all costs and will underestimate individuals' WTP to avoid health impacts. Conversely, if the additional effect is positive, then averting behavior measures will overestimate individuals' WTP. Third, averting behavior implies that individuals change their behavior to reduce their exposure to pollution. These behavior changes can distort estimates from epidemiological models that link pollution exposure to health risks. For instance, an individual who takes averting behavior is exposed to less pollution than is assumed in the epidemiological model. This can lead epidemiological studies to underestimate the true impact of pollution exposure on health. This impacts on the accuracy of averting behavior measures by underestimating the health impact that people are taking averting behavior to avoid (Dickie, 2017).

4.5 Cost of illness method

Death and illness impose an economic burden on individuals and society. The cost of illness method aims to measure the direct and indirect financial costs of death and illness. This method is also referred to as the *human capital approach*. The financial costs are separated into direct and indirect costs (Pervin et al., 2008). Direct costs can be further separated into direct costs of health-care use such as ambulance, medical, hospital, and health-care professional costs and direct costs not related to health-care use such as informal and social care costs (Pervin et al., 2008; Pimpin et al., 2018). Indirect costs are those not related to care and include the present value of an individual's forgone lifetime earnings and productivity losses to firms.

A cost of illness study can either focus on the health-care system or the individual. Studies that focus on the health-care system use the average cost of treating an illness within a given health-care system to calculate population-based costs of different diseases and health conditions (Heijink et al., 2006; Pimpin et al., 2018). An epidemiological model of how pollution affects disease incidence is used to calculate the health-care system costs that are due to pollution exposure (see Chapter 3: Health impact assessment: quantifying the health benefits and costs). For instance, Pimpin et al. (2018) estimate the cost of illness due to air pollution in the United Kingdom using data from the National Health Service (costs of primary care, prescriptions, and secondary care) and publicly provided social care. Studies that focus on the individual measure the exposure to pollution first and then use surveys to assess the individual's experience of symptoms and the individuals' use of health-care resources (Alberini and Krupnick, 2000).

Cost of illness is neither a stated nor revealed preference method. The cost of illness method provides a conservative estimate cost of pollution to the health-care system, individual or both. The estimate is conservative because it neither accounts for averting behavior, the disutility of illness for those affected, nor the intangible effects of being alive (Harrington and Portney, 1987; Alberini and Krupnick, 2000). The cost of illness method cannot be used to compare different environmental policies. A policy will reduce the risk or incidence of an illness but typically will not eradicate the illness. The method suffers from a de facto bias because cost of illness studies allocate the current health-care costs to a typical case of illness based on the current situation, but it do not provide the information about how health-care costs will change if the incidence of illness changes (Shiell et al., 1987). Furthermore, cost of illness studies equate the value of avoiding an illness with how much it costs the health-care system to treat that illness. Health-care system costs will be lower in countries with more efficient health-care systems, but this does not mean people in these countries place a lower value on avoiding illness. Cost of illness studies report substantial variation in estimated health-care system costs for the same illnesses (Bloom et al., 2001).

4.6 Benefits transfer

Stated preference and revealed preference studies are needed but are expensive to undertake. Robinson and Hammitt (2015) find that by 2015 there were approximately 200 studies that estimate a VSL in a diverse set of countries and contexts. It would save research resources if existing studies could be used to value new policies rather than paying for a new research study for each new policy that is proposed. Despite the overall high number of existing studies, it seems unlikely that researchers or policymakers will find a single study that matches *exactly* the policy and population they want to examine (Robinson and Hammitt, 2015). *Benefit transfer* has been proposed as a solution. This method takes values from existing studies and assesses (after adjustments) a new policy (Johnston et al., 2015; Navrud, 2017; Robinson et al., 2019).

While intuitively appealing, studies that compared transferred values with the results of new studies find *transfer error*. There have been several proposals to address transfer error. First, researchers can *adjust* the transferred value to take into account that the transferred values are several years old or were measured in a different currency. Second, researchers can use meta regression methods to pool transferred values from a range of studies and, in doing so, compensate for the limitations of any one study (Rosenberger and Loomis, 2017). Metaregression assumes that there is a true WTP function that is represented imperfectly in each individual study, but which can be found by averaging over the results of all studies. Lindhjem et al. (2011) report in detail the steps that a meta regression takes to transfer estimates of VSL from stated preference studies to a new situation. Despite these efforts to improve the accuracy of benefit transfer studies values—it is unlikely that the results will be more accurate than a well-conducted primary stated preference or revealed preference study (Krupnick, 2004).

4.7 Household versus individual valuation

The welfare economic framework in Section 4.2 focuses on the WTP or WTA of individuals. In the applications of stated and revealed preference studies, it may be the household that is represented, however. It is important to know whether a study measures individual or household values because different total values will be calculated depending on whether the researcher aggregates over individuals or households to measure the total value of the health impact to society (Lindhjem and Navrud, 2009).

In a stated preference survey, it should be clear to respondents if they should answer from their own or their household's perspective. However, studies are not always explicit about the perspective respondents should take (Bateman and Munro, 2009; Lindhjem and Navrud, 2009) and respondents may not heed the survey instructions. Studies find differences in WTP elicited in stated preference surveys from an individual perspective and a household perspective (Bateman and Munro, 2009; Lindhjem and Navrud, 2009; Adamowicz et al., 2014).

In revealed preference studies, the perspective measured will depend on the method used. Hedonic regression studies of wage differentials measure individuals' trade-offs between their wage and their own risk. Hedonic regression studies of house prices measure households' trade-offs between the cost of their home and risks to the health of the entire family, or particular members of the family. For instance, in Davis (2004) the preferences of the caring parents were estimated. Averting behavior studies may measure individual or household valuations depending on the type of averting behavior taken and who benefits from this behavior. For instance, when a household installs an air purifier all members of the household will benefit.

4.8 The effect of age on health values

While stated preference studies and revealed preference data may have socioeconomic information on individuals, this is not always used for the estimation of WTP for health impacts. WTP estimates are therefore averages for the sample and it is not always clear what this average represents. An individual's age affects their life expectancy and therefore the length of life that is at risk. Theoretical models suggest that VSL should decrease with age if consumption is constant over the lifetime (Shepard and Zeckhauser, 1984). However, theoretical predictions become less clear if consumption varies over the lifetime because such consumption variations influence risk-money trade-offs (Johansson, 2002). Studies find that the VSL estimated using wage-risk trade-offs decreases with age (Viscusi and Aldy, 2003). However, when occupational wage-risk data allow for variations in risk across age-groups an inverted U-shaped relationship between VSL and age is found. This implies that VSL increases to a point and then falls.

Viscusi (2010) reviews the literature on heterogeneity in VSL estimates in both stated preference and revealed preference studies. Many VSL studies are based on hedonic wage-risk trade-offs and therefore calculate VSL for the subset of the population who are economically active. Stated preference studies have been used to test if the VSL differs across the population, and if people value reducing mortality risks for children and adults differently. Studies find that people are willing to pay more for risk reductions for small children than they are willing to pay for older children or adults (Viscusi, 2010). Similarly, studies have found people are willing to pay more to avoid illness for children compared to adults, and for young children compared to older children (Liu et al., 2000; Dickie and Messman, 2004; Prosser et al., 2005, 2011).

It is difficult to measure children's WTP for their own health using stated preference methods. It is not clear that children are able to complete a stated preference survey reliably (Prosser et al., 2007; Alberini et al., 2010). For instance, children may not be familiar with money and lack independent financial means. Many studies avoid these difficulties by asking adults to complete stated preference studies either by placing themselves into the child's perspective (proxy preferences) or by reporting the adults' own WTP for the child (Alberini and Ščasný, 2011). An exception is Guerriero et al. (2018) who measure children's own WTP to reduce the risk of an asthma attack. The children who took part in the study were aged between 7 and 19 years of age. Guerriero et al. (2018) found children were able to complete a CV question and their ability improved with age. Children's WTP reduced with their age and was less than the WTP of their parents.

4.9 Summary

In this chapter, we have summarized the methods that are used to measure WTP or WTA for changes in health impacts that arise from environmental health interventions. We presented a brief overview of welfare economics to motivate what researchers aim to value in cost–benefit analyses. We briefly summarize the steps taken in both stated preference and revealed preference methods and discuss the strengths and weaknesses of both methods. Throughout the chapter we refer the reader to sources of more detailed information. We explained the cost of illness method and why this is neither a stated nor a revealed preference method. We have summarized some methodological issues that should be considered when valuing health impacts. This is not an exhaustive list of methodological considerations.

References

Adamowicz, W., Dickie, M., Gerking, S., Veronesi, M., Zinner, D., 2014. Household decision making and valuation of environmental health risks to parents and their children. J. Assoc. Environ. Resour. Economists 1, 481−519.

Alberini, A., Krupnick, A., 2000. Cost-of-illness and willingness-to-pay estimates of the benefits of improved air quality: evidence from Taiwan. Land Econ. 76, 37−53.

Alberini, A., Ščasný, M., 2011. Context and the VSL: evidence from a stated preference study in Italy and the Czech Republic. Environ. Resour. Econ. 49, 511−538.

Alberini, A., Bateman, I., Loomes, G., Ščasný, M., 2010. Valuation of Environment-Related Health Risks for Children. OECD, Paris.

Arrow, K., Fisher, A., 1974. Environmental preservation, uncertainty and irreversibility. Q. J. Econ. 88, 312−319.

Baron, J., 1997. Confusion of relative and absolute risk in valuation. J. Risk Uncertain. 14, 301−309.

Bateman, I.J., Munro, A., 2009. Household versus individual valuation: what's the difference? Environ. Resour. Econ. 43, 119−135.

Bloom, B.S., Bruno, D.J., Maman, D.Y., Jayadevappa, R., 2001. Usefulness of US cost of illness studies in healthcare decision making. Pharmacoeconomics 19, 207−213.

Boadway, R., Bruce, N., 1984. Welfare Economics. Blackwell.

Bockstael, N., McConnell, K., 2007. Environmental and Resource Valuation With Revealed Preferences: A Theoretical Guide to Empirical Methods. Springer, Amsterdam.

Cameron, T.A., 2014. Valuing morbidity in environmental benefit-cost analysis. Annu. Rev. Resour. Econ. 6, 249−272.

Carson, R.T., Groves, T., List, J.A., 2014. Consequentiality: a theoretical and experimental exploration of a single binary choice. J. Assoc. Environ. Resour. Economists 1, 171−207.

Champ, P., Boyle, K., Brown, T., 2017. A Primer on Non-Market Valuation, second ed. Springer, Amsterdam.

Corso, P.S., Hammitt, J.K., Graham, J.D., 2001. Valuing mortality-risk reduction: using visual aids to improve the validity of contingent valuation. J. Risk Uncertain. 23, 165−184.

Cropper, M.L., Deck, L.B., McConnell, K.E., 1988. On the choice of functional form for hedonic price functions. Rev. Econ. Stat. 70, 668−675.

Davis, L.W., 2004. The effect of health risk on housing values: evidence from a cancer cluster. Am. Economic Rev. 94, 1693−1704.

Dickie, M., 2017. Defensive behavior and damage cost methods. In: second ed. Champ, P., Boyle, K., Brown, T. (Eds.), A Primer on Non-Market Valuation, 2017. Springer, Amsterdam.

Dickie, M., Messman, V.L., 2004. Parental altruism and the value of avoiding acute illness: are kids worth more than parents? J. Environ. Econ. Manage. 48, 1146−1174.

Freeman, A.M., Herriges, J., Kling, C., 2014. The Measurement of Environmental and Resource Values, third ed. Routledge.

Greenstone, M., 2017. The continuing impact of Sherwin Rosen's "Hedonic prices and implicit markets: product differentiation in pure competition". J. Polit. Econ. 125, 1891−1902.

Guerriero, C., Cairns, J., Bianchi, F., Cori, L., 2018. Are children rational decision makers when they are asked to value their own health? A contingent valuation study conducted with children and parents. Health Econ. 27, e55−e68.

Haab, T., McConnell, K., 2002. Valuing Environmental and Natural Resources: The Econometrics of Non-Market Valuation. Edward Elgar.

Hammitt, J.K., Graham, J.D., 1999. Willingness to pay for health protection: inadequate sensitivity to probability? J. Risk Uncertain. 18, 33−62.

Hanemann, W.M., 1984. Welfare evaluations in contingent valuation experiments with discrete responses. Am. J. Agric. Econ. 66, 332−341.

Harrington, W., Portney, P., 1987. Valuing the benefits of health and safety regulation. J. Urban Econ. 22, 101−112.

Heijink, R., Koopmanschap, M., Polder, J., 2006. Cost-of-Illness Studies: An International Comparison. Report, Erasmus MC.

Hess, S., Daly, A., 2014. Handbook of Choice Modelling. Edward Elgar.

Johansson, P.-O., 2002. On the definition and age dependency of the value of a statistical life. J. Risk Uncertain. 25, 251−263.

Johnson, F.R., Lancsar, E., Marshall, D., Kilambi, V., Mühlbacher, A., Regier, D.A., et al., 2013. Constructing experimental designs for discrete-choice experiments: report of the ISPOR conjoint analysis experimental design good research practices task force. Value Health 16, 3−13.

Johnston, R., Rolfe, J., Rosenberger, R., Brouwer, R., 2015. Benefit Transfer of Environmental and Resource Values. Springer, Amsterdam.

Johnston, R., Boyle, K., Adamowicz, W., Bennett, J., Brouwer, R., Cameron, T., et al., 2017. Contemporary guidance for stated preference studies. J. Assoc. Environ. Resour. Econ. 4, 319−405.

Jones-Lee, M.W., 1994. Safety and the saving of life. The economics of safety and physical risk. In: Layard, R., Glaister, S. (Eds.), Cost-Benefit Analysis. Cambridge University Press, Cambridge.

Kanninen, B., 2007. Valuing Environmental Amenities Using Stated Choice Studies: A Common Sense Approach to Theory and Practice. Springer, Amsterdam.

Kling, C.L., Phaneuf, D.J., Zhao, J., 2012. From Exxon to BP: has some number become better than no number? J. Econ. Perspect. 26, 3—26.

Kochi, I., Hubbell, B., Kramer, R.A., 2006. An empirical bayes approach to combining and comparing estimates of the value of a statistical life for environmental policy analysis. Environ. Resour. Econ. 34, 385—406.

Krupnick, A.J., 2004. Valuing health outcomes: policy choices and technical issues. In: RFF Report.

Krutilla, J., 1967. Conservation reconsidered. Am. Econ. Rev. 57, 777—789.

Kuminoff, N.V., Parmeter, C.F., Pope, J.C., 2010. Which hedonic models can we trust to recover the marginal willingness to pay for environmental amenities? J. Environ. Econ. Manage. 60, 145—160.

Lindhjem, H., Navrud, S., 2009. Asking for individual or household willingness to pay for environmental goods? Implications for aggregate welfare measures. Environ. Resour. Econ. 43, 11—29.

Lindhjem, H., Navrud, S., Braathen, N., Biausque, V., 2011. Valuing mortality risk reductions from environmental, transport and health policies: a global meta-analysis of stated preference studies. Risk Anal. 31, 1381—1407.

Lipkus, I.M., 2007. Numeric, verbal, and visual formats of conveying health risks: suggested best practices and future recommendations. Med. Decis. Mak. 27 (5), 696—713.

List, J., Gallet, C., 2001. What experimental protocol influences disparities between actual and hypothetical state values? Environ. Resour. Econ. 20, 241—254.

Little, J., Berrens, R., 2004. Explaining disparities between actual and hypothetical stated values: further investigation using meta-analysis. Econ. Bull. 3, 1—13.

Liu, J.T., Hammitt, J.K., Wang, J.D., Liu, J.L., 2000. Mother's willingness to pay for her own and her child's health: a contingent valuation study in Taiwan. Health Econ. 9, 319—326.

Manski, C.F., 1977. The structure of random utility models. Theory Decis. 8, 229—254.

McFadden, D., 1974. Conditional logit analysis of qualitative choice behavior. In: Frontiers in Econometrics, pp. 105—142.

Mitchell, R.C., Carson, R.T., 1989. Using Surveys to Value Public Goods: The Contingent Valuation Method. RFF.

Murphy, J., Allen, P., Stevens, T., Weatherhead, D., 2005. A meta-analysis of hypothetical bias in stated preference valuation. Environ. Resour. Econ. 30, 313—325.

Navrud, S., 2017. Possibilities and challenges in transfer and generalisation of monetary estimates for environmental and health benefits of regulating chemicals. OECD Environment Working Papers, No. 119. OECD Publishing, Paris.

Pervin, T., Gerdtham, U.-G., Hampus Lyttkens, C., 2008. Societal costs of air pollution-related health hazards: a review of methods and results. Cost Effectiveness Resour. Allocat. 6, 19.

Pimpin, L., Retat, L., Fecht, D., de Preux, L., Sassi, F., Gulliver, J., et al., 2018. Estimating the costs of air pollution to the national health service and social care: an assessment and forecast up to 2035. PLoS Med. 15 (7), e1002602.

Prosser, L.A., Bridges, C.B., Uyeki, T.M., Rêgo, V.H., Ray, G.T., Meltzer, M.I., et al., 2005. Values for preventing influenza-related morbidity and vaccine adverse events in children. Health Qual. Life Outcomes 3, 18.

Prosser, L.A., Hammitt, J.K., Keren, R., 2007. Measuring health preferences for use in cost-utility and cost-benefit analyses of interventions in children. Pharmacoeconomics 25, 713—726.

Prosser, L.A., Payne, K., Rusinak, D., Shi, P., Uyeki, T., Messonnier, M., 2011. Valuing health across the lifespan: health state preferences for seasonal influenza illnesses in patients of different ages. Value Health 14, 135—143.

Robinson, L.A., Hammitt, J.K., 2015. Research synthesis and the value per statistical life. Risk Anal. 35, 1086—1100.

Robinson, L., Hammitt, J., O'Keeffe, L., 2019. Valuing mortality risk reductions in global benefit-cost analysis. J. Benefit-Cost Anal. 10, 15—50.

Rosen, S., 1974. Hedonic prices and implicit markets: product differentiation in pure competition. J. Political Economy 82, 34—55.

Rosenberger, R., Loomis, J., 2017. Benefit transfer. In: second ed. Champ, P., Boyle, K., Brown, T. (Eds.), A Primer on Non-Market Valuation, 2017. Springer, Amsterdam.

Shepard, D., Zeckhauser, R., 1984. Survival versus consumption. Manage. Sci. 30, 423—439.

Shiell, A., Gerard, K., Donaldson, C., 1987. Cost of illness studies: an aid to decision-making? Health Policy 8, 317—323.

Small, K., Rosen, H., 1981. Applied welfare economics with discrete choice models. Econometrica 49, 105—130.

Train, K., 2003. Discrete Choice Methods With Simulation. Cambridge University Press, Cambridge.

Viscusi, W.K., 2010. The heterogeneity in the value of a statistical life: Introduction and overview. J. Risk Uncertain. 40, 1—13.

Viscusi, W.K., Aldy, J.E., 2003. The value of a statistical life: a critical review of market estimates throughout the world. J. Risk Uncertain. 27, 5—76.

Visschers, V.H., Meertens, R.M., Passchier, W.W., De Vries, N.N., 2009. Probability information in risk communication: a review of the research literature. Risk Anal. 29, 267—287.

Vossler, C.A., Watson, S.B., 2013. Understanding the consequences of consequentiality: testing the validity of stated preferences in the field. J. Econ. Behav. Organ. 86, 137—147.

Wooldridge, J.M., 2013. Introductory Econometrics. A Modern Approach, fifth international ed. Cengage Learning, South-Western.

CHAPTER 5

Health benefit analysis: monetization of health impacts and its use in environment and health

Marco Martuzzi and Frank George
World Health Organization, Regional Office for Europe, European Centre for Environment and Health, Bonn, Germany

Contents

5.1 Environmental health determinants

Study and knowledge on the ways through which human health is shaped, influenced, promoted, and damaged by the environment go back to a very distant past, spanning over centuries. The onset of the modern, prevailing view on environment and health (EH), however, is relatively recent. Only in the last few decades, in fact, have we clarified the role of numerous environmental factors and accumulated solid evidence on their health implications, which represent a sound basis for the formulation of public policies in this domain. Such a substantial body of knowledge has developed, by and large, thanks to observations of health effects following high exposures, for example, in the occupational settings, followed by other observational studies on populations exposed to variable levels of noxious agents. Besides epidemiology, several other disciplines, such as biomedicine, toxicology, biostatistics have contributed to this process.

Cost-Benefit Analysis of Environmental Health Interventions
DOI: https://doi.org/10.1016/B978-0-12-812885-5.00005-6

This work has resulted in a reliable picture of the most important environmental health determinants, where "importance" typically refers to the magnitude of the measurable health impacts on the population. This comprises excess mortality and/or morbidity for causes of death or occurrence of diseases causally attributable to the considered risk factors. The metric of burden of disease (BoD) has also been developed to this end. BoD combines mortality and morbidity into one indicator, through summing up the amount of time by which lives of the affected people are shortened and the time they live with diseases. This combination is done using comparative weights, established through expert consensus.

The resulting overall picture of the health effects and impacts of environmental risk factors, despite a number of open questions, provides a sound basis for policy response and interventions and can guide priority settings; such picture draws from many established pieces of evidence, from ambient air pollution to radiation, from noise to second-hand smoking, from vector-borne diseases to asbestos.

Emphasis has long been on environmental hazards and single agents, but more recently, there has been growing interest in "salutogenic" factors, such as vicinity to green or blue space, or active transport involving physical activity. This tendency is one of the aspects of an increasing attention paid to the policy dimension, that is, to how evidence-informed policies can contribute to better health, essentially through primary or even so-called primordial prevention (Etzel, 2016). This represents a departure from a view of the environment as a set of risk factors, each entailing a raised level of mortality and morbidity, with the EH profession and community mainly charged to provide a "body count" and inform reactive policies, focused on keeping risks below acceptable levels.

As this earlier state of affairs showed important limitations, a more direct connection between assessors and the policymaking sphere has been developing. A stronger focus on the policy implications of available evidence has promoted more research into "upstream" or distal, rather than proximal, health determinants, which is needed to support the so-called health in all policies agenda. So for example, besides continuing research on the health effects of air pollution, important progress has been made on the role of activities and sectors that influence air pollution, such as transport or power generation and related policies, for health (Martuzzi, 2006).

This approach has made a mark on the EH community in Europe. Inter alia, it is reflected in the evolution of the European Environment and Health Process (EHP), an initiative first promoted by WHO in the late 1980s and involving since the 53 WHO European member states, through their ministries of health and ministries of environment, together with a variety of other entities and stakeholders (WHO Regional Office for Europe, 2018).

The EHP is marked by a series of ministerial conferences on EH, producing consensus-based positions, expressed by member states of the WHO Regional Office for Europe, on priorities for action in EH. The last conference, the 6th in the series and held in Ostrava, Czechia, in June 2017, identified the following priority areas:

- Improved air quality
- Water use, sanitation, and hygiene
- Chemical safety
- Waste and contaminated sites
- Sustainable and healthy cities
- Environmentally sustainable health systems
- Climate change adaptation, resilience

For all these areas, the underlying available evidence and policy needs were used to develop a set of possible policy and response actions, for member states to consider, prioritize, and undertake in order to address the most urgent challenges in EH.

The EHP reflects the aspirations of many engaged in contemporary EH science and practice, that is, to identify and implement evidence-informed decisions and policies, applying approaches that are not only mindful of stakeholders' needs and values but also effective. Efforts are being made to develop frameworks, resources, methods, and tools to facilitate a dialog at the interface between science and policy; remarkable progress has been made, especially with regard to clarifying the shortcomings of a simplistic model, long-prevailing, based on a rigid demarcation between supposedly value-free "facts" and policy decisions. These shortcomings have become all too evident as the focus of the questions asked to research has shifted from "what is the evidence that X causes Y, and how large is its impact?" to "what is the best course of action for maximizing health?" (Saltelli and Giampietro, 2017).

The hard evidence of the health effects of proximal risk factors (e.g., urban ambient air pollution) can first be shaped as a piece of rigorous, self-contained information, such as a set of relative risks; next, it can be used to assess the health impact through various health outcomes as a function of hypothetical or measured levels of concentration or exposure;

finally, the potential health gains from, say, cleaner transport policies can be assessed building on data on emissions and diffusion, considering a broader spectrum of health outcomes as well as cobenefits.

Thus, in many ways the debate has become more focused on concrete action and decisions, on factors with direct and indirect health consequences, often involving substantial uncertainties. In this context, much has been clarified on how to deal with the manifold complications that arise as the distance from the controlled setting of a laboratory, or a randomized clinical trial, increases. The entire domain of health impact assessment, with its very broad spectrum of methods and tools, has flourished in the last couple of decades as a response to these needs (O'Mullane et al., 2012).

5.2 The economic dimension

In such an increasingly policy-relevant debate the economic question arises naturally: evidence-informed, health-promoting policies are desirable, but should they not be worth their cost, that is, cost-effective, too? Obviously, the answer is a resounding "yes" (although some qualification is needed), and it is no surprise that a whole discipline has flourished, dedicated to the very issue of addressing the economic dimension of the relationship between environment and human health.

From the viewpoint of public health (which is the standpoint of this chapter), the reasoning is simple: given the expanding knowledge on the role of the environment to shape human health, and given the finite and often limited availability of resources for the environment, where are these best allocated so as to maximize health returns? Although the framing implied by this question is somewhat restrictive, for reasons discussed below, it is also often faced by many in public policy and can be addressed as follows.

Suppose environmental intervention or policy A costs C_A and is likely to improve health by gain G_A, and intervention B has cost $C_B < C_A$ and gain $G_B < G_A$. Which one is preferable? Simply put, the preferable intervention is the one that has a higher G/C ratio. Assuming that the costs C_A and C_B are known, this exercise requires nothing else than being able to quantify the health gains G_A and G_B, in a monodimensional metric such as a number of deaths, or disability-adjusted life years (DALYs). This is one case of cost-effectiveness studies.

The model above does not include the common case where option B is just non-A, that is, nonimplementation of A, that is, inaction. C_B being zero, the simple comparison above is impossible. Public health advocates will argue that A is preferable to B, simply because G_A is greater than G_B (equal to zero as well). If B is inaction, intervention A will thus be supported on public health grounds because of its health benefits. But is the intervention justified, regardless of its costs? The real-life answer to this question is clearly "no": there is certainly a limit in the intervention cost, beyond which the intervention would not be promoted. However, it is not uncommon that this evaluation is made only implicitly, for example, in the form of generic feasibility considerations. When, on the other hand, the economic dimension is explicitly addressed, a counter-argument is often formulated in a way that if intervention A is considered too costly, alternative ways to allocate the same resources will be suggested that produce a higher health gain (typically, health-promoting interventions affecting health determinants stronger than environmental ones, such as tobacco smoking). This, in turn, introduces another (hypothetical) intervention, C, with $C_C = C_A$, which means that the cost-effectiveness exercise reduces to estimating G_A and G_C—the policy producing the bigger health gains is selected.

So far, with this argument, the "economic dimension" of decision-making looks relatively simple. Costs and benefits, in cost-effectiveness analysis, are measured in their natural metrics, money and health impacts, respectively. In principle, cost-effectiveness analysis would be sufficient, through comparisons, for the identification of environmental interventions that are good value for money. In principle the evaluation of the monetary value of health impacts and gains is not needed, for this purpose. After all, this kind of logic, explicitly or implicitly, is applied by individuals when facing alternative options, for example, when buying a new house: the typical buyer weighs pros and cons of different properties, somehow establishing a single metric, compares scores to the price (without assigning a dollar value to the unit of the metric), and draws their conclusions. While this process can take place implicitly at the individual level, public policies often make efforts to make it explicit, for example, applying multicriteria analysis.

In any case the above does not entail a need to convert health impacts, or degree of preference for a property, to money. Yet, a whole discipline has developed, in the last couple of decades, on cost–benefit analysis, revolving around the notion of the monetary worth of health events and leading to the development of a whole range of methods for dealing with its complexity. Why is it so, that is, why cost-effectiveness was not sufficient for the job?

There are several reasons for this. Some have to do with intrinsic technical difficulties, for example, concerning the fact that benefit estimates can have different values for different interventions. An intervention that prevents catastrophic events such as road crashes and saves 1000 lives per year may be considered preferable to one that decreases air pollution by a small amount, also preventing 1000 premature deaths, regardless of the costs involved, because the victims are identified individuals, dying of a horrific, unexpected death (Ackerman and Heinzerling, 2004). Other reasons stem from the difficulty of conducting a policy negotiation where one of the options is hypothetical, or artificially introduced, such as the comparison intervention C in the previous section.

More in general, the assumption that policy decisions are univocally determined by maximizing a well-defined utility is flawed (Saltelli and Giampietro, 2017). In reality, decision makers, unlike the house buyer, are rarely if ever faced with a discrete set of options, presented as a finite menu, to choose from; rather, they must engage in complex negotiation processes where options are often shaped as the discussion goes on, and alternative courses of action are gradually identified. Consider, for example, the case of the proposed creation of a local waste disposal facility; at the onset the available options may appear to be a handful of solutions or even a simple yes/no alternative, but it is typically the case that a negotiation between opposing views produces more options, for example, on the exact location for the facility, on the kind of technology to be employed, on distribution of the benefits (jobs, income), on investments on mitigation, and other variants that could not be identified and considered in the first place. Most importantly, any underlying utility function to be maximized such as the quantifiable BoD, if it exists, will most likely be but one of the considerations, as stakeholders holding variable levels of power and leverage will try to influence the decision-making process to their advantage.

Experience with the "health in all policies" agenda, where the health sector promotes consideration of health in the development of policies in other sectors (e.g., transport, industry/energy, and agriculture), has taught that health considerations do not necessarily prevail over others. When it comes to environmental interventions, while health advocates may assume that improving health is a kind of moral imperative trumping other priorities, they soon find themselves in discussions where other questions, for example, protection of jobs or of shareholders' interests, are regarded as equally compelling. In some cases, these other constraints may have a health relevance, for example, it is obvious that employment and income are, generally speaking, good for health—so that in any case a broad and inclusive definition of health, including well-being, is appropriate. However, in other cases the competing considerations may be of different nature and have no bearing with human health. In these circumstances an argument must be presented, for example, to government officials from the economic sector, to make the case that a given environmental intervention benefitting health is, per se, good value for money. Comparisons are not between alternative environmental interventions and not even between intervention and no intervention, but rather between different allocations of public and private budgets. The hybrid metric of any G/C ratio will not enable such a negotiation. What is needed is then a dimensionless ratio between the monetary value of G (the benefit) and the cost of the intervention. The higher the ratio, the better, especially if it is significantly higher than other proposals.

5.3 Quantifying the monetary value of health

Thus the need to quantify the monetary value of health outcomes such as mortality and morbidity has emerged very strongly in recent years. This has involved challenging discussions between economists and epidemiologists; both using full-fledged, rigorous methodologies, the conversation requires clarity on assumptions, uncertainties, underlying values in each expert domain; efforts are needed for establishing a common language and in identifying shared goals. The journey can be sometimes bumpy, but highly instructive.

A conceptually more approachable avenue to undertake a cost—benefit type analysis is the cost-of-illness (CoI) concept. If, for example, an environmental intervention is assessed in a yes/no scenario, the CoI's goal is to estimate the direct expenditures of the health system for the care of the health conditions that would be prevented (or increased) through the intervention. Once the number of events of the relevant outcomes are estimated, the cost associated with treatment, surgery, hospital stay, therapies, medicines, etc. are derived. In addition to this, broader, usually direct, societal costs can be included, such as loss of productivity or workdays lost due to absenteeism, also expressed in money units. There will be, most likely, uncertain coefficients, and accuracy may be an issue on both sides of the equation (although uncertainties in costs are often underestimated), but the exercise produces an estimate of the cash that the intervention will save to the health system, some employers, and some affected individuals. This amount of money, the monetized benefit, can be then compared to the cost of the intervention, to gauge its worth.

CoI produces easily understandable information, as it predicts how much bank balances will change as a result of an intervention. This is of course valuable information, for example, in negotiations across different government sectors, where a minister of health and a minister of environment can argue in favor of certain interventions, providing hard facts not only about the health benefits but also about its economic virtues. Transport is an area where this kind of analysis has been often applied, probably because many of the health implications of transport policies, that is exposure to air pollution and noise, road injuries, physical activity, involve substantial, and costly burden on health systems through their chronic disease impacts. It is not by chance that the transport sector has joined forces with EH in THE PEP program (UNECE, 2014), and it is hoped that other sectors will follow soon.

Critiques to the CoI, however, are leveled both in the health community as well as by economists. To start with, CoI tends to quantify a subset of the direct societal costs, mainly those borne by the health systems; so what about an intervention that, although recommended by EH advocates, demanded by local communities, and preventing sizeable amounts of ill health and disease, seems to cost more than it saves, when this can be due to assessing only a part of the benefits? Also, what about outcomes such as shortening of life expectancy, which cost little to health systems and are therefore discarded (and taking the argument to the extreme of a paradox, can even involve savings to the welfare system)?

The latter concern exposes the main shortcoming of CoI: specular to its quality of estimating concrete savings in cash expenditures, it does not capture the nonmarket value of pain and suffering involved with discomfort, disease, and mortality. A death due to a road collision may be much less expensive for the health system compared to a chronic cardiovascular condition due to air pollution but is hardly less valuable for society. CoI can consequently be criticized for looking only at the tip of the iceberg (Byford et al., 2000).

Willingness to pay (WTP) methods for economic assessments, described in detail in Chapter X, is a different approach, where this limitation does not apply. By assessing people's preferences and priorities through rather sophisticated techniques, WTP studies set out to attach a monetary value to events such as death and disease, quantifying the extent to which people would hypothetically be prepared to spend in order to prevent them. As these preferences are individual and are influenced by cultural norms, level of education, gender, and age, the estimated values are not constant but rather country- or even community-specific; in addition, they are proportionate to the level of income and the purchasing power of the local currency.

Clearly, WTP threads a more slippery terrain than CoI: while CoI is based on the fairly rigorous and inescapable accountancy of expenditures in health systems, WTP ventures in the realm of people's opinions and values. However, rigorous methodologies have been developed to this effect, and bodies such as the OECD have been producing authoritative estimates of country-specific so-called values of statistical life (VSL) for many years (OECD, 2012). Combined with estimates of health impacts and BoD routinely produced by WHO and others, these data have been used for countless exercises. Air pollution being one of the most studied area, we summarize below the results from a WHO-OECD assessment of its economic costs in Europe and discuss it as an example.

VSLs represent a one-dimensional synthesis of the efforts that society is prepared to make in order to avert a death, expressed in money, which is a metric in common with other spheres of the policy discourse and therefore suitable for negotiations across sectors. Because VSL's goal is to quantify such societal value, the WTP approach is considered by some a kind of quintessential economic analysis, in contrast with CoI, which focuses on hard expenditures. One downside is that the money estimates produced by WTP studies are not "real" cash: following a given environmental intervention, the predicted benefit, typically valued at much higher levels than the CoI, will not materialize in bank accounts as a positive balance. Rather, it will be a measure of the societal gain in terms of health and wellbeing, due to the prevention of death and disease.

Somewhat paradoxically, the frequent reluctance of health professionals to attribute a monetary value to health outcomes, typically mortality and morbidity, is sometimes more pronounced for WTP than for CoI, despite the fact that WTP aims at being more inclusive and to capture the full set of adverse health consequences of ill health. This reluctance may reflect underlying ethical models attaching an essentially incommensurable nature to health outcomes. For some in public health, using an ordinal scale for comparing the gravity of, say, an incident cancer with a heart attack is an awkward exercise—so much so that even BoD metrics such as DALYs are at times criticized (Li, 2014). And if anything, throwing money into the equation may make matters worse.

The discipline, on the other hand, did itself no favor in coining the expression "value of a statistical life": despite the disclaimer built into the word "statistical," VSLs are occasionally dismissed on the ground that one cannot attach a price tag to life and death, or that it is inconceivable that VSLs vary by country. Attempts to change the expression were made (e.g., with "Value of an avoided/prevented fatality," or "Statistical value of the risk reduction of premature death") but none was successful.

5.4 Quantifying the monetary value of health: the case of ambient air pollution in Europe

An area where economic evaluations in the EH domain have been repeatedly made, applying a variety of approaches and methods, is air pollution. As described in Chapter X, the epidemiology of air pollution-related disease is very well developed. In the environmental field, few, if any, other risk factors have been so extensively studied. The available evidence on the health effects of many different air pollutants is nowadays very solid: the causal link between several pollutants and multiple health endpoints including mortality and morbidity is established; the magnitude of these association is reliably and accurately estimated, including through detailed concentration-response functions; air pollution is constantly monitored in many cities and countries worldwide; even where air pollution is not measured, remote sensing or model-based estimates based on land use and emission information provide concentration estimates with a fair degree of reliability. This has allowed reliable estimation not only of the impact of air pollution in many different settings, but also of how these impacts are predicted to vary as a function of variable concentrations resulting from the implementation of policies or interventions. In turn, this has led to the formulation of guideline values (WHO Regional Office for Europe, 2006) and evidence-informed policies at various levels. Given the direct engagement with the policy domain and the relevance of the evidence for multiple sectors, the issue of costs and cost—benefit ratios arose soon, as a natural question that decision makers had to face when considering different interventions.

In the air pollution domain the notion of *counterfactuals*, that is scenarios under which hypothetical concentrations or exposures are compared to those actually observed, has become a standard approach for evaluating health impacts. Such impacts are often "negative," in that typical scenarios and counterfactuals describe an improvement of air quality compared to the existent, for example, thanks to an abatement of emissions, which would result in a reduction of the health burden. While the plain vocabulary can be a source of confusion (the "health impact of X" tends to imply an adverse event in common parlance), the underlying methodology and simple algebra is of course the same, bar a minus sign.

WHO has long been interested in economic assessments in EH (WHO Regional Office for Europe, 2004). Having been at the forefront in promoting intersectoral work, WHO has been facing, since early days, the need to support the health sector not only by providing evidence on health effects and impacts of environmental determinants, but also with arguments to promote preventive, cost-effective action. In the case of air pollution the WHO Regional Office for Europe collaborated with OECD to estimate the economic costs of the health impacts of air pollution in its 53 member states (WHO Regional Office for Europe, 2015). The assessment, carried out for 2010, adopted the WTP approach and focused on long-term mortality from PM2.5 exposure, using previously existing WHO estimates of number of excess deaths per country. These were combined with OECD-produced estimates of VSLs, so as to derive the monetary measure of what people in each country are willing to pay to prevent the mortality due to air pollution. Costs were estimated for two sets of VSLs: those from 2005, deriving from multiple national surveys and those extrapolated to 2010. The latter are of course more realistic, as the extrapolation takes into account economic growth and the changing purchasing power at national level. In all member states, 2010 VSL are greater than 2005 ones, by 30.8% on average; the increase ranges from 1.9% to 119%, mainly reflecting very different levels of economic growth. Once these VSLs are used in combination with country-specific data on the impact of air pollution on long-term mortality, an estimate of the economic costs is derived for each country. These costs range across countries from USD 62 mio to 154,382 mio in 2005, and from USD 96 to 144,715 mio in 2010, amounting to a total USD 1.4 trillion. To put the country-specific figures in context, they were also expressed as a proportion of the national GDP, which ranged from 0.58% to 34.9% in 2005 and from 0.3% to 35.2% in 2010. The findings, fully in line with comparable estimates (OECD, 2012), describe a very large economic cost, reaching a staggering one-third of the national GDP in countries with high levels of air pollution and comparatively smaller economy size.

5.5 Discussion

The value and use of these estimates to stimulate preventive policies and interventions on the ground is a matter of intense debate. Somehow masked by the technical intricacies, the questions underlying these assessments reach the very core of the science—policy interface. In the following, we refer to three such questions.

A first point pertains the value of the mere availability of these estimates, independently of the numbers they carry: the fact that health impacts and their costs can be reliably quantified, and that there is some consistency between different assessments, represents a compelling reason, a specific piece of evidence reinforcing the sense of urgency to act, both for the sake of public health and for society's prosperity, regardless of the actual estimates. This may be due to a general acceptance of the fact that health impact estimates are often built following an "at least" principle, that is, using only the part of the evidence that allows quantitative modeling, bound to be a part of a larger total (Künzli et al., 2000).

A second, closely related point, also pertaining the value of accuracy, is in connection with the magnitude of the estimates. For a nonspecialized audience, possibly including one with policy responsibilities, billions (in any currency) are daunting figures, and the order of magnitude (i.e., the "number of zeros" involved), rather than the actual estimate, becomes the main dimension that a reader may try to grasp. This brings the said reader on unfamiliar grounds: when these large numbers are translated into proportions of GDPs, and when such proportions are in the order of 20% or 30%, some skepticism may emerge and the various disclaimers about the meaning of a VSL and the logic of the WTP approach can be questioned. GDP proportions are very helpful for putting large monetary figures in the right perspective but may suggest a mistaken direct connection with actual economic performance and more available liquidity. Almost paradoxically, economics, teaming up with public health to provide money-based factual arguments for preventive policies, may bring the debate into an even more value-rich terrain, where the monetary metric is applied to societal preferences, and the supporters of the health and economic cases may find themselves on the defensive.

On the other hand, it is sometimes observed that a proliferation of estimates (of mortality, morbidity, BoD, economic costs, multiplied by different air pollutants and other variables) can be detrimental and damage their credibility. Indeed the availability of data and richness of methods stimulate the production of many such assessments, not always easy to compare, thereby potentially confusing the users.

Lastly, and perhaps most troubling, a question, already mentioned above, arises in connection not only with economic assessments of air pollution and health, but virtually to all environmental interventions: what if a proposed intervention, beneficial for public health, does not pass the cost−benefit test or an equivalent threshold?

Admittedly, this "what-if" question, what to do when the economics of an environmental intervention is not favorable, is a difficult one for public health advocates. The argument that the same resources would be spent more effectively elsewhere and bring better health benefits, as discussed above, can be logically appealing. However, it is not very practical, in that the alternative, more cost-effective interventions may not be so readily available after all. Also, when a decision is needed on a certain proposed intervention that will bring health benefits to some identified community, few decision makers will be at ease rejecting it on the ground that the health benefits for the people are not worth the expense.

Dubious assumptions, however, underlie the what-if question, suggesting that it is ill-posed, and problematic due to its poor framing. One implicit assumption is that society operates in a way that maximizes a utility function linked to the common good, which is hardly defensible. Another one is that interventions are a matter of binary decisions, a yes or no decided on the basis of factual, preferably quantitative information. In contrast, as argued above, environmental interventions and policies are, more often than not, defined by a variety of variables and parameters, effectively creating multiple choices and options. Far from being binary, the decision space is more likely multidimensional, with some discrete variables (e.g., what are the alternative kinds of available technologies that can be deployed for the intervention? What are the main pollutants of concern?) and some continuous axes (how much can impacts be mitigated, by which adjustments?). In many cases the decision-making process is a dynamic and iterative negotiation, in that the outcome of a health impact assessment exercise can lead to the identification of further options or adjustments in the intervention.

Finally, and probably most importantly, a fallacy is in the notion that an economic assessment such as a cost—benefit exercise should have the last word in a policy decision. Attributing a "traffic light" role to these assessments is at odds with the necessary approach to evidence-informed decision-making in EH. Such approach hinges on the need to embrace complexity through the consideration of multiple kinds of evidence, mediated by relevant stakeholders. Economic evidence can and must contribute to such pool of evidence, with limitations and assumptions of all pieces being made explicit. If the health impact assessment of an intervention is complemented with an assessment of the economic costs, this process can also lead to identifying and choosing not only a health-friendly course of action, but also a cost-effective one—that is the ultimate goal of an alliance of public health and economics.

In conclusion, economic assessments of environmental interventions, where health impacts are involved, have been playing an increasingly important role in EH. In many cases, they proved very useful for supporting policy decisions, by adding further evidence to the mix. The dialog between economists and public health experts and advocate requires preparation, time, the establishment of a common language, and harmonization of approaches and methods. This investment is not negligible but can be very profitable.

References

Ackerman, F., Heinzerling, L., 2004. Priceless: On Knowing the Price of Everything and the Value of Nothing. The New Press, New York.

Byford, S., Torgerson, D.J., Raftery, J., 2000. Cost of illness studies. BMJ 320, 1335.

Etzel, R.A., 2016. Children's environmental health—the role of primordial prevention. Curr. Probl. Pediatr. Adolesc. Health Care 46, 202—204. Available from: https://doi.org/10.1016/j.cppeds.2015.12.008.

Künzli, N., Kaiser, R., Medina, S., Studnicka, M., Chanel, O., Filliger, P., et al., 2000. Public-health impact of outdoor and traffic-related air pollution: a European assessment. Lancet 356, 795—801.

Li, V., 2014. The rise, critique and persistence of the DALY in global health. J. Global Health.

Martuzzi, M., 2006. Environment and health: perspectives from the intersectoral experience in Europe. In: Stahl, T., Wismar, M., Ollila, E., Lahtinen, E., Leppo, K. (Eds.), Health in All Policies: Prospects and Potentials. Ministry of Social Affairs and Health, Helsinki, pp. 129—144.

OECD, 2012. Mortality Risk Valuation in Environment, Health and Transport Policies [WWW Document]. <http://www.oecd.org/env/tools-evaluation/mortalityrisk valuationinenvironmenthealthandtransportpolicies.htm> (accessed 20.01.19.)

O'Mullane, M., Martuzzi, M., Martin-Olmedo, P., Kvakova, M., 2012. Health impact assessment: present and future directions. Eur. J. Public Health 22, 48.

Saltelli, A., Giampietro, M., 2017. What is wrong with evidence based policy, and how can it be improved? Futures 91, 62–71. Available from: https://doi.org/10.1016/j. futures.2016.11.012.

UNECE, 2014. Transport, Health and Environment Pan-European Programme [web site] [WWW Document]. <http://www.unece.org/thepep/en/welcome.html> (accessed 09.10.14.)

WHO Regional Office for Europe, 2004. Declaration: fourth Ministerial Conference on Environment and Health, Budapest, Hungary, 23–25 June 2004. WHO Regional Office for Europe, Copenhagen.

WHO Regional Office for Europe, 2006. Air quality guidelines. Global update 2005. Particulate matter, ozone, nitrogen dioxide and sulfur dioxide. Copenhagen.

WHO Regional Office for Europe, 2015. Economic Cost of the Health Impact of Air Pollution in Europe: Clean Air, Health and Wealth. Copenhagen. <http://www. euro.who.int/__data/assets/pdf_file/0004/276772/Economic-cost-health-impact-air-pollution-en.pdf>.

WHO Regional Office for Europe, 2018. European Environment and Health Process (EHP). <http://www.euro.who.int/en/health-topics/environment-and-health/pages/european-environment-and-health-process-ehp> (accessed 26.10.18.)

CHAPTER 6

Costing environmental health intervention

Carla Guerriero
Department of Economics and Statistics, University of Naples Federico II, Naples, Italy; Centre for Studies in Economics and Finance (CSEF), Naples, Italy

Contents

6.1 Introduction

Depending on the type of perspective adopted and the spillover effects associated with environmental health intervention(s) (EHIs), the range of the costs items as well as the type of cost analysis to adopt vary significantly. For instance, a financial analysis can be conducted if the perspective adopted is the one of a private firm willing to invest in a new infrastructure project. More frequently, however, the intervention(s) considered in the cost—benefit analysis (CBA) affects society as a whole and

Cost-Benefit Analysis of Environmental Health Interventions
DOI: https://doi.org/10.1016/B978-0-12-812885-5.00006-8
111

Table 6.1 Example of financial analysis.

	Year 1	Year 2	Year 3	Year 4	Year 5–20
Start-up cost	1200		400		
Fixed cost	450				
Investment cost	1650		400		
Direct production cost	5000	2000		600	600
Administrative cost	1500	300	300	300	300
Sales and distribution expenditures		200	200	200	200
Operating cost	6500	2500	500	1100	1100
Revenues			10,000	10,000	15,000

an economic analysis accounting for shadow prices[1] need to be adopted. Another issue to consider in costing a new intervention is the size of its effects. If the intervention affects a single market or a small number of markets, a partial equilibrium analysis is the preferred and easier approach. Alternatively, if the intervention is expected to impact many sectors, its costs should be estimated employing a general equilibrium model (GEM) that evaluates the effects on the entire economy.

6.2 Financial and economic analysis

Depending on the perspective adopted, either a financial or an economic type of analysis can be employed to estimate the total cost associated with an EHI. The main objective of this section is to describe with examples these two types of cost analysis.

6.2.1 Financial analysis of cost

The main objective of a financial analysis is to provide an ex ante estimate of a project cash flow and to determine its performance and profitability. The costs involved in the financial analysis are tangible costs and they can be grouped into three macro categories: total investment cost, total operating cost, and revenues (Table 6.1).

The first component of financial analysis, total investment cost, can be divided into fixed investment costs, which are usually the largest component of the total investment cost (e.g., land, equipment, and building costs fall within this category) and start-up costs that are defined as "all the costs

---

[1] A shadow price is the estimated price for a commodity or service that is not normally priced and/or sold in the market.

that are incurred in view of the effects that will accrue beyond the financial period in which the relative disbursements were made" [European Commission (EC), 2014]. Examples of start-up costs are preparatory studies, consulting studies, initial training expenses, etc. [European Commission (EC), 2014]. Given the information asymmetries between the intervention provider (e.g., government) and the intervention supplier (e.g., contractors of the remediation activities), initial start-up costs estimated a priori may be overestimated or underestimated compared with the final cost incurred to implement the policy (OECD, 2006a, 2006b; Tonin, 2014). Predicting the start-up costs ex ante is even more difficult when the intervention is new, and there are no previous cost estimates available (OECD, 2006a, 2006b).

The second cost component of financial analysis is the operating costs associated with the intervention(s) [European Commission (EC), 2014]. The operating costs are all those costs associated with the acquisition of those goods and services that do not have an investment nature such as labor, electric power, and raw materials. In general, in the estimation of operating costs, all cost that is not associated with a real monetary expenditure should not be included in the financial estimation. To facilitate their analysis, operating costs can be classified using the following categories: direct production costs (e.g., materials and services used during the production, personnel labor costs); administrative costs, and sales and distribution expenditures. Each of these three costs components are usually divided into fixed (do not vary with the volume of goods consumed) and variable costs (costs that depend on the volume of goods being employed) [European Commission (EC), 2014].

EHIs such as congestion charge or environmental taxes may also be a source of revenue (e.g., revenues from selling the energy produced with the incinerator plant). The revenues are simply estimated by multiplying the quantity of the X good produced by its price P_X. The net revenues are estimated each year until the end of the time horizon considered. The final row of the financial analysis quantifies for each year the net revenues of the project.

Once the total investment cost, operating costs, and revenues have been estimated, the last step of financial analysis is to estimate the financial sustainability of a project. A project is said to be financially sustainable when "it does not incur in the risk of running out of cash in the future" [European Commission (EC), 2014]. Given a time span selected for the cash outflows and inflows, the sustainability is reached if in each year the

Table 6.2 Example of financial sustainability (million Euros).

	Years		
	1	2	3
Total financial resources	165	25	0
Total operating revenues	0	42	115
Total inflows	165	67	115
Total operating cost	0	−56	−75
Total investment cost	−165	−4	−4
Interest	0	0	0
Loans	0	0	0
Taxes	0	−6	−7
Total outflows	−165	−66	−86
Total cash flows	0	1	29
Cumulated net cash flow	0	1	30

Source: Modified from EU (2014).

net flow of the cumulative cash generated is positive. The outflows included in the calculation of the financial sustainability will consider the operating, investment, and interest costs, as well as the loan, reimbursements, and the taxes. An example of a financial sustainable project is reported in Table 6.2. As observed, after the first year, the project starts generating a positive net cash flow.

6.2.2 Economic analysis of costs

When the objective of CBA is to estimate the impact of an intervention to the society, observed prices of inputs and outputs (also referred to as explicit costs) may either not represent the total opportunity cost, because the market is inefficient, or the market itself may not exist for the commodities considered. Economic analysis is based on the concept of "opportunity cost" that is here defined as the value forgone by not using the same resource in the best alternative activity [European Commission (EC), 2014; HM Treasury, 2018].

Compared to explicit/financial cost, the opportunity cost considers all the positive and negative externalities associated with an asset/resource (HM Treasury, 2018). In the case of EHIs the social opportunity costs are often nonnegligible and as a result, the economic analysis considering the social opportunity costs associated with EHIs is preferred to a financial analysis which is based exclusively on market prices. The standard methodology to account for the social opportunity costs of inputs and outputs is to convert market prices to shadow prices using an appropriate conversion factor or, when prices are not available (e.g., costs of asthma cases associated with PM_{10} exposure), to monetize them using the stated or revealed preference techniques described in Chapter 5, Costing environmental health interventions.

One of the differences between financial and economic analyses of cost is the treatment of capital assets such as buildings and land [HM Treasury, 2018; European Commission (EC), 2014]. Buildings no longer incurring in a depreciation in the financial analysis will still have a cost in the economic analysis. This cost can be estimated with two alternative approaches: one approach would use the annualized value of the building—the cost of constructing the same building today depreciated by the annualization factor plus the interest rate associated with the asset [European Commission (EC), 2014]. The alternative approach uses the current rental value of a similar asset (assuming that the rental market is not distorted) [European Commission (EC), 2014].

A second difference between financial and economic analysis is the estimation of labor cost and the overall employment effects. If wages do not reflect the true opportunity cost, prices must be adjusted to account for distortions (e.g., true opportunity cost of skilled health workers in Cuba are underestimated because the government control salaries). One of the most debated issues about EHIs is the measurement of the consequences of more stringent regulation on unemployment. As suggested by the EPA Guidelines for CBA, "the social cost of the new intervention includes the value of lost output associated with the reallocation of resources including labor away from production of output towards pollution abatement" (EPA, 2010). In the EC guidelines for CBA of investment projects the effects in terms of employment used by the project should be captured by applying the Wage Conversion Factor to the labor cost. The effects on employment arising from the intervention should be quantified by the additional profits or costs created.

According to Sustain (2018), "If regulation creates serious job losses, it will have significant negative impact on individuals' wellbeing, even if CBA does not recognize or capture that fact." The author suggests for large EHIs, such as national regulations, to complement CBA analysis with an analysis of the unemployment effects. It is important to highlight that the time horizon assumed for the analysis can significantly affect labor costs. The net consequences on employment of new environmental interventions are likely to be negative in the short run but the net benefit is usually positive in a longer time frame. Even small interventions (e.g., the creation of a pedestrian area in the historical center) despite the initial skepticism are usually associated with increase in revenues and jobs in the affected area (Garrett-Peltier, 2011). Whether employment costs are included directly in CBA or not, the appropriate way of doing so is to account for the shadow pricing of labor (EPA, 2010). In contexts where there is a high unemployment rate the project would create employment for individuals, otherwise be jobless. In this case the shadow pricing of labor is well below the wage paid employed labor. In contexts in which the unemployment rate is low the shadow pricing rule still applies, but the cost of created labor will be at the ruling wage. As suggested by OECD (2006a,b), in many cases, employment cost is not relevant for CBA but are very important for politicians willing to justify government interventions. If this is the case, an impact analysis assessing the consequences for employment of proposed EHIs may inform evidence complementary to the source provided by CBA.

Another important issue to consider when conducting an economic analysis is that in many settings, current market prices diverge from their opportunity costs. Due to monopoly power, taxes, import tariffs, or competitive strategies (e.g., dumping), prices can be higher or lower than their real opportunity costs. These distortions are more common in developing countries or in isolated economies because the market is more likely to be constrained by managerial and political issues.

When real prices are distorted because of market failure (e.g., restricted competition) or because governmental tariffs do not reflect the cost of public services, a standard conversion factor (SCF) approach can be used to transform market prices in accounting prices [European Commission (EC), 2014]. The SCF can be estimated as the ratio of the value of traded goods and services at the international price level to the value of traded goods and services at the domestic price level or can be approximated by the weighted average import tariff [European Commission (EC), 2014].

For example, if the average tariff was 25%, the SCF would be 0.8. In the case of distorted prices for tradable goods (e.g., natural resources such as oil and gas) the easiest solution is the adoption of border prices. Border price is the minimum price of the good right when the good passes through the border. For EU countries, the external border may be used for most tradable goods.

In cases of nontradable goods an SCF[2] approach is used. An example of specific conversion factors by sector is reported in Table 6.3.

Conversion factor represents the factor at which the market price has to be multiplied to obtain inflows values reflecting the total social opportunity cost.

The formula to translate market price p for the good i into its shadow price v using the conversion factor k is the following [European Commission (EC), 2014]:

$$k_i = \frac{v_i}{p_i} \Leftrightarrow k_i \times p_i$$

Conversion factors should be made available at a national level by a planning office. However, as suggested by EU Guidelines for CBA, when SCF by sector are not available they at least need to be consistent across research projects of similar objectives.

In the cases of the negative impacts for which a market value does not exist the willingness to pay (WTP) approach described in Chapter 5, Costing environmental health interventions, is the preferred method to monetize health externalities and to integrate them in the analysis. In addition to the health cost, EHIs can also be associated with other externalities such as noise increase, landscape degradation, and decreased resilience to climate change.

Table 6.4 reports some example of environmental externalities.

In the recent years an increasing attention has been paid to the valuation of the ecosystem services. The valuation of natural capita including elements of nature such as forests, rivers, and biodiversity whose existence is extremely valuable to the society should be included in CBA (Barbier and Markandya, 2013).

Stocks of natural capital alone or in combination with other types of capital such as human and social capital provide a wide range of benefits (HM Treasury, 2018). These benefits include values such as the use of natural stock as inputs to production (e.g., timber, minerals, or water) or for nonmarket purposes (e.g., leisure activities) (Fig. 6.1).

Individuals also value the simple existence of the natural stock as demonstrated by previous studies investigating WTP for the existence of particular habitat or species. The value of the natural stock can and should be

---

[2] SCF measures the average difference between world and domestic prices of a given economy.

Table 6.3 Example of specific conversion factors (CFs) by sector.

Sector	Details
Land	Assume the SCF is 0.8. Government provides the land at a price reduced by 50% compared with market prices. So, the market price is double the current one. The selling price should be doubled to reflect the domestic market and, as there is no specific conversion factor, the conversion factor to turn market prices into border prices is the SCF. CF = 2 × 0.6 = 1.6
Building	The total cost consists of 30% of nonskilled workforce (CF of nonskilled workforce is 0.48), 40% of imported material cost with import tariffs of 23% and sales of 10% (CF = 0.75), 20% of local materials (SCF = 0.8), 10% of profits (CF = 0). Conversion factor is (0.3 × 0.48) + (0.4 × 0.75) + (0.2 × 0.8) + (0.1 × 0) = 0.6
Machinery	Imported without taxes and tariffs (CF = 1)
Stock of raw material	Only one traded material is supposed to be used; the item is not subject to taxes and the market price is equal to the free on board price. CF = 1
Output	The project produces two outputs. A, imported and B, a nontraded intermediate item. To protect domestic firms, the government has imposed an import tax of 33% on item A. The CF for A is 100/133 = 0.75. For item B, as there is no specific conversion factor, the SCF = 0.8 is used
Raw materials	No significant distortions. CF = 1
Electricity	There is a tariff that covers only 40% of the marginal supply cost of electricity. There is no disaggregation of cost components, and it is assumed that the difference between international and domestic prices for each cost component used to produce a marginal unit of electricity is equal to the difference between all traded items considered in the SCF. CF = 1/0.4 × 0.8 = 2
Skilled labor force	The market is not distorted. Market wage reflects the opportunity cost for the economy
Nonskilled labor force	Supply exceeds demand but there is a minimum wage of $5 per hour. Nonetheless, in this sector, the last employed workers come from the rural sector where the wage is only $3 per hour. Only 60% of nonskilled workforce wage reflect the opportunity cost. The SCF is used to turn the opportunity cost of nonskilled work into border price. CF = 0.6 × 0.8 = 0.48

CF, Conversion factor; *SCF*, standard conversion factor.
Source: Modified from European Commission (EC) (2008). Guidelines to cost−benefit analysis of investment projects. Economic Appraisal Tool for Cohesion Policy 2008−2014. <https://ec.europa.eu/inea/sites/inea/files/cba_guide_cohesion_policy.pdf> [European Commission (EC), 2008].

Table 6.4 Examples of environmental externalities.

Noise. Any increase or decrease of noise emissions affects activities and health

Air pollution. Emissions of localized air pollutants such as nitrous oxide, sulfur dioxide, or small particulate matters. Have negative impacts on human health, generate material damages, loss of crops, and affect the ecosystem

GHG emissions. Interventions can emit or reduce GHGs into the atmosphere. GHG have a worldwide impact due to global scale of the damage caused, thus there is no difference on where the GHG emission is taking place

Soil contamination. This is caused by the presence of human-made chemicals or other alternations in the natural soil environment, typically because of industrial activity, agricultural chemicals, or improper disposal of waste. Its effects on production, consumption, and human health can be deferred over time

Water pollution. Water pollution is the contamination of human bodies such as lakes, rivers oceans, aquifers, and groundwater. This occurs when pollutants are discharged directly or indirectly into water bodies without adequate treatments to remove the harmful compounds

Ecosystem degradation. New infrastructure projects can deplete water sources, increase habitat fragmentation, and contribute to the deterioration of biodiversity, loss of habitats, and species. The economic costs come in the form of lost services when an ecosystem is degraded and loses its functions

Landscape deterioration. This usually involves a loss of recreational and aesthetic value

Vibrations. Mainly from transport-related projects, vibrations affect health, and the quality of urban life

GHG, Greenhouse gas.
Source: Modified from European Commission (EC), 2014. Guidelines to cost—benefit analysis of investment projects. In: Economic Appraisal Tool for Cohesion Policy 2014—2020. <https://ec.europa.eu/inea/sites/inea/files/cba_guide_cohesion_policy.pdf>.

systematically accounted for in CBA using either stated or revealed preference techniques described in Chapter 5, Costing environmental health interventions. Failing to assign a monetary value to the costs (and benefits) of natural stock degradation (improvement) could lead to dramatic reductions in present and future-ecosystem services.

Given the mounting evidence on the present and future catastrophic effects of climate change, consideration of the effects of EHIs on greenhouse gas (GHG) emission is essential. The most commonly adopted approach to integrate climate change externalities in CBA of EHIs is the one developed by the European Investment Bank Carbon Footprint Methodology. The approach consists of three steps:

1. First step: To quantify the volume of additional or saved emissions associated with the EHI. Emissions refers to carbon dioxide (CO_2), but they also include significant increases or decreases of nitrogen dioxide and methane. All these elements have a long lifetime in the atmosphere, and present emissions can contribute to dramatic events associated with climate change in the distant future.
2. Second step: To convert all emissions to CO_2 values other than CO_2 (e.g., tons emitted of nitrogen dioxide) into CO_2 by multiplying them with a factor equivalent to their global warming potential.
3. Third step: To assign a monetary value to CO_2 emissions. The total quantified tons of CO_2 emissions are multiplied by the unit cost of GHG emissions (Table 6.5). If the change in carbon cost is significant,

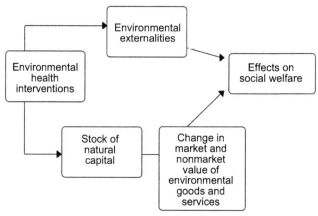

Figure 6.1 From EHIs to effects on social welfare. *EHIs*, Environmental health intervention(s).

Table 6.5 Unit cost of greenhouse gas emissions.

	Value in 2010 (Euro/t-CO$_2$e)	Annual adders 2011−30
High	40	2
Central	25	1
Low	10	0.5

Note: estimates are reported using 2006 prices and need to be adjusted at the price level of the year of the analysis.
Source: Modified from European Commission (EC), 2014. Guidelines to cost−benefit analysis of investment projects. In: Economic Appraisal Tool for Cohesion Policy 2014−2020. <https://ec.europa.eu/inea/sites/inea/files/cba_guide_cohesion_policy.pdf>.

it is recommended to estimate a carbon switching price defined as the price for which the decision maker is indifferent between one or more projects.

All the discussion above pertaining financial and economic analysis is applied if the costs estimate are elicited from the setting in which the analysis is conducted. If the cost/price information for the analyst's setting is not available, unit cost can be transferred from other settings and used to populate the analysis. In particular, a distinction should be made between traded and nontraded goods. Traded goods should be valued in their international price as described above, and purchasing power parity could be used. Nontraded goods estimates (e.g., WTP estimates for reducing the risk of an asthma attack) should be converted using the benefit transfer procedure described in Chapter 5, Costing environmental health interventions.

6.3 General versus partial-equilibrium analysis

The second main challenge when costing EHIs is to determine whether their costs and benefits will be confined to a single or multiple markets.

Large scale EHIs can be associated with effects that go beyond the targeted sector. Partial-equilibrium analysis, as suggested by its name, is conducted when the scope of the intervention is mainly concentrated in a single market and/or is negligible to a small number of sectors. For marginal/small interventions, for example, the introduction of a new pedestrian area in proximity of a primary school or the creation of new cycle lanes in the city center, using a partial equilibrium analysis to estimate the total social cost and benefit is appropriate and easier. For major interventions, such as large infrastructure projects or new national regulations on air quality, the adoption of a partial-equilibrium analysis may lead to significantly underestimating the total societal cost and benefit. Partial-equilibrium analysis may also fail to accurately model the consequences of large change in a single-regulated market.

Large environmental interventions as, for example, those associated with a new tax on fossil fuels (e.g., on coal-fired power plants) will not affect only the market interested by the policy but also other sectors, such as industries, that must buy energy inputs at higher prices or the general population living close to coal-fired plants that benefit from a reduction in air pollution exposure and subsequently will experience fewer respiratory health problem (OECD 2006a,b). When the "spillovers" of an

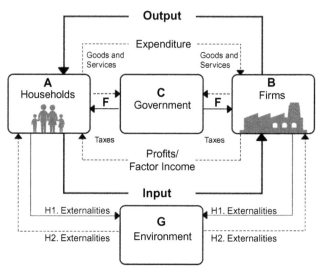

Figure 6.2 General equilibrium model.

intervention to other markets are not negligible the adoption of a wide perspective, also referred to as GEM, is envisaged (OECD 2006a,b). General equilibrium analysis assumes that an exogenous shock in the price of one commodity leads to changes in the relative prices faced by economic agents in different markets of the economy.

General equilibrium analysis is based on the Arrow−Debreu model[3] of Walrasian Equilibrium in a competitive market calibrated on economy specific data. In the model the economy(ies) is represented using the same basic structure with three possible agents: a set of producers, consumers (households), and government(s). The framework of GEM is represented in Fig. 6.2. Households/Consumers are assumed to generate income by

---

[3] The Arrow−Debreu model specifies a competitive economy in which there are finite numbers of consumers, commodities (some being used as production inputs), and production units. Consumers have a set of well-defined preferences (continuous, no satiated, and convex), and each consumer holds an initial endowment of the commodities, with a positive quantity of at least one commodity. The technology that converts inputs into outputs is either nonincreasing returns to scale or constant returns to scale. In this economy, every producer maximizes profit and every consumer maximizes utility over their budget sets. The equilibrium of the economy is characterized by a set of prices at which the excess demand is zero for every commodity, and producers make zero profit. These market-clearing prices are reached through a atonement process, in which "a fictitious price-setter" facilitates the price adjustment following a set of rules that resembles the way in which prices are reached in the real competitive economy.

renting factors to the firms and using income to purchase factor commodities, producers that produce goods purchased by households, and other firms and government(s) that produce commodities consumed by both firms and households.

The starting point of GEM is constructing an input—output table/matrix in which columns and rows indicate the purchases of inputs and the sales of output by each sector in the economy. Given an initial base case scenario, GEM simulates the consequences of a new intervention (e.g., introduction on a new fossil fuels tax) on the relative prices faced by the different economic agents (households, firms, and government) in the economy. Using the ex ante and ex post sets of value, GEM quantifies the expected net benefit of a given intervention and provides evidence on the consequences for the agents of the circular flow displayed in Fig. 6.2 of policies improving environmental qualities (Conrad, 2002).

Funded by the Commission of the European Communities1, DG Research, 5th Framework programme and by national authorities, the GEM for energy, environment, and economic interactions (GEM-E3) is a recursive dynamic computable GEM that covers the interactions between the economy, the energy system, and the environment (GEM-E3, 2018). It is developed to assess energy, climate, and environmental policies. The model, freely accessible and constantly updated, can compare the economic effects of various cost-efficient climate policy instruments, such as taxes, auctioning, various forms of pollution permits and command-and-control policy in the context of climate and energy policies. GEM-E3 can also be used to quantify the revenue from different recycling technologies.

A remarkable practical example of the general equilibrium analysis of EHIs is provided by the CBA of Clean Air Act routinely conducted by the US EPA. This CBA examines in detail the consequences of new air pollution regulations in the US economy considering a range of markets affected by the new regulation.

The main disadvantage of the general equilibrium analysis is its complexity. To determine a priori the size of the effects and the markets affected by a new intervention is difficult and time-consuming. In addition, simulating the linkages between sectors using realistic assumptions requires a high degree of interdisciplinary expertise and increases the cost of carrying out a CBA. As suggested by the EPA Guidelines for preparing economic analysis in both partial and general equilibrium, analysis is essential to select the appropriate estimates of social costs. Especially in General

Equilibrium Analysis (GEA), there is the risk to overestimate the total social costs because of double counting the same price effects in two separate intermediate markets. Including changes in the final demand for goods and excluding intermediate goods can significantly minimize this issue.

6.4 For how long should costs be considered?

The third main challenge in costing EHIs is the cost time horizon. As for benefits, there is not a gold standard for the cost time horizon. Existing guidelines for CBA are not consistent on the time frame suggested for the analysis. According to the EC Guidelines (2014), for the majority of the infrastructure projects, the assumed time horizon should be 20 years, while for productive investments, the time frame should be 10 years. Although, in practice, the investment time horizon is indefinite for many infrastructural projects, it is essential to assume that in a given point in time, all the liabilities have been liquidated. The HM Treasury (2018) suggests that costs and benefits should be estimated over the entire lifetime of the intervention. This guideline suggests as baseline a 10-year horizon 10; however, it also specifies that in some cases, a time horizon as long as 60 years may be suitable (e.g., infrastructure projects). Some guidelines for cost time frame are provided from the European Commission (EC) (2014) and reported in Table 6.6.

Table 6.6 European Commissions reference periods.

Sector	Reference period (year)
Railways	30
Roads	25−30
Ports and airports	25
Urban transport	25−30
Water supply/Sanitation	30
Waste management	25−30
Energy	15−25
Broadband[a]	15−25
Research and innovation[a]	15−25
Business and infrastructure	10−15
Other sectors	10−15

[a]This sector is unlikely to be relevant for EHIs.
Source: Modified from European Commission (EC), 2014. Guidelines to cost−benefit analysis of investment projects. In: Economic Appraisal Tool for Cohesion Policy 2014−2020. <https://ec.europa.eu/inea/sites/inea/files/cba_guide_cohesion_policy.pdf>.

In the financial analysis the investment cost can span several initial years and some more routine or replacement costs can be assumed to occur in more distant years. It is essential when making a financial analysis to define a realistic time horizon (maximum number of years for which forecasts are provided. Forecasts should be formulated according to the intervention duration and the time horizon adopted should be long enough to include mid and long-term impacts. If a GEM is adopted, it is also important to consider that the effects of many EHIs are not static and may have a significant impact even after several years. If the intertemporal effects of new intervention affecting multiple markets are not negligible, a dynamic GEM can be adopted. Using, for instance, the simulated trajectory of the economy without the regulation, the dynamic GEM quantifies the incremental costs and benefits of the regulation at different future points in time. Given the high degree of uncertainty associated with this type of analysis, an extensive sensitivity analysis is recommended.

6.5 Other types of costs to consider

While social costs are the most comprehensive types of costs and the preferable measure to use in CBA of EHIs, there are other categories/terms used to qualify the costs associated with EHIs. In this section, alternatives terms are described to facilitate the reader's interpretation of the existing literature on CBA (EPA, 2010).

6.5.1 Direct versus indirect costs

Direct costs are defined as those that fall directly in the market affected by the intervention. Indirect costs are those costs that accrue to secondary market/households or agencies not affected by the regulation. These two types of costs will be clarified in the following section covering partial and general equilibrium analysis.

6.5.2 Private and public-sector cost

The total cost associated with a new intervention can also be divided in costs that are born by private bodies, such as households and firms versus public costs that accrue to different national or regional governments.

6.5.3 Incremental costs

The incremental costs are all those costs incurred because of the new intervention versus the status quo scenario. For instance, the incremental cost of a regulation is estimated by subtracting the total cost of the new regulation and the total cost of the environmental regulation already in place.

6.5.4 Abatement cost

The abatement cost is the cost for the industry/firms to reduce or prevent pollution following a new regulation. Abatement cost can be divided into four subcategories: treatment-the cost to capture and remove pollution after its generation during the production process (e.g., air pollution car filter); recycling cost: the cost or processing waste after production for an alternative use; disposal cost: the cost of placing or destroying the waste produced during production; and finally prevention cost: which is the cost of any method/device/process to reduce the amount of pollution/waste generated during production.

6.5.5 Government regulatory costs

The government regulatory costs are the costs to the government for implementing the policy. Regulatory costs are often substantial, especially if the project involves a large area (e.g., European regulation) and/or a large number of industries.

6.5.6 Distributional costs

Since CBA focuses on maximizing net benefits to the whole society, it can create winners and losers by imposing higher costs to different socioeconomic groups/entities. These costs will be discussed in the conclusion of this book.

6.6 Conclusion

The objective of this chapter is to provide an overview of the main issues associated with costing EHIs. Section 6.2 outlines the two approaches: financial and economic analysis to quantify the costs to EHIs. Section 6.3 is devoted to examining the differences between a partial equilibrium analysis and a general equilibrium analysis. Section 6.4 provides suggestions on selecting an appropriate time frame for estimating costs-summarizing suggestions from exiting CBA guidelines.

References

Barbier, E.B., Markandya, A., 2013. A New Blueprint for a Green Economy. Routledge, p. 2013.

Conrad, K., 2002. Computable general equilibrium models in environmental and resource economics. In: Tietenberg, T., Folmer, H. (Eds.), The International Yearbook of Environmental and Resource Economics 2002/2003. Edward Elgar, pp. 66–114.

Environmental Protection Agency (EPA), 2010. Steps in Conducting Benefits Analysis. 2010. <http://www.epa.gov/ttn/ecas/econdata/Rmanual2/7.2.html>.

European Commission (EC), 2008. Guidelines to cost–benefit analysis of investment projects. In: Economic Appraisal Tool for Cohesion Policy 2008–2014. <https://ec.europa.eu/inea/sites/inea/files/cba_guide_cohesion_policy.pdf>.

European Commission (EC), 2014. Guidelines to cost–benefit analysis of investment projects. In: Economic Appraisal Tool for Cohesion Policy 2014–2020. <https://ec.europa.eu/inea/sites/inea/files/cba_guide_cohesion_policy.pdf>.

Garrett-Peltier, H., 2011. Pedestrian and Bicycle Infrastructure: A National Study of Employment Impacts. Political Economy Research Institute University of Massachusetts, Amherst, MA. <https://www.peri.umass.edu/publication/item/427-pedestrian-and-bicycle-infrastructure-a-national-study-of-employment-impacts>.

GEM-E3, 2018. EU Science HUB. The European Commission's Science and Knowledge Service. <https://ec.europa.eu/jrc/en/gem-e3>.

HM Treasury, 2018. The Green Book. Appraisal and Evaluation in Central Government. <https://www.gov.uk/government/publications/the-green-book-appraisal-and-evaluation-in-central-governent>.

OECD, 2006a. Economic Evaluation of Environmental Health Risks to Children. OECD Publishing, Paris, p. 2006.

OECD, Pearce, D., Atkinson, G., Mourato, S., 2006b. Cost-Benefit Analysis and the Environment, OECD OECD, Geneva, 2006.

Sustain, C.R., 2018. The Cost-Benefit Revolution. The MIT Press.

Tonin, S., 2014. Assessing the impact of the remedial actions taken at a contaminated Italian site: an ex-post valuation analysis. Rev. Environ. Sci. Biotechnol. 13, 121. Available from: https://doi.org/10.1007/s11157-014-9332-8.

Further reading

European Commission (EC), 2001. Recommended Interim Values for the Value of Preventing a Fatality in DG Environment Cost Benefit Analysis 2001. <ec.europa.eu/environment/enveco/others/pdf/recommended_interim_values.pdf>.

Environmental Protection Agency (EPA), 1993. Policy for Use of Probabilistic Analysis in Risk Assessment. <http://www.epa.gov/spc/2probana.htm>.

Environmental Protection Agency (EPA), 2011. Benefits and Costs of the Clean Air Act 1990–2020, the Second Prospective Study. <https://www.epa.gov/clean-air-act-overview/benefits-and-costs-clean-air-act-1990-2020-second-prospective-study>.

CHAPTER 7

Discounting benefits and costs

Carla Guerriero[1] and Antonia Pacelli[2]

[1]Department of Economics and Statistics, University of Naples Federico II, Naples, Italy; Centre for Studies in Economics and Finance (CSEF), Naples, Italy
[2]Department of Economics and Statistics, University of Naples Federico II, Naples, Italy

Contents

7.1 Introduction

The consistency and robustness of intertemporal preferences[1] are meaningful features of the cost—benefit analysis (CBA) framework. The appraisal of intertemporal preferences matters because economic evaluation passes through the lenses of preferences for being more reliable and for predicting the behavior of the economic agents. Understanding in detail the structure of the preferences is central to the use of scarce resources.

Choices are affected by the time in which an event is expected to occur: generally, receiving goods or services today is worth more than receiving them in the future. Discounting implies measuring the intertemporal preferences, and it allows the analyst to compare costs and benefits that occur at different times. CBA discounting is an essential step when

---

[1] The rate at which consumption and public spending are discounted over time.

Cost-Benefit Analysis of Environmental Health Interventions
DOI: https://doi.org/10.1016/B978-0-12-812885-5.00007-X
129

choosing between different programs and assessing their attractiveness: the project or the policy with the higher present value is the one that, following the CBA rule, should be chosen.

There exist different discounting methods for providing a realistic weight to the future, and the selected approach (e.g., zero discounting vs constant discount rate) can significantly affect the CBA results. Depending on the model adopted, the main issues associated with discounting are related to time inconsistency and an excessive care of the needs of the current generation against the interests and the welfare of future generations. The analyses on the relevance and the weight of those problems are discussed in this chapter together with the explanation of the different discounting models.

The following section classifies the types of discount rates based on the perspective of the agents considered, individuals, or society. The third section illustrates discounting methods together with the Collard alternative approach. The fourth section focuses on the main models of intergenerational discounting used in the literature. Finally, the last section of the chapter describes the effects of uncertainty as an assumption of the models and the issue of intergenerational equity. Given the focus of this book, specific references are made to environmental and healthcare interventions throughout the chapter.

7.2 Individual versus social discount rate

Private discounting refers to discounting from a specific limited perspective of private individuals or firms while social discounting, as the name suggests, considers the point of view of the society as a whole (Environmental Protection Agency, 2010).

Individual intertemporal preferences are influenced by subjective factors such as probability of death, savings, consumption, and borrowing habits. Social discount rate is defined as a normative concept: it tells what the society components should do; it gives a price to time and can be interpreted as the minimum required rate of return from a socially desirable project. The social discount rate is the rate at which the society is willing to trade present versus future consumption, and, as a result, it is not affected by individual characteristics.

The adoption of individual versus societal discount rate can bias the CBA results influencing policy makers in their decisions. The volume of the wedge between social and individual discounting depends on the set of assumptions made in the analysis. In the benchmark case (a first best world considering perfect capital markets and without any type of distortion), the social discount rate does not differ from the individual rate.

On the other hand, the closer the model is to the real-world complexity, the larger the wedge between the individual and societal discount rates (OECD, 2006).

Other important elements impacting CBA results are the different factors (e.g., time horizon considered in the analysis) affecting the decisions of individuals and communities. Individual choices are shorter term run and based on concerns that are relevant at a private level. For instance, knowing their probability of death can influence the behavior of the individuals affecting their consumption choices. This might not be the case when the agent is not a private individual but a society that has longer-term objectives and a wider perspective (Environmental Protection Agency, 2010).

The choice of the appropriate discount rate has critical implications for the CBA results and depends on the perspective adopted in the analysis. If a narrow perspective is adopted, as in the case of small private company and/or small short intervention(s), an individual discount rate may be used. Regarding future health events, the relationship between individual and social preferences over future events and the related discount rate is a point of discussion: in general, the health economists concentrate their studies on a period coincident with the lifetime of the treated individual; therefore the discount is mainly an individual discounting framework.

Most of the times, however, CBA is conducted using a societal perspective, and a social rate of time preferences is recommended. The perspective from which the costs and benefits are analyzed and discounted in this chapter is a societal one considering the welfare of the society and not the limited point of view of private individuals. The social discount rate is considered the rate that better represents preferences because the individual perspective involves misleading information, giving most of the power to the present compared to the future welfare.

7.3 Measurability of time preferences

In an intertemporal framework, to associate a numerical value to individual and social preferences is not a straightforward procedure. Economic evaluation is based on the value of costs and benefits taken into consideration the preferences of the agents.

Two are the most common approaches to quantify intertemporal preference: revealed and stated preferences methodologies. As the name suggests, revealed preferences approaches are based on data of actual behavior of the agents, whereas the stated preferences refer to the answers of the individuals considering hypothetical circumstances. Surely, choices made by individuals are more reliable than what they say that they would do in an hypothetical situation. However, a limitation of the revealed preference methods is the complexity of the estimation of the time preference rate, since it is not possible to control for potential confounding factors as in the stated preference methods.

Another issue associated with revealed preferences is that it is not always possible to obtain valuations from observed behavior: this is the case, for instance, for the time preferences over future health events. Trading health is much more complicated than trading wealth over time due to so many confounding and endogenous factors that affect health decisions. This is one of the reasons why often economists apply stated preference methods instead of the more reliable revealed preference methodology. The relationship between time preference and health-related behaviors has been the subject of several studies that found that agents that are more patient have lower rates of time preference, so they might be more willing to bear short-term costs for obtaining long-term benefits (e.g., they would sacrifice their wealth or conduct a healthier lifestyle to be better off/healthier in the future) (Cairns, 2006).

Another feature of the measurability of future health events is that the economic evaluation of health choices done in monetary terms generally use a discount rate which is equal to the discount rate of the costs. The problems occur when the health outcomes are expressed in monetary terms and the discount rate is considered not consistent. Nevertheless, in most of the cases, health outcomes are not valued in money terms but quantified in terms of years of life gained or QALYs gained, and in this case, they should be discounted at a different rate that is generally lower than the one applied for the costs (Cairns, 2006).

As it will be shown in the next sections, in a CBA, the process of assigning a weight to the future with respect to the present is made through the discount rate. Analysts utilize this procedure for evaluating costs and benefits in a common metric that leads to the present value of the net benefits of the policy or the project. Different methodologies lead to different results and different ethical concepts: intergenerational equity is the most difficult achievement because the trade offs between the long-term benefits for future generation and the short term costs for current generations are difficult to measure.

The remaining part of this section will describe the different approaches to discounting including the alternative model proposed by Collard (1978).

7.3.1 Zero discounting

"Zero discounting" considers a discount rate equal to zero and a discount factor equal to one. If a zero discount is assumed, everyone is "equal" now and in the future. This outcome has very important implications for CBA results. As suggested by Pearce et al. (2003), the first unrealistic consequence of using a zero-discount rate is "that we care as much for someone not just one hundred years from now as we do for someone now, but also someone one thousand years from now, or even one million years from now."

The rejection of the rationale behind the zero discounting is also based on the resulting impoverishment and increasing sacrifices until substantial levels of current generations[2] caused by saving and investment choices. This principle would be true for every generation, even future ones, so in practice, every generation will found itself impoverished to benefit future generations.

For this reason, the zero discounting approach goes in the opposite direction of the Rawls criterion, which takes care of the welfare of the poorest individuals in the society having as a scope of maximizing their welfare. Under a zero discounting scenario the sacrifice would be made by the poorest generations. In conclusion, from an ethical perspective, zero discounting does not solve the discounting dilemma, but it creates other contradictions.

7.3.2 Standard approach: constant discount rate

Following the methodological structure utilized the most in the economic analysis, the further in the future an event is going to occur, the lower is its weight. The standard approach considers the discount rate invariant constant in time. This concept is not exempted from criticisms and dilemmas that will be described later.

In a constant discount rate framework the discount factor is computed as follows:

[2] Olson and Bailey (1981).

$$w_t = \frac{1}{(1+s)^t}$$

where w_t is the discount factor, s is the discount rate, and t is the time period. This method is also called "discounted utilitarianism" model. The consistency of a constant discount rate has been an important focus of discussion, because it generates some issues especially in terms of equity.

Indeed, this approach does not make any difference between intergenerational and intragenerational social discounting, ignoring the eventual changes in preferences, economic system, and income of future generations. It is a representative-agent approach, where the welfare of future generations is considered an extension of the welfare of the current generation.

Therefore these are the reasons that led some studies to denominate it as the "tyranny of discounting": it is not acceptable that current generations do not consider the wellbeing of future generations, holding a position of dictators with respect to the future human beings.

An interesting example can be made about environmental damages: a waste of environmental resources that would create an environmental cost in 100 years is valued much less if the cost would occur today. For this reason, this discounting method seems inconsistent with the values and objectives of sustainable development path, which is a global priority in this historical period.

Another limitation of the constant discount rate approach is that it assumes economic growth being constant over time. The assumption that future generations are going to be richer in the future could not be realistic, and, in the same way, constant discount rate does not fit properly the reality since a lot of important parameters are a function of economic growth (as, for instance, the interest rates).

Nevertheless, the constant discount rate model is commonly used in standard practice. An example is the United Kingdom. In its HM Treasury (2018), the United Kingdom specifies social time preference rate (STPR) equal to 3.5% and computed estimating time preferences and wealth effect components. A peculiarity of this system is that the discount rate is not the same in the case of risk to health and life values, which is 1.5%, due to the absence of wealth effect. This is the case because the preferences of future health are not easily measurable in monetary terms, because in general, the method for quantifying them are the years of life gained or quality-adjusted life-years (QALYs) gained.

In addition, when the time-horizon is particularly long, the STPR should decline due to uncertainty about its parameters. In practice the United Kingdom implemented an extension of the constant discount rate approach, utilizing a step function. This means that the approach of the United Kingdom to the discounting models tries to perform variations of the constant discount rate to render the results more reliable by internalizing some of the issues generated by the latter approach.

7.3.3 Time declining rates

In the recent years, economists are trying to set a discounting model that better describes how people behave and make decisions about their consumption over time. A significant body of evidence shows that people do not have a constant discount rate, but it is likely to be time-declining. Therefore the discount rate s of the previous equation varies over time, s_t: the more t is high, the smaller is the discount rate.

From empirical studies a declining discount rate, also referred as hyperbolic discount rate, is the rate that better describes the behavior of agents (Frederick et al., 2002). The most commonly used formulas to express the hyperbolic discount rates utilized in the literature are

$$w_t = \frac{1}{(1 + gt)} \, w_t = \frac{1}{(1+t)^h}$$

where w_t is the discount factor, g and h are the discount rates, and t is the time period.

Evidences show that hyperbolic discounting models are more realistic than the others, especially when the object considered are the monetary outcomes. Indeed, under uncertainty and other market imperfections, time-decline rate models are considered the discounting models that better performs with these complications.

However, this method carries with it several limitations; one of the most relevant and well-known is the time inconsistency problem: policy formulated in the present might not be optimal in the moment where it should be implemented using a different discount rate, and it will be contradicted by future behavior. Some economists argue that time inconsistency is not an issue that invalidates the results, because they found the process of changing the path of discount rates conditional to a new situation and different set of preferences of individuals in the future legitimate

(Henderson and Bateman, 1995). From this point of view, time consistency is a "most unnatural requirement," as defined by Heal (2000).

Following this approach, it is also possible to maximize the discounted value of net benefits accomplishing the sustainability requirement, which involves the care of future generations' welfare.

7.3.4 An alternative to discounting: the Collard approach

In a long-time horizon framework the use of any positive discount rate produces small present value, even though the discount rate is low. Thus long-term costs and benefits have a small impact on current choices affecting negatively the intertemporal fairness of the choices. In circumstances in which the costs (or benefits) of some actions must be borne by a different generation, it represents a relevant problem, which led economists to formulate alternative methods that could replace the logic of discounting.

Collard (1978), in his paper "Altruism and Economy," proposes a method for disentangling intergenerational discounting and equity. The idea is to discount the streams of costs and benefits considering each generation in its own present, obtaining a stream of present values. Then, the weighted combination of these present values attached to different generations gives the net present value (NPV) of the project or policy. The method for weighing reflects the altruism of the current generation toward the future generations, rather than discounting. The complexity of the main assumption made by the Collard approach: to represent future generation in their own present, makes this approach difficult to apply in real practice.

7.4 Intergenerational social discounting

Policies that are designed to address long-term environmental and health problems such as climate change, radioactive waste disposal, and biodiversity loss will involve, given the length of their time horizon, discounting the benefits and costs of multiple generations. In the literature, this approach to discounting is also referred as intergenerational discounting. Independently from the discounting method adopted (e.g., constant, hyperbolic), the length of the time horizon has a significant effect on the estimated present value. The standard approach with constant discount rates is defined unfair from most of the recent studies that tried to develop different approaches for discounting in a more fairly and consistent way.

However, as mentioned, a long-time horizon even with decreasing discount rates will generate small present values. This is an important issue of intergenerational fairness since future generations will bear costs (or benefit) from actions of previous generations. As showed before, Collard (1978) is an example of an alternative method for disentangling this issue, combining present values and a weight that incorporates the "rate of altruism" instead of properly discounting.

The length of the time horizon implies that a small change in the social discount rate leads to significant differences in the present value of future net benefits. The present value of large but distant future net benefits are rendered insignificant by discounting.

An assumption of discounting is that future generations will be better off with respect to the present and that current generations care less about future welfare. However, the criticisms are based on the potential catastrophic changes and risks that future generations would suffer if the environmental degradation will follow the current unsustainable path. Therefore it is unavoidable to examine the environmental impacts on future generations since the effects of actions undertaken today have consequences in the long run. Indeed, a crucial analysis on intergenerational concerns has to be made about the current environmental crisis due to climate change. The trade-off between the short-term benefits for the current generation and the costs that will be paid by the future generations should be measured to promote a rapid and global response to this issue.

Properly discounting the future to predict the global impacts and effects of these choices, avoiding excessive sacrifices of current and future generations, is the central focus of the economic models in the next paragraph.

7.4.1 Economic models

Included in this paragraph are the most common economic models studied by economists in recent years: the Ramsey model and Dynamic Integrated model of Climate and Economy (DICE) proposed by the Yale economist William Nordhaus. The first is an optimal growth model, which is more general and has its fundamentals in a strict set of assumptions; the second model investigates the effects of climate catastrophes and the effects of the environmental crisis. Both have the scope of finding the correct discount rate to avoid damages for current and future generations.

7.4.1.1 Ramsey model

Policies and projects with a long-time horizon need a process of discounting that should be realistic, considering the welfare of current and future generations. The Ramsey framework discusses the assumptions made in optimal growth models and the conventional discounting procedures developed in their applications. Indeed, in the Ramsey model the economy as a whole is assumed to behave as a "representative agent" choosing consumption and savings in each point of the time in order to maximise his NPV. The Ramsey model assumes perfect competition and full information, under these assumptions the social discount rate equals the market interest rate.

As the discount rate, the market interest rate incorporates the changes in marginal utility of consumption over time due to different levels of consumption and the impact of time preferences that the agents apply on their own utility functions.

The Ramsey equation allows to estimate the market interest rate (r), and it can be written as

$$r = \eta g + \rho$$

where the first term is called wealth effect, which is composed by the aversion to inequality (η) multiplied by the income growth (g); the second term refers to the pure rate of time preference or utility discount rate (ρ).

There exist two types of approaches for providing values to the parameters of this equation: a descriptive and a prescriptive approach. The distinction between them consists in the choice of assigning the figures based on what is the actual behavior of the individuals or societies or instead evaluating what should be the ethically correct behavior of the agent. Therefore the descriptive approach tries to predict the actual behavior estimating the parameters starting from what empirically happens. This consideration holds for the first term of the formula: marginal utility of consumption and changes in the growth rate. For the ρ, which is the pure rate of time preference, it is inferred since it is not possible to provide a direct estimation of that.

Instead, the second approach is called "perspective" because its aim is to find in this equation an ethical benchmark, chosen by the economists. One of the mostly debated issues is whether is appropriate to assign a lower weight to the welfare and consumption of future generations (ρ greater than zero); hence, if it is exact to assign a lower weight to the welfare and consumption of future generations. However, if consumption continues to grow over time, future generations are going to be richer than the current generation, but the decreasing marginal utility and higher consumption levels are worth less than they would be valued today. Consequently, in a growing economy, beside the value of the pure rate of time preference, the future consumption is discounted and has a lower weight than the consumption today. Following this approach, some economists argue that a low discount rate would lead to an overinvestment in environmental protection, reducing the resources for investments that have more direct consequences on the welfare of future generations and have positive impacts on current generations. A very low discount rate, for those who believe in this point of view, leads to huge and unethical sacrifices of current and close generations. Examples of these investments are the interventions for the mitigation of climate change.

The Ramsey model is very common and intuitive, but it is not exempted from limitations: it ignores the difference in income within generations, and over a long-time horizon, the assumptions made could bring to misleading results.

7.4.1.2 Dynamic integrated climate-economy model

The intergenerational comparison in the context of climate change is unavoidable, because the slow pace of climate system's response to emissions of greenhouse gases causes trade-off that last several decades making the time horizon long and uncertain. This is an important argument in the discussion about the methods to adopt in order to reduce polluting emissions.

Most climate economists adopt the Ramsey model through a descriptive approach. The model estimates the underlying parameters of the equation on actual behavior. Indeed, Nordhaus (1992) with his Dynamic Integrated Climate-Economy Model (DICE) shows that economic models should be based on actual behavior and able to predict this behavior. So, Nordhaus used the Ramsey equation and then calibrated the parameters around the market interest rate, using empirical estimates of its first term (ηg).

DICE considers the standard cases, in the absence of any action, and the cases of climate catastrophes. For the aggregate consumption, in the first case, Nordhaus assumes the standard hypothesis that future generations will grow richer: it leads to an increasing function; instead, in the case of climate catastrophe (a very realistic scenario in this historical period), the welfare of future generations is compromised and the slope of the function from positive becomes negative.

Analyzing the net benefits of global emissions path, if the policy-makers want to avoid 2°C of global warming, this model clarifies that current and close generations should sacrifice income and consumption to mitigate climate change. However, under the assumptions of the conventional discounting approach, the present value of the long-term benefits is lower than the short-term costs. This means that the social discount rate that should be used is lower than the one extrapolated by the conventional approach, otherwise it fails the CBA because it does not increase the social welfare (the social discount rate suggested is 3%). The robustness of the results of this model to keep global warming under 2°C with a more appropriate social discount rate is consistent in both economic and ethical terms.

7.5 Uncertainty and intergenerational equity

Preferences can change over time, and this characteristic makes very difficult for the analysts to assess whether current generations' preferences reflect those of communities that are not born yet. The issues related to this consideration are about uncertainty and equity among generations. Uncertainty about the future complicates the dynamic optimization problem of maximizing the lifetime welfare of individuals and communities, because the conditions of the future are unknown, and it is hard to determine the optimal level of saving and consumption based on uncertain estimations of future utility of wealth. The issue of intergenerational equity is strongly emphasized in the discounting framework: current generations assign weights to benefits and costs that will affect people belonging to future generations. In the moment of the evaluation, future individuals cannot provide their contribution to the decisions that are going to be made, and as we saw in the previous sections, even with declining discount rates, costs and benefits in the late future approximate to zero.

Future generations cannot contribute to the choices of current generations, even though the impacts of these choices are particularly relevant on their lives—sometimes, these are larger for future generations than current and close generations (e.g., climate change). When costs and benefits are distributed on a long-time period, it is hard to choose a fair path for the future welfare, because most of the time it requires sacrifices today.

Uncertainty and equity issues are interrelated: considering uncertainty in the models should reduce equity problems, choosing a lower discount rate that makes society care more about future welfare. Without uncertainty the discount rate is equal to the average market interest rate. If uncertainty is accounted for, the discount rate, independently from the discount model adopted, is lower than the average market interest rates. This phenomenon occurs because uncertainty it is internalized in the NPV of the policy or of the project analyzed; with a long-time horizon, uncertainty and risks increase, and this causes the decline of the discount rate. Adjusting the previous models by involving considerations about uncertainty clarifies the implications of using different models for evaluating real life circumstances.

Weitzman (1998) gives a theoretical justification for implementing the declining discount rates models, considering uncertainty and risk neutral policy makers. Utilizing discount rates lower than the average market interest rate is based on the estimation of the certainty-equivalent discount rate, under uncertainty the analyst should consider the average of the discount factors instead of the average of the discount rates.

Indeed, in the standard approach, it is intuitive that a model considers a constant discount rate; it treats in the same way current and future generations, regardless of changes in preference and economic growth, which strictly and positively depends on the discount rate. So, comparing the standard approach and the model involving uncertainty, as the study of Newell and Pizer (2001) about US interest rates, constant discount rates approach could undervalue the NPV, using a discount rate in the future which is higher than the discount applied in the uncertainty case.

The models that imply the downward sloping structure of discount rates present other types of problems due to the presence of uncertainty, as the generation of inconsistency policy ranking between NPV and net future value (NFV). The NPV is the stream of current and future net benefits, computed as benefits minus costs of each period, multiplied by their weight, which is the discount factor.

$$NPV = \sum_{t=0}^{n} d_t NB_t$$

where NB_t is the net benefit at time t, and d is the discount factor, which negatively depends on the discount rate (r):

$$d_t = \frac{1}{(1+r)^t}$$

Instead, the NFV is estimated in a point of time in the future, n, corresponding to the end of the project. The formula is the same, but the discount factor positively depends on the discount rate.

$$d_t = (1+r)^{(n-t)}$$

Therefore the NPV and NFV can be written in relative terms with respect to each other.

Studies conducted from economists as Gollier and Hammitt (2014) demonstrate the economic significance in long-time horizon policies of this structure on policy evaluation, in particular regarding long-term environmental policies such as mitigation of climate change.

7.6 Conclusions

The objective of this chapter is to illustrate the different methodologies developed for discounting. The discussion of the discounting models and Collard's alternative made clearer the issues related to the long-term assessments of costs and benefits in CBA. This lead the analysis on intergenerational fairness, which is one of the main issues related to the discount rates. The assumption made in intergenerational studies is that future people will have the same preferences as those living today. However, as many authors suggest, it is likely present adult preferences will be different from those of future generations. In the future, some natural resources may not exist anymore. If the resources still exist, changes in their quantity/quality will affect their intrinsic value. Even for present abundant resources, the continuous loss in natural asset cannot be compensated forever as there will be a critical point of degradation (e.g., the issue of plastic in the oceans).

In conclusion the presence of uncertainty in the discounting methodology would make the CBA results more reliable, because many future events are unforeseeable, and, as mentioned, preferences are likely to change over time within and between generations.

References

Cairns, J., 2006. Developments in discounting: with special reference to future health events. Resour. Energy Econ. 28, 282–297.

Collard, D., 1978. Altruism and Economy. Martin Robertson, Oxford.

Environmental Protection Agency, 2010. Chapter 6: Discounting future benefits and costs. Guidelines for Preparing Economic Analyses. United States Environmental Protection Agency, Washington, DC.

Frederick, S., et al., 2002. Time discounting and time preference: a critical review. Journal of Economic Literature 40 (2), 351–401.

Gollier, C., Hammitt, J., 2014. The long run discounting controversy. Annu. Rev. Resour. Econ. 6, 273–295.

Heal, G., 2000. Valuing the Future: Economic Theory and Sustainability. Columbia University Press.

Henderson, N., Bateman, I., (1995). Empirical and public choice evidence for hyperbolic social discount rates and the implications for intergenerational discounting. Environmental & Resource Economics. vol. 5, issue 4, 413—423.

HM Treasury, 2018. The Green Book

Newell, R., Pizer, W., 2001. Discounting the distant future: how much do uncertain rates increase valuations? In: Resources for the Future.

Nordhaus, W., (1992), "The 'DICE' Model: Background and Structure of a Dynamic Integrated Climate-Economy Model of the Economics of Global Warming", Cowles Foundation for Research in Economics, Yale University.

OECD, 2006. Cost-Benefit Analysis and the Environment: Recent Developments. Discounting. OECD Publishing, Chapter 13.

Olson, M., Bailey, M. J., (1981). Positive Time Preference. Journal of Political Economy vol. 89, 1—25.

Pearce, D., Groom, B., Hepburn, C., Koundouri, P., 2003. Valuing the future. World Econ. 4 (2).

Weitzman, M.I., 1998. Why the far-distant future should be discounted at its lowest possible rate. J. Environ. Econ. Manage. 36, 201—208.

Further reading

Arrow, K., Cropper, M., Gollier, C., Groom, B., Heal, G., Newell, R., et al., 2013. Determining benefits and costs for future generations. Science 341 (6144), 349—350.

Boardman, A., Greenberg, H., et al., 2006. Cost-Benefit Analysis, Concepts and Practice, third ed. Pearson Prentice Hall, Upper Saddle River, NJ.

Dietz, S., Groom, B., Pizer, W.A., 2016. Weighing the costs and benefits of climate change to our children. Children and Climate Change. Princeton-Brookings, volume 261.

Gollier, C., 2011. Pricing the Future: The Economics of Discounting and Sustainable Development. Princeton University Press.

Van der Pol, M., Cairns, J., 2002. A comparison of the discounted utility model and hyperbolic discounting models in the case of social and private intertemporal preferences for health. J. Econ. Behav. Organ. 49, 79—96.

CHAPTER 8

Quantifying uncertainty in environmental health models

Zaid Chalabi[1,2]
[1]Institute of Environmental Design and Engineering, Bartlett School of Environment, Energy and Resources, University College London, London, United Kingdom
[2]Department of Public Health, Environments and Society, Faculty of Public Health and Policy, London School of Hygiene and Tropical Medicine, London, United Kingdom

Contents

8.1 Introduction

The development of environmental health models for risk assessment has increased considerably over the years. Notable examples of such models are those developed by the US Environmental Protection Agency, such as 3MRA, SHEDS, ERDEM, MENTOR, CalTox, MMSOILS, TRIM, PRESTO, BEAM (Williams et al., 2010), among many others developed elsewhere. With the increasing use of such models to support policy making particularly in relation to the evaluation of the cost−benefits of environmental health interventions, it is imperative to quantify the uncertainty in the models to ensure the robustness of any decision based on their predictions.

Cost-Benefit Analysis of Environmental Health Interventions
DOI: https://doi.org/10.1016/B978-0-12-812885-5.00008-1

In general, environmental health models consist of a series of linked models. For example, in the case of the evaluation of an environmental intervention to reduce the health impact of a point source of pollution, the cost–benefit analysis would be based on several connected models consisting of (1) the generation of the pollutant; (2) the spatiotemporal dispersal of the pollutant in the environment away from the source; (3) the exposure of the affected population to the pollutant, pre- and postintervention; (4) the exposure–health outcome relationship(s); (5) population health dynamics; (6) direct cost of the intervention from different perspectives; and (7) indirect cost of the intervention such as healthcare and social care costs associated with the disease burdens averted or incurred.

Environmental health models represent an extension of environmental models in which an additional modeling component on health risk assessment is included. The methods which have been developed to quantify uncertainty in environmental models—and complex models in general—are equally applicable to quantify the uncertainty in environmental health models. There has been much interest in the development and use of quantitative methods for uncertainty analysis of environmental models (Ziehn and Tomlin, 2009; Gan et al., 2014; Uusitalo et al., 2015), environmental exposure models (Bennett et al., 1998; Semple et al., 2003; Ciffroy et al., 2016), and environmental health risk assessment models (McKone and Bogen, 1992; Yokota and Thompson, 2004; Mesa-Frias et al., 2014; Lam, 2012; Chalabi et al., 2015; Dong et al., 2015; Dutta, 2017; Stewart and Hursthouse, 2018).

The methods described in the abovementioned studies span a suite of uncertainty analysis approaches ranging from the screening of noninfluential parameters before embarking on detailed analysis, Monte Carlo (MC) simulations and efficient variations of it, global sensitivity analysis, Bayesian methods, fuzzy set methods, among many others. Congruent with the increasing use of such methods, and to facilitate their use in practice, generic software toolboxes have been developed for uncertainty analyzes (e.g., Tong, 2005; Ziehn and Tomlin, 2009).

The aim of this chapter is to describe the very basics of some of the mathematical methods for quantifying the uncertainty in models used to evaluate environmental health interventions. More detailed reviews of generic methods of uncertainty analysis and their applications in environmental health risk assessment can be found in several review articles (e.g., Dong et al., 2015; Uusitalo et al., 2015; Stewart and Hursthouse, 2018).

The chapter is divided into six sections including the "Introduction" and "Conclusion." The second section outlines the main types of uncertainty. The third section describes the propagation of uncertainty, from both theoretical and computational perspectives. The fourth section outlines the application of these methods to handling uncertainty in cost—benefit analyses. The fifth section outlines briefly risk-sensitive and robust methods of estimation in the face of model uncertainty. The sixth section discusses practical approaches for performing uncertainty analysis and summarizes more comprehensive methods for handling uncertainty. The final section concludes. All numerical simulations and symbolic processing and were conducted in *Mathematica* version 11.3 (https://www.wolfram.com/mathematica/)

8.2 Types of uncertainty

There are two main types of uncertainty in any model: parametric and structural. Parametric uncertainty is concerned with the uncertainty in the parameters of the model, whereas structural uncertainty is concerned with the uncertainty in the structure of the model. In practice, a model has both parametric and structural uncertainties.

8.2.1 Parametric uncertainty

Starting with parametric uncertainty, consider a parameter p in a model. The uncertainty in this parameter can be represented in three main ways:

1. Deterministically, for example, as an interval $[p_{min}, p_{max}]$ where p_{min} and p_{max} are respectively the minimum and maximum possible values of the parameter. This means that the only information available on the uncertainty in the parameter is that it is bounded between a minimum and a maximum value.

2. Probabilistically, for example, in terms of a probability density function $f(p)$. As an example, $f(p) = \frac{1}{\sqrt{2\pi\sigma^2}} exp\left(-\frac{(p-\mu)^2}{2\sigma^2}\right)$ expresses the uncertainty in p as a normally distributed variable with mean μ and variance σ^2. Fig. 8.1 shows the probability density function of a parameter whose uncertainty is characterized by a normally distributed random variable with zero mean and variance 1. The area underneath the probability density function curve between two given points is the probability that the value of the parameter is between those points.

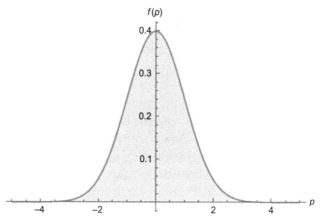

Figure 8.1 Probability density function of a normally distributed parameter with zero mean and variance unity.

3. As a fuzzy variable where the parameter is defined in terms of its degree of membership of a set. An example of a fuzzy parameter from the built environment is a dwelling's ventilation rate. From the perspective of health and wellbeing, ventilation rate can be defined as "low," "medium," or "high," The relationship between ventilation rate and air exchange rate is uncertain and can be shown in Fig. 8.2. If we denote air exchange rate by u and ventilation rate by v, then

$$a_1 \leq u \leq a_3; v = low$$

$$a_2 \leq u \leq a_4; v = medium$$

$$a_3 \leq u \leq a_5; v = high$$

The categories "low," "medium," and "high" are represented, respectively, by the sets Φ, Ψ, and Ω.

The above set of equations can be represented by:

$$a_1 \leq u \leq a_3; v \in \Phi$$

$$a_2 \leq u \leq a_4; v \in \Psi$$

$$a_3 \leq u \leq a_5; v \in \Omega$$

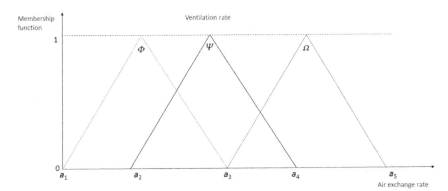

Figure 8.2 An example of a fuzzy variable whose membership function is defined by a trapezoidal rule.

where the symbol "$\in$" means belongs to, that is, $\nu \in \Phi$ means that ventilation rate belongs to the set Φ. In Fig. 8.2 the x-axis represents the air exchange rate and the y-axis the membership function of each set. The membership function is the degree to which the parameter belongs to the set. If it is zero, it means the parameter does not belong to the set; if it is unity, it means it fully belongs to the set. It is obvious that a parameter can belong to more than one set. This fuzzy set representation is an alternative to the probability representation. In this example the membership functions are defined in triangular form, which are simplest to use.

Other forms of membership functions can also be used (Zimmermann, 2001), but the trapezoidal membership function is simplest to use and process. There are several examples of the use of fuzzy mathematics in environmental health risk assessment (e.g., Ghomshei and Meech, 2010; Mofarrah and Husain, 2011; Mesa-Frias et al., 2014).

8.2.2 Structural uncertainty

In terms of structural uncertainty the source of the uncertainty is the structure of the model. Consider for illustrative purposes three different possible pathways connecting an exposure variable x to a health outcome variable y (Fig. 8.3). The first is formulated as a linear relationship (*dotted line*), the second as a continuous nonlinear relationship (*dot-dashed*), and the third as a discontinuous nonlinear relationship (*dashed line*). Each of these relationships defines a possible model structure.

Another example illustrating high-level structural uncertainty is shown in Figs. 8.4 and 8.5. Fig. 8.4 shows an abstract model connecting a set of

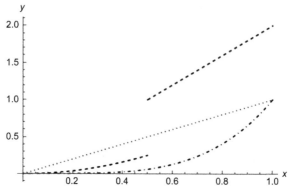

Figure 8.3 Three alternative model structures. *Dotted*, linear; *dot-dashed*, nonlinear; *dashed*, nonlinear and discontinuous.

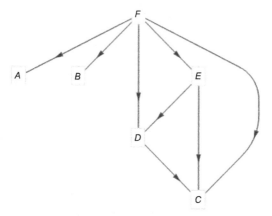

Figure 8.4 An abstract model shown in terms of links connecting nodes. The direction of arrow represents the impact pathway.

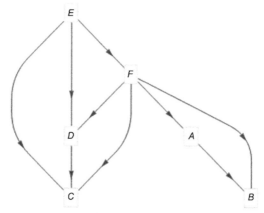

Figure 8.5 An alternative model configuration to that in Fig. 8.4. A new link is added ("A" impacts "B" directly), and a link is reversed ("E" impacts "F" directly).

nodes or variables. The direction of the arrow indicates the impact pathway. In this model, node "F" is assumed to impact nodes "A," "B," "C," "D," and "E" directly; node "E" impacts nodes "D" and "C" directly; and node "D" impacts node "C" directly.

Fig. 8.5 represents an alternative model structure linking the nodes. It differs from the model configuration in Fig. 8.4 in two ways: (1) there is an additional link connecting node "A" to node "B" where "A" impacts "B" directly, (2) the impact direction between "F" and "E" is reversed.

The quantification of structural uncertainty is not as straightforward as that of parametric uncertainty, because any model structure is also characterized by parameters, and hence, in theory, it is not possible to disentangle structural uncertainty from parametric uncertainty.

In its simplest form, structural uncertainty can be characterized by simulating the alternative model structures and then measuring the variation in the outputs. For example, assume that we have n alternative deterministic models $M_i, i = 1 \ldots n$, and each model M_i produces the output of interest y_i giving the spread of model outputs $\{y_i, i = 1 \ldots n\}$. The variance, higher order moments, or the empirical probability density function can be deduced from the model outputs $\{y_i, i = 1 \ldots n\}$ to characterize the uncertainty in the model output. If the output is a time-varying variable, the spread of outputs is referred to as a multimodel ensemble (which is quite common in climate models).

If data observations are available, there are statistical methods, such as Bayesian model averaging, which can be used to produce a combined model output by weighing the outputs of the alternative models based on how well they perform against the data and thus provide a better estimate of the uncertainty in the model output (Hoeting et al., 1999; Georgakakos et al., 2004; Duan et al., 2007; Tebaldi and Knutti, 2007). Bayesian model averaging has also been used to quantify structural uncertainty in decision models (Jackson et al., 2011).

8.3 Propagation of uncertainty

This section is divided into two parts and is outlined using simple illustrative examples. The first part covers very basic theoretical concepts in propagation of uncertainty in deterministic and probabilistic space. The second part outlines classical deterministic and probabilistic methods for propagating parametric uncertainty in models.

8.3.1 Theoretical perspective

The concept of propagation of uncertainty is fundamental to dealing with uncertainty in environmental health models. An illustrative example is shown next:

$$x \longrightarrow y = f(x) \longrightarrow z = g(y)$$

where x could be the pollutant concentration at a pollution source, y the pollutant level to which individuals are exposed to, and z is the health outcome associated with exposure level y. The functions f and g represent, respectively, the models associating the variable x and y, and y and z. The key point here is to propagate the uncertainty in x to that in z, conditional on knowing the uncertainties in x, f, and g.

Let us consider a very simple example of uncertainty propagation: $z = x + y$ where x and y are independent random variables. If we know the uncertainty in x and y, what is the uncertainty in z? We can approach the solution to this problem in three ways: deterministic, probabilistic, and fuzzy set theoretic. In this discourse, only the first two techniques are explored. In both techniques, we will assume that the uncertainty in x and y can be presented as simple bounds.

From the deterministic perspective, this takes the form of $\tilde{x} = [x_{min}, x_{max}]$ and $\tilde{y} = [y_{min}, y_{max}]$, where x_{min} and x_{max} are, respectively, the minimum and maximum possible values of x, and likewise, y_{min} and y_{max} are, respectively, the minimum and maximum possible values of y. The symbol $\sim$ above the variable name indicates that the variable is an interval.

Using operations in interval mathematics, the uncertainty in z is given by $\tilde{z} = [z_{min}, z_{max}] = [x_{min} + y_{min}, x_{max} + y_{max}]$ where z_{min} and z_{max} are, respectively, the minimum and maximum possible values of z. For example, if $\tilde{x} = [0, 1]$ and $\tilde{y} = [0, 1]$, then $\tilde{z} = [0, 2]$. Other operations in interval mathematics such as multiplication and division can also be defined (Nickel, 1980).

The counterpart operations in probability space are as follows. Here x and y are represented, respectively, by uniformly distributed random variables in the ranges $[x_{min}, x_{max}]$ and $[y_{min}, x_{max}]$, which means that their probability density functions are given, respectively, by

$$f(x) = \left\{ \begin{array}{l} 1/(x_{max} - x_{min}); x_{min} \leq x \leq x_{max} \\ 0; x < x_{min}, x > x_{max} \end{array} \right\}$$

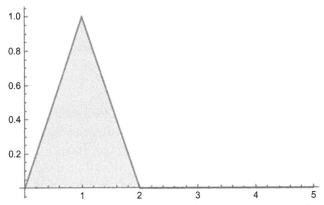

Figure 8.6 Probability density function of the sum of two standard uniformly distributed random variables.

$$f(y) = \left\{ \begin{array}{c} 1/(y_{max} - y_{min}); \, y_{min} \leq y \leq y_{max} \\ 0; \, y < y_{min}, \, y > y_{max} \end{array} \right\}$$

The probability density function of z, $f(z)$, is given by the convolution of $f(x)$ and $f(y)$. It is beyond the scope of this chapter to derive or explain this relationship (Argawal and Elmaghraby, 2001); however, a solution is given next. If x and y are independent uniformly distributed variables between 0 and 1, the probability density function of their sum is given by (Fig. 8.6):

$$f(z) = \left\{ \begin{array}{c} z; \, 0 \leq z \leq 1 \\ 2 - z; \, 1 \leq z \leq 2 \\ 0; \, z < 0, z > 2 \end{array} \right\}$$

It is interesting to note that the sum of two uniformly distributed random variables is not a uniformly distributed random variable, and this shows that the propagation of uncertainty is not intuitive. Using *Mathematica*, Rose and Smith (2002) were able to derive the analytical expressions for the sum of two or more uniformly distributed random variables as well as the sums and products of random variables of few other well-known probability distributions.

8.3.2 Computational perspective

When a model has many parameters, it is imperative that any uncertainty analysis should consider the uncertainty in all the parameters simultaneously. Two methods will be outlined: deterministic and probabilistic. To simplify the exposition of the methods, it will be assumed that the parameters are independent (and thus uncorrelated).

8.3.2.1 Deterministic approach

Starting with the deterministic approach, consider a model which has two parameters: α and β, and denote the model output by u. Assume that (1) the best estimates of the parameters are $\widehat{\alpha}$ and $\widehat{\beta}$, and (2) the only information available on characterizing the uncertainty in these parameters is that each parameter is bounded, that is, $\alpha_{min} \leq \alpha \leq \alpha_{max}$ and $\beta_{min} \leq \beta \leq \beta_{max}$ where the subscripts "min" and "max" on a variable mean, respectively, the lower and upper bounds of the variable. For many environmental health models, it is insufficient to evaluate the uncertainty of a model output caused by the uncertainty on one parameter at a time because of the nature of the nonlinear relationship between the model output and the model parameters and their interactions. The uncertainty in the model output should be evaluated against the uncertainty in all the parameters of the model simultaneously.

One very simple form of deterministic uncertainty analysis is to evaluate the model output for the best estimates of the parameters and then for each permutation of the parameters at their respective lower and upper bounds as shown in Table 8.1.

In Table 8.1 the first and second columns give, respectively, the values of the α and β parameters, and the third column gives the corresponding model output. This means that the model should be run five times to get all the variations in the model outputs corresponding to the combination of the parameter values at their bounds. If we denote by u_{min} and u_{max} to be lowest and highest values of the set of model outputs $\{\widehat{u}, u_1, u_2, u_3, u_4\}$ then the uncertainty in the model output is expressed as

Table 8.1 Permutation of parameter values at their bounds and baseline estimates.

α	β	u
$\widehat{\alpha}$	$\widehat{\beta}$	$\widehat{u}$
α_{min}	β_{min}	u_1
α_{min}	β_{max}	u_2
α_{max}	β_{min}	u_3
α_{max}	β_{max}	u_4

a bounded interval: $u_{min} \leq u \leq u_{max}$. Variance and higher order moments of u can also be used to characterize the uncertainty in model output.

Note that if the number of parameters in a model is n, the number the computer model runs, which would be required, is $2^n + 1$ where 2^n is the number of permutations of parameters at their lower and upper bounds. This approach is very impractical if the model has more than a few parameters. For example, if $n = 20$, the number of computer-runs required to cover all the permutation of parameter values at their bounds (in addition to the nominal values of the parameters) is $1048,576$, which is computationally prohibitive. There is another disadvantage to this method. In nonlinear models the sensitivity of the model to the parameters at their bounds is not necessarily the same as that in other regions of the parameter space. In other words, in relation to the example in Table 8.1, there could be internal regions in the parameter space for which the model output is less than u_{min} or greater than u_{max}.

8.3.2.2 Probabilistic approach

In the probabilistic approach the uncertainty in each of the parameters is defined by its probability density function. The simplest approach—but not necessarily the most efficient—is the MC approach. In the MC approach the model is run many times where each run is executed with different permutations of the model parameters selected randomly based on their probability density functions. From the model outputs, the variance or the high-order moments are calculated and used to characterize the uncertainty in the model output induced by the uncertainty in the model parameters. For a complete characterization of the uncertainty in the model output, an empirical probability density function of the model output can be constructed.

For illustrative purposes, assume a model has m independent parameters $\alpha_1 \ldots \alpha_m$. Assume also that the uncertainty in each parameter $\alpha_i, i = 1 \ldots m$ is characterized by its probability density function $f(\alpha_i)$. The steps of the MC approach can be conceptualized by the following pseudo-algorithm:

Step 1. Select the number of model computer runs, r

Step 2. For each model computer run $j = 1 \ldots r$

    Step 2.1. Sample each parameter $\alpha_i, i = 1 \ldots m$ from its probability density function $f(\alpha_i)$ and denote the sample value of the parameter by $\alpha_i^{(j)}$

Step 2.2. Run the model with the sampled parameters $\alpha_i^{(j)}, i = 1 \ldots m$

Step 2.3. Collate the r model output runs $y^{(j)}, j = 1 \ldots r$ where $y^{(j)}$ is the model output corresponding to the parameter combination $\alpha_i^{(j)}, i = 1 \ldots m$

Step 3. Construct the empirical probability density function of the model output $f(y)$ from $y^{(j)}, j = 1 \ldots r$.

As an illustrative example, consider the following simple algebraic model:

$$d = a^2 + b^3 c$$

where d is the output. Assume that the uncertainty in a is characterized by a normally distributed variable of mean 0 and standard deviation 3, that in b by a uniformly distributed random variable bounded between -5 and $+5$, and in c by a normally distributed variable with mean -1 and standard deviation 4.

The uncertainty in d can be characterized using the MC method. The results are shown next: Figs. 8.7−8.9 show, respectively, the probability density functions of the input parameters a, b and c, and Fig. 8.10 shows the probability density function of the model output, d.

In this simulation the model was run 10^6 times. This was feasible because the model is very simple and the computer processing time (CPU) per model run is very short. If the model however is complex and the CPU per model is long or very long, the MC method would be

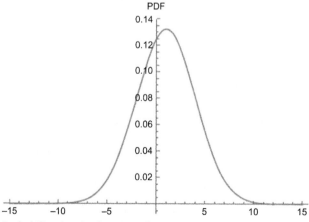

Figure 8.7 Probability density function of a.

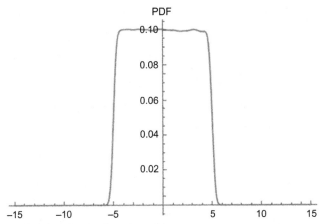

Figure 8.8 Probability density function of *b*.

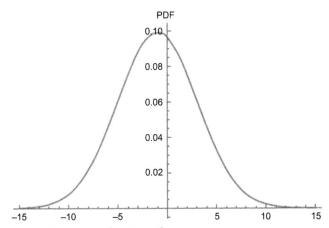

Figure 8.9 Probability density function of *c*.

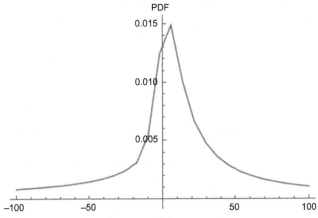

Figure 8.10 Probability density function of *d*.

impractical. In this case a stratified form of MC sampling can be used such as Latin hypercube sampling (Helton and Davis, 2003). Examples of using MC in environmental health risk assessment are given in Smith (1994) and Qu et al. (2012). Examples of comparing the MC approach to other approaches in environmental health risk assessment are given in Kental and Aral (2005) and Chalabi et al. (2015).

8.4 Uncertainty in cost–benefit analysis

Once the uncertainty in the costs and benefits of environmental health interventions have been quantified separately using models, the uncertainty in the cost–benefit metric can be calculated using probabilistic approaches. Denote by c the cost of the intervention, b the health benefit of the intervention, λ the monetary value of health, then the monetized net benefit is given by

$$\phi = \lambda b - c$$

Assuming that λ is fixed, then the uncertainty in ϕ is a function of the uncertainty in b and c. If we represent the uncertainty in b and c, respectively, by their variances v_b and v_c, and assuming the benefits and costs of the intervention are independent (which is usually the case), the uncertainty in ϕ is given by

$$v_\phi = \lambda^2 v_b + v_c$$

If the interest is the cost–benefit ratio

$$\delta = c/b$$

then the uncertainty in cost–benefit ratio can be determined using the methods described in Section 8.3.2.2. In some cases, analytical solutions can be obtained. For example, if b and c can both be expressed as normally distributed variables, for some scenarios an analytical expression of the probability density function of δ can be obtained (Pham-Gia et al., 2006). In health economics where the cost-effectiveness analysis is based on epidemiological models only, more tailored methods for uncertainty analysis have been developed (e.g., Stinnett and Mullahy, 1998, Briggs, 2000).

8.5 Risk-sensitive and robust methods of estimation

There are several mathematical methods which can handle uncertainty in ways to incoporate the attitude of policy makers to risk and uncertainty.

A simple example will be illustrated here. Denote by y the output of interest, the health burden of an environmental intervention. Normally, decision makers would be interested in the expected value of y, $\bar{y}$, and make their decision based on that value.

An engineering-based approach called risk-sensitive optimal control can be used to provide a "risk-sensitive" estimate of y (Whittle, 1990; Whittle, 2002). Denote the risk-sensitive value of y by $\tilde{y}$ and define it as

$$\tilde{y} = -\frac{1}{\psi} log\left(\overline{e^{-\psi y}}\right)$$

where ψ is the risk parameter and the overbar over a variable denotes its expected value.

It can be shown that (Whittle, 1990; Whittle, 2002)

$$\tilde{y} = \bar{y} - \frac{\psi}{2}\nu_y + h_{y,\psi}$$

where ν_y is the variance in y, and $h_{y,\psi}$ is a function of high-order moments of y and polynomial powers in ψ. In other words the risk-sensitive value of a model output is equal to its expected value minus the risk parameter multiplied by the variance of the output (i.e., uncertainty of output) plus high-order terms. The value of the risk parameter can be chosen to reflect the attitude of the decision maker. Assuming $h_{y,\psi}$ is negligible, the interpretation of $\tilde{y}$ from the preceding equation is as follows:

If the value of ψ is chosen such that
1. $\psi = 0$ (default value), then $\tilde{y} = \bar{y}$, that is, the risk-sensitive value of the estimated health burden is the same as the expected value of the burden. This means that the decision maker is risk-neutral.
2. $\psi > 0$, then $\tilde{y} < \bar{y}$. This means that the decision maker is risk seeking: he/she is gambling that the uncertainty is in their favor and that the true burden is likely to be less than the expected burden.
3. $\psi < 0$, then $\tilde{y} > \bar{y}$. This means that the decision maker is risk averse: he/she is gambling that the uncertainty is not in their favor and that the true burden is likely to be more than the expected burden.

Another approach which is widely used to make robust decisions under uncertainty is that of robust optimization (Ben-Tal and Nemirovski, 2002; Beyer and Sendhoff, 2007; Bertsimas et al., 2011). In cost–benefit analysis, it is often required to determine the optimal environmental intervention which maximizes the net health benefit. Denote by $\theta_i, i = 1 \ldots m$ the m feasible interventions, Γ the net health benefit, and ω the set of disturbances.

Determining the optimal intervention can be defined by the following mathematical problem:

$$\max_{\theta_i} \min_{\omega} \Gamma(\theta_i, \omega)$$

The above mathematical problem can be explained simply as a game between two operators. The "max" operator is maximizing the net benefit, whereas the "min" operator is minimizing the net benefit. In other words, "uncertainty" is attempting to hinder the maximization. Solving the above mathematical problem would give you a robust solution, because the maximization is sought under all types of uncertainties.

8.6 Discussion

The methods of uncertainty analysis are generic and apply to many types of models. The specific issue pertaining to environmental health models is that they consist of a series of models of different orders of complexity. There is uncertainty (parametric and structural) in each of the models, and the challenge is to characterize the uncertainties in all the models and then propagate the uncertainties through the series of models to the final model output. If, however, all the uncertainties are considered simultaneously, there is a risk of very large uncertainty at the final output in whatever representation the uncertainty is expressed. It is more practical therefore to apply a suite of methods in a step-wise manner to screen different types of uncertainties before using the more extensive methods (e.g., Gan et al., 2015).

The field of uncertainty analysis is rich and there are many thorough and powerful mathematical methods which are beyond the scope of this chapter. Prominent among these methods are global sensitivity analysis (GSA), polynomial chaos expansion (PCE), and Gaussian process emulation (GPE). GSA decomposes the total variance of the output (uncertainty) into the sum of the variances (uncertainties) of the input parameters and all orders of their interactions (Saltelli et al., 1993, 1999, 2004, 2010; Homma and Saltelli, 1996; Sobol, 2001; Sobol and Kucherenko, 2009). In PCE, the uncertain parameters and the model output are expressed as orthogonal polynomial expansions of random variables and the coefficients of expansion of the model output are determined from those of the inputs (Surdet et al., 2008; Crestaux et al., 2009). To alleviate the time required to carry out MC-based uncertainty analysis of large-scale models, which take very long time to run, metamodeling methods are used to approximate a large-scale model by a surrogate empirical model, which takes much shorter time to execute (Schultz et al., 2006; Ratto et al., 2007). GPE is a metamodeling nonparametric regression approach that approximates a model using Gaussian processes (Haylock and O'Hagan, 1996; Conti et al., 2009; Fricker et al., 2011). GPE has been used in quantifying uncertainty in health economic models (Stevenson et al., 2004).

8.7 Conclusion

The field of uncertainty quantification is wide-ranging ,and inevitably, this chapter will not do it justice. The chapter outlined some very basic principles of uncertainty analysis in relation to the characterization of uncertainty and the propagation of uncertainty. Three main approaches were outlined for characterizing uncertainty: deterministic, probabilistic, and fuzzy. The fundamentals of uncertainty propagation were explained analytically and illustrated through using simple numerical examples. In the last section the readers are referred to more comprehensive methods for uncertainty analysis.

References

Argawal, M.K., Elmaghraby, S.E., 2001. On computing the distribution function of the sum of independent random variables. Comput. Oper. Res. 28, 473−483.

Bennett, D.H., James, A.L., McKone, T.E., Oldenburg, C.M., 1998. On uncertainty in remediation analysis: variance propagation from subsurface transport to exposure modelling. Reliab. Eng. Syst. Saf. 62, 117−129.

Ben-Tal, A., Nemirovski, A., 2002. Robust optimization − methodology and applications. Math. Program. Ser., B 92, 453−480.

Bertsimas, D., Brown, D.B., Caramanis, C., 2011. Theory and applications of robust optimization. SIAM Rev. 53, 464−501.

Beyer, H.-G., Sendhoff, B., 2007. Robust optimization − a comprehensive review. Comput. Meth. Appl. Mech. Eng. 196, 3190−3218.

Briggs, A.H., 2000. Handling uncertainty in cost-effectiveness models. Pharmacoeconomics 17, 459−500.

Chalabi, Z., Das, P., Milner, J., Davies, M., Hamilton, I., Jones, B., et al., 2015. Risk analysis of housing energy interventions under model uncertainty. Energy Build. 109, 174−182.

Ciffroy, P., Alfonso, B., Altenpohl, A., Banjac, Z., Bierkens, J., Brochot, C., et al., 2016. Modelling the exposure to chemicals for risk assessment: a comprehensive library of multimedia and PBPK models for integration, prediction, uncertainty and sensitivity analysis—the MERLIN-Expo tool. Sci. Total Environ. 568, 770—784.

Conti, S., Gosling, J.P., Oakley, J.E., O'Hagan, A., 2009. Gaussian process emulation of dynamic computer codes. Biometrika 96, 663—676.

Crestaux, T., Le Maître, O., Martinez, J.-M., 2009. Polynomial chaos expansion for sensitivity analysis. Reliab. Eng. Syst. Saf. 94, 1161—1172.

Dong, Z., Liu, Y., Duan, L., Bekele Naidu, R., 2015. Uncertainties in human health risk assessment of environmental contaminants: a review and a perspective. Environ. Int. 85, 120—132.

Duan, Q., Ajami, N.K., Gao, X., Sorooshian, S., 2007. Multi-model ensemble hydrologic prediction using Bayesian model averaging. Adv. Water Res. 30, 1371—1386.

Dutta, P., 2017. Modelling variability and uncertainty in human health risk assessment. MethodsX 4, 76—85.

Fricker, T.E., Oakley, J.E., Sims, N.D., Worden, K., 2011. Probability uncertainty analysis of an FRF of a structure using a Gaussian process emulator. Mech. Syst. Signal Process. 25, 2962—2975.

Gan, Y., Duan, Q., Gong, W., Tong, C., Sun, Y., Chu, W., et al., 2014. A comprehensive evaluation of various sensitivity analysis methods: a case study with a hydrological model. Environ. Modell. Softw. 51, 269—285.

Gan, Y., Liang, X.-Z., Duan, Q., Choi, H.I., Dai, Y., Wu, H., 2015. Stepwise sensitivity analysis from qualitative to quantitative: application to the terrestrial hydrological modeling of a conjunctive surface-subsurface (CSSP) land surface model. J. Adv. Model. Earth Syst. 7, 648—669.

Georgakakos, K.P., Seo, D.-J., Gupta, H., Schaake, J., Butta, M.B., 2004. Towards the characterization of streamflow simulation uncertainty through multi-model ensembles. J. Hydrol. 298, 222—241.

Ghomshei, M.M., Meech, J.A., 2010. Application of fuzzy logic on environmental risk assessment: some thoughts on fuzzy sets. Cybern. Syst. 31, 317—332.

Haylock, R., O'Hagan, A., 1996. On inference for outputs of computationally expensive computer models with uncertainty on the inputs. In: Bernado, J.M., Berger, J.O., Dawid, A.P., Smith, A.F.M. (Eds.), Bayesian Statistics 5. Oxford University Press, Oxford, UK, pp. 629—637.

Helton, J.C., Davis, F.J., 2003. Latin hypercube sampling and the propagation of uncertainty in analyses of complex systems. Reliab. Eng. Syst. Saf. 81, 23—69.

Hoeting, J.A., Madigan, D., Raftery, A.E., Volinsky, C.T., 1999. Bayesian model averaging: a tutorial. Stat. Sci. 14, 382—417.

Homma, T., Saltelli, A., 1996. Importance measures in global sensitivity analysis of nonlinear models. Reliab. Eng. Syst. Saf. 52, 1—17.

Jackson, C.H., Bojke, L., Thompson, S.G., Claxton, K., Sharples, L.D., 2011. A framework for addressing structural uncertainty in decision models. Med. Decis. Making 31, 662—674.

Kental, E., Aral, M.M., 2005. 2D Monte Carlo versus 2D fuzzy Monte Carlo health risk assessment. Stochastic Environ. Res. Risk Assess. 19, 86—96.

Lam, N.S.-N., 2012. Geospatial methods for reducing uncertainties in environmental health risk assessment: challenges and opportunities. Ann. Assoc. Am. Geogr. 102, 942—950.

Mesa-Frias, M., Chalabi, Z., Foss, A.M., 2014. Quantifying uncertainty in health impact assessment: a case-study example on indoor housing ventilation. Environ. Int. 62, 95—103.

McKone, T.E., Bogen, K.T., 1992. Uncertainties in health-risk assessment: an integrated case study based on tetrachloroethylene in California groundwater. Regul. Toxicol. Pharmacol. 15, 86—103.

Mofarrah, A., Husain, T., 2011. Fuzzy based health risk assessment of heavy metals introduced into the marine environment. Water Qual. Exposure Health 3, 25−36.

Nickel, K.L.E., 1980. Interval Mathematics. Elsevier.

Pham-Gia, T., Turkkan, N., Marchand, E., 2006. Density of the ratio of two normal random variables and its applications. Commun. Stat. Theory Methods 35, 1569−1591.

Qu, C., Sun, R., Wang, S., Huang, L., Bi, J., 2012. Monte Carlo simulation-based health risk assessment of heavy metal soil pollution: a case study in the Qixia mining area, China. Hum. Ecol. Risk Assess. 18, 733−750.

Ratto, M., Pagano, A., Young, P., 2007. State dependent parameter metamodelling and sensitivity analysis. Comput. Phys. Commun. 177, 863−876.

Rose, C., Smith, D., 2002. Mathematical Statistics with Mathematica. Springer-Verlag.

Saltelli, A., Andres, T.H., Homma, T., 1993. Sensitivity analysis of model output. An investigation of new techniques. Comput. Stat. Data Anal. 15, 211−238.

Saltelli, A., Trantola, S., Chan, K.P.S., 1999. A quantitative model-independent method for global sensitivity analysis of model output. Technometrics 41, 39−56.

Saltelli, A., Tarantola, S., Campolongo, F., Ratto, M., 2004. Sensitivity Analysis in Practice. A Guide Addressing Scientific Models. John Wiley & Sons.

Saltelli, A., Annoni, P., Azzini, I., Campolongo, F.M., Tarantola, S., 2010. Variance based sensitivity analysis of model output. Design and estimator for the total sensitivity index. Comput. Phys. Commun. 18, 259−270.

Schultz, M.T., Small, M.J., Fischbeck, P.S., Farrow, R.S., 2006. Evaluating response surface designs for uncertainty analysis and prescriptive applications of a large-scale water quality model. Environ. Modell. Assess. 11, 345−359.

Semple, S.E., Proud, L.A., Cherrie, J.W., 2003. Use of Monte Carlo simulation in exposure modelling. Scand. J. Work Environ. Health 29, 347−353.

Smith, R.L., 1994. Use of Monte Carlo simulation for human exposure assessment at a superfund site. Risk Anal. 14, 433−439.

Sobol, I.M., 2001. Global sensitivity indices for nonlinear mathematical models and their Monte Carlo estimates. Math. Comput. Simul. 55, 271−280.

Sobol, I.M., Kucherenko, S., 2009. Derivative based global sensitivity measures and their link with global sensitivity indices. Math. Comput. Simul. 79, 3009−3017.

Stevenson, M.D., Oakley, J., Chilcott, J.B., 2004. Gaussian process modelling in conjunction with individual patient simulation modeling: a case study describing the calculation of cost-effectiveness ratios for the treatment of established osteoporosis. Med. Decis. Making 24, 89−100.

Stewart, A.G., Hursthouse, A.S., 2018. Environment and human health: the challenge of uncertainty in risk assessment. Geosciences 8 (1), 24.

Stinnett, A.A., Mullahy, J., 1998. Net health benefits. A new framework for the analysis of uncertainty in cost-effectiveness analysis. Med. Decis. Making 18, Suppl: S68-Suppl: S88.

Surdet, N., 2008. Global sensitivity analysis using polynomial chaos expansions. Reliab. Eng. Syst. Saf. 93, 964−979.

Tebaldi, C., Knutti, R., 2007. The use of the multi-model ensemble in probabilistic climate projections. Philos. Trans. R. Soc., A 365, 2053−2075.

Tong, C., 2005. Problem Solving Environment for Uncertainty Analysis and Design Exploration (PSUADE) User's Manual. Lawrence Livermore National Laboratory (LLNL), Livermore, CA, p. 109.

Uusitalo, L., Lehikoinen, A., Helle, I., Myberg, K., 2015. An overview of methods to evaluate uncertainty in deterministic models in decision support. Environ. Modell. Softw. 63, 24−31.

Williams, P.R.D., Hubbell, B.J., Weber, E., Fehrenbacher, C., Hardy, D., Zartarian, V., 2010. Chapter 3: An overview of exposure assessment models used by the US Environmental Protection Agency. In: Hanrahan, G. (Ed.), Modelling of Pollutants in Complex Environmental Systems. ILM Publications, pp. 61−131.

Whittle, P., 1990. Risk Sensitive Optimal Control. Wiley, Chichester.

Whittle, P., 2002. Risk sensitivity, a strangely pervasive concept. Macroecon. Dyn. 6, 5−18.

Yokota, F., Thompson, K.M., 2004. Value of information analysis in environmental health risk management decisions: past, present, and future. Risk Anal. 24, 635−650.

Ziehn, T., Tomlin, A.S., 2009. GUI-HDMRI − a software tool for global sensitivity analysis of complex models. Environ. Modell. Softw. 24, 775−785.

Zimmermann, H.J., 2001. Fuzzy Set Theory and Its Applications, fourth ed. Kluwer Academic Publishers, Boston, MA.

CHAPTER 9

Alternatives to cost–benefit analysis for economic evaluation

John S. F. Wright
Institute for Public Policy and Governance, University of Technology Sydney, Sydney, NSW, Australia

Contents

9.1 Introduction

Cost–benefit analysis (CBA) is an appraisal and assessment technique commonly applied across a wide range of contemporary policy sectors, including health care, planning, public transport, development, and the environment. At the fundamental level the application of CBA within each of these policy domains rests on the assumption that any increase in human well-being represents a "benefit," and conversely, that any decrease in human well-being represents a "cost." In sectors such as health care the environment, public transport, and development, a project, program, or policy is deemed "efficient" under CBA where the derived social benefit or aggregated level of individual well-being outweighs any associated loss of social well-being (Pearce et al., 2006).

Cost-Benefit Analysis of Environmental Health Interventions
DOI: https://doi.org/10.1016/B978-0-12-812885-5.00009-3

CBA has intellectual roots in 19th century European welfare economics. However, it has only recently become a regular feature of contemporary policy development and appraisal. The utilization of CBA within policy processes follows from the conclusion of the Second World War and the transition from corporate to market-style bureaucracies. By the late 1970s the old-style Weberian hierarchical bureaucracies of the prewar era, with their systems of program coordination and policy activity grounded in rules, statutes, protocols and accepted practices, had fallen from favor. In an increasingly complex and interconnected world, policy development needed more dynamism and greater sensitivity to external pressures (Considine and Lewis, 1999). In the 1950s and early 1960s the development of corporate bureaucracies on the model of the RAND corporation and under the guidance of important figures, such as US Secretary of State Robert MacNamara, had already seen the introduction of CBA, together with other mechanisms such as program budgeting, for the purpose of delivering "efficiency in government" and ensuring the effective use of public funds in major investment strategies. By the late 1980s, however, the transition from corporate bureaucracies to market-style bureaucracies would see CBA become the major appraisal technique for the deployment of public resources and the formulation of public policy in general.

The development of market bureaucracy was a distinguishing feature of advanced North Atlantic economies toward the end of the 20th century. Arguably, market-oriented public-sector organizations were indebted to the intellectual thrust of Osborne and Gaebler's (1992) "market-oriented government" and also to formal policy initiatives such as the "reinvention laboratories" of the Gore (1993) and the Thatcher and Major governments' "Next Steps" program. CBA seemed to thrive within these new organizational environments. Its notions of individual well-being, measures of total economic value, and the willingness to pay (WTP) for the maintenance of public assets such as transport, health, and the environment synergized with the new public-sector emphasis on competition and negotiation, market incentives, and regulatory mechanisms consolidated beneath a wider umbrella of public ownership and control. By the 21st century, CBA had become a powerful bureaucratic tool for inducting "market rationality" into policy development and for providing transparency and thereby ensuring the accountability of organizational activity on the basis of market friendly principles, both to the government and the wider public.

In many ways, CBA is analytical statement of the new organizational economics on which market-style bureaucracies of the 1980s and 1990s were founded. In this context, CBA is important to policy development across a wide range of sectors insofar as it enables political elites inside public-sector organizations to replace central planning and avoid responsibilities for associated failures, with a system of market incentives and mechanisms that allow rational choice making to determine appropriate policy ends. Under the rubric of CBA, available policy options become a continuum of initiatives differentiated according to differential levels of cost, quality, and benefit. For public sector elites, CBA enables the reimagination of responsibility for policy-making, and the associated potential for failure, as a talent for public administration. Under CBA, policy-making becomes decision-making, the requirement for senior public-sector managers to select from menu of available initiatives, shielded from responsibility for failure, insofar as decision-making activity proceeds on the basis of business plans, quotes, quality assurances, work practices and contracting skills. With the organizational reform of the public sector and corporate bureaucracies into quasi-business operating within quasi-markets, CBA has become centrally important to contemporary public administration in the 21st century (Considine and Lewis, 1999).

9.1.1 Why is cost—benefit analysis relevant to health and environmental policy?

At the fundamental level the relevance of CBA to health and environmental policy-making is its ability to force the issues of the environment and human health into the mainstream of rational calculation. In the context of environmental policy-making, CBA is a prospective or retrospective means for appraising interventions ultimately aimed at the prevention of environmental harms. It is also a mechanism for assessing the levels of benefit and harm involved in productive activities. Further, CBA can also function as mechanism for projecting the benefits of reclamation, or cleanup, initiatives with regard to environmental hazards that already exist. In all these roles, CBA is relevant to environmental policy-making as a corrective to the ordinary market situation, under which environmental goods have no immediate and obvious market value. Indeed, in the ordinary market situation, the impacts of productive activity on the environment are often ignored, and the implicit price of the environment is set at zero. At this point, CBA is relevant to environmental policy making insofar as it postulates the existence of a third party, or externality, that the policy activity or initiative either beneficially or detrimentally affects. In the ordinary market situation, industry has no incentive to calculate the cost of the by-products of production process, such as toxic waste, on third parties. But under CBA, the profits of industry are measured against an external third party, or the damage to the environment, with the benefits and the damages calculated in monetary terms. By doing so, CBA forces the issues of health and the environment to forefront. Where the environmental damage exceeds the profits of production, the industry's activities are deemed nonefficient. And where government intervention is required, environmental policy-making thus becomes simple public administration within an environmental context.

Overall, CBA is relevant to health and environmental policy-making in the same way it is relevant to other policy sectors. It is essentially a decision-making tool. In the particular case of environmental reclamation, for example, CBA enables decision-makers to differentiate between a menu of interventions on the basis of higher net benefits and thereby prioritize individual sites and also select between the various means for their reclamation. Specifically, a CBA conducted for these purposes would quantify the health outcomes associated with waste exposure before and after the intervention; would fix monetary values to the averted health impacts of exposure; would quantify the cost of the intervention; and, accounting for uncertainties, would compare results and prioritize options (Guerriero and Cairns, 2011, 406). In this way, CBA enables decision-makers to place environmental and health concerns at the center of their decision-making activity by deferring rationality to the system of prescribed market values and incentives for action that characterize both the CBA process and the new organizational context within which public sector elites necessarily operate. CBA enables elites to understand themselves as operating within a world of limited resources and beset with the possibilities for market failure. And, by attending to the process of CBA, they can ascertain the benefits of their interventions. They can prioritize competing alternatives. They can fix the levels of uncertainty associated with their activity. And, ultimately, they can comprehend and justify their efforts as attempts to correct the failures of the ordinary market situation with the production of verifiable and defensible data. As such, CBA is relevant to health and environmental policy-making because it gifts the decision-makers with both the capacity and the confidence to act.

9.1.2 What does cost—benefit analysis require from health and environmental policy-makers?

As a scientific measure of costs and benefits assessed against WTP, CBA requires more than a market-orientated bureaucratic context to function successfully as a decision-making tool. Indeed, CBA produces verifiable data regarding the impacts of environmental degradation on human biology based on defensible scientific methods. But, even to function in this capacity, CBA requires policy-makers to cultivate a wider environment in which the public accepts that decision-making activities, and any associated interventions, are undertaken on the basis of an appropriate balance between political judgment and science-based expertise.

This is no easy task. Science and politics have a tumultuous relationship. And there is no guarantee that any defensible and verifiable data that CBA might produce in relation to health and environmental interventions will have an impact on policy. As such, the conduct of CBA requires policy-makers to develop an understanding of the conditions under which the knowledge that CBA produces is likely to receive uptake. In other words, utilizing CBA requires an understanding of the science-policy relationship, or the science/policy nexus.

Typically, experts have attempted to understand the conditions under which the products of decision-making tools, such as CBA, are accommodated in policy via best practice models, or ideal types, of the science/policy nexus. All of these models, however, involve the important assumption that scientific knowledge should have uptake in policy. As such, the fact that CBA might very probably have no effect on policy at all should not necessarily discourage its application to policy questions.

As maintained, CBA is relevant to environmental policy on the basis that it forces consideration of human health to the forefront of calculation. By the same token, policy-makers must make equal efforts to force the role of scientific research to the forefront of political consideration. At the very least, this requires the assumption in favor of the science/policy relationship even where science is ignored in particular cases. Put another way, the use of CBA requires policy-makers to create an environment in which all parties accept that the application of scientific data and methods to policy questions delivers more sophisticated, sustainable, and beneficial outcomes. Under this assumption, policy-makers can facilitate easier long-term means of exchange and collaboration between science and policy regardless of, however, many short-term set-backs they may endure. Assuming in favor of the science/policy relationship opens the potential for greater communication between CBA and political decision-making. Rather than frustration regarding the lack of uptake, the issue becomes about understanding and improving the CBA-policy relationship and discovering the conditions under which scientists and policymaker can cooperate.

Given the importance of the environment to human health, and the emerging threat of climate change, the useful application of CBA to environmental health interventions may require the construction of guides and models through which CBA experts and policy-makers can understand how to operate across each other's borders.

In comparison with other policy sectors the border between CBA experts and environmental policy-makers has received significantly less attention. CBA experts need to recognize that the translation of defensible and verifiable scientific data into policy initiatives is by no means straightforward. They need to understand that even the relationship that CBA cultivates with policy-makers is subject to characterization. Across the range of other policy sectors, for example, a common media representation of the cross-border relationship is one of "business-as-usual." Despite appearances to the contrary, politics is safely "on top" and that CBA experts are always "on tap." In other words, politics is in charge. CBA experts are ready to provide advice, but only on request. Under this characterization the implication is that the relationship between CBA and the environment is about clever, inventive, but powerless environmental health economists "speaking environmental truths to power."

Especially today, there are also other and much more cynical representations of the relationship. In a world that has had enough of experts, scientific advisers are perceived to follow their own independent interests. Where they received sufficient funding, they will follow the interests of their funders. Similarly, CBA experts might themselves cynically characterize the relationship in terms of policy-makers commissioning their advice in the interests of legitimizing preformed decisions. The conduct of CBA requires both policy-makers and health-economists to avoid such easy characterizations of each other's position. Where these representations hold sway, both policy-makers and the CBA experts lose credibility in both each other's eyes and those of the public. Ultimately, the environment and human health is left to suffer the negative impacts.

If CBA is to enjoy influence, both the policy-makers charged with responsibility for making environmental decisions and the health economists involved in the conduct of research and production of data need to recognize that their relationship exists on more complex foundations. In other policy sectors, analysts of the science/policy nexus make reference to so-called collisions between science and politics (Hoppe, 2005). Under this notion the policy uptake of the knowledge produced via devices such as CBA involves a situation of mutual transgression of the boundaries between the field of knowledge utilization (KU) in policy studies (KU-PS) and the wider field of science, technology, and society (STS). By theorizing the development of the nexus between KU-PS and STS in the contemporary era, both environmental policy-makers and environmental health economists can build an understanding of how they can make their relationship work (Hoppe, 2005).

For environmental health economists, theorizing the nexus involves understanding the "scientization" policy. Today, we ordinarily think of policy as a position taken on an issue by an organization or individual in a position of authority (Hogwood and Gunn, 1984). But it was not always so. In the 1950s and 1960s, policy was the output of processes within political institutions. In the 1970s and 1980s, however, political scientists began distinguishing between functionally and temporally distinct subprocesses through which policies were made. Or, they began modeling the policy process, initiating a line of inquiry that would lead to the "scientization" of policy itself. In the 1980s the important implication of their work was that policy gained an ontological dimension. It became an object of study in its own right. The new models of the policy process were applied, in the same way, across the wide variety of political institutions and the different sectors of the economy. By the 1990s the new field of PS had become a business of marking-out the content, the development, and the impact of policy processes with a view to explaining variations over time, across sectors, and between national contexts. The point is that, in the new millennium, there are tangible and exploitable links between knowledge of policy sciences and KU in policy. Mobilizing the uptake of CBAs in policy is easier where policy-makers and health economists understand how policies come into being. Indeed, environmental health economists need to understand that policy-makers have an interest in grappling with the issues on the political agenda, which often demands engagement with the best available knowledge. At some point, policy will require high-quality scientific input (Hoppe, 2005).

In the 21st century context, devices such as CBA are undeniably important to policy-making regardless of their uptake or nonuptake in specific circumstances. The sheer complexity of issues that capture the contemporary political agenda gives need for the continued use and development of scientific methods and data in the policy-making process (Stoutenborough et al., 2015). The utilization of CBA in environmental policy requires both decision-makers and experts to recognize that the former will regularly turn to the latter for assistance in framing policy problems and their potential solutions. The relationship will not always succeed. But the complexity of contemporary policy problems also makes the relationship inevitable. For each party the challenge is to understand the conditions on which it can succeed, and through which these two different communities can work together.

In breaking through, environmental health economists must appreciate that policy is already "scientized" (Hoppe, 2005). Equally, they must also understand that policy sciences deal with complex multidimensional problems that do not always respect the safe disciplinary boundaries of the social and environmental sciences. For these reasons, policy makers are defensively minded. The policy world they inhabit is risk averse. Policymakers fear uncertainty, and they are almost pathologically reluctant to experiment. Outside the laboratory environment the policy initiatives for which they necessarily take responsibility have unknowable consequences. The careers of policy-makers often rest on whether the initiatives they choose to sponsor will work in a world of both known–unknowns and unknown–unknowns. Conversely, science just is not like this. The social sciences, such as environmental health economics, is a world of innovation and excitement, a field in which new and unexpected things regularly occur. The sciences are built on experimental evaluation designs. Knowledge is produced on the basis of falsification. For scientists to build knowledge, things need to go wrong. Policy-makers cannot afford "things-going-wrong." Policy-makers want quick results. They want administrative and political accountability. Alternatively, social scientists are about time and patience; they seek rigor and quality control (Hoppe, 2005).

9.1.3 What do health and environmental policy-makers require from cost–benefit analysis?

Policy-makers position themselves toward the political agenda. But when the issues that appear on the agenda involve matters of environmental concern, what do policy-makers require from tools such as CBA? What are they looking to achieve through their engagements with environmental health economists and the methods they employ? What contributions do they expect health economists to make? For the CBA experts, answers to these questions would appear relatively straightforward. CBA offers policy-makers reliable methods of data collection. Their analysis of the collected data facilitates improved knowledge of negative environmental externalities. And by assigning monetary values to health risks associated with externalities, CBA enables the formal quantification of the impacts of policy initiatives on human health, which empowers policy-makers to design and deliver "optimal policies" aimed at reducing environmental harms and the associated costs on wider society (Guerriero and Cairns, 2009). Certainly, CBA brings these valuable contributions to the table. And there are strong grounds for interpreting the value of CBA to policy in terms of a "read-across" from CBA outputs to the design of optimal policies. But the growing involvement of environmental health economists in contemporary policy processes is also important to decision-making in a more substantive and, arguably, cultural sense.

Since the early 1990s, an "evidence based" movement has developed within the policy sciences. The movement has its origins in the practice of evidence-based medicine (EBM) in the United Kingdom, which sought to regulate the practice of medicine and the standards of health care delivery throughout the country. Under EBM, health care would be delivered on the basis of the systematic review of available therapies and not the experiential knowledge of clinical professionals. The success of EBM in delivering higher and more consistent standards of care encouraged policy-makers to pursue the technique in other policy sectors. The movement for evidence-based policy (EBP) stresses that the usable and relevant knowledge must inform decision-making, policy development, or in fact any generalized effort to address and resolve issues on the political agenda. Today, policy-makers are broadly concerned to utilize knowledge and research evidence to formulate policy to the major issues of the contemporary political agenda such as juvenile crime, domestic poverty, poor educational performance, drug and alcohol abuse, preventable diseases, systemic disadvantages of indigenous communities, and indeed health and environmental degradation and harms.

EBP is about rational problem-solving. It involves making the effort to diagnose the causes of these issues, develop accurate knowledge of the relevant linkages, on the basis of the evidence. Considered broadly, CBA is part of this movement for including evidence in policy. In addition to the valuable knowledge products they offer, environmental health economists can be thought of as assisting policy-makers in taking a strategic position in relation to major social problems and helping them to develop informed responses. As such, CBA holds an obvious capacity to shape and deliver optimal environmental health policy. But the movement for EBP also has the capacity to shape wider social sciences such as health and environmental economics. Consistent with the needs of policy-makers, EBP will likely prioritize some kinds of disciplinary methods above others on a case-to-case basis.

The EBP movement is mostly a creature of the mature democracies of the developed world. Its grip over policy-making extends from government agencies, through bureaucracies and even into legislatures. At all these levels, the pursuit of EBP presents both a challenge and an opportunity to public officials and social researchers alike. Environmental health economists are no exception. The prospect of developing optimal environmental policies, making continuous improvements to population and environmental health, on the basis of rational evaluation and well-informed knowledge of available options is exciting to decision-makers. Equally, the prospects of having the recommendations of research endeavors formally recognized in practical policy interventions is alluring to social researchers. But, this excitement and allure also holds consequences. In order to exploit these opportunities, political leaders and public-sector managers recognize the need to make major investments in the applied social sciences.

From the public-sector perspective, investment in social sciences is about providing resources and ensuring means for the routine production and collection of input, output, and impact data. Public sector investment is a cyclical process of producing, analyzing, managing, and further reinvesting in the "bank" of useable and useful knowledge. Today, public-sector managers ordinarily take responsibility for the systematic collection of large data sets. In the private sector too, large organizations are engaged in developing "knowledge-management" strategies, processes through which they carryout the complex business of data collection, analysis, and dissemination (Saunders and Walter, 2005). Health and environmental economists depend on these strategies. Knowledge production mechanisms such as CBA refine and analyze the implications of these large data sets. They transform routinely collected data into usable knowledge and information.

In terms of the strategies that large organizations adopt and the data sets that collect, some academic disciplines are more useable and valuable to policy-makers than others. For example, methods of financial accounting, risk auditing, and CBA are more able to engage with the investments that large organizations make in the social sciences than the hermeneutic approaches of history and sociology. The organizational investments made in the social science chime with the relative utility of different means of knowledge production. EBP orientations within public-sector organizations and institutions make government the major investor in the social sciences. Governments do not gratefully wonder at and enthusiastically utilize the knowledge products that CBA and environmental health economists bring to policy processes. Governments are both knowledge-takers and knowledge-makers. Their investments in public-funded research strategies and organizations shape the kind of knowledge they receive as interest on their investment. By exercising their capacity to manage internal policy research and external research tenders, government influence the processes and the products of the social science at multiple levels.

9.2 Are there alternatives to cost–benefit analysis?

In a world of EBP and market-oriented bureaucracy, of course there are. Moreover, if the use of research evidence generated through CBA in decision-making proceeds on the basis of a relationship, or nexus, between science and policy, then it stands to reason that other forms of knowledge production are equally relevant to the relationship. Further still, if government is able to structure the nexus through indirect means at multiple levels, the question of what health and environmental policy-makers require from CBA becomes an issue of additional means of evidence production health, and environmental economist might be able to contribute to the decision-making process. Generally speaking, EBP orientations within government make prescriptions for methodological rigor on the basis of "what works" in a specific policy sector (Davies, 2004; Percy-Smith, 2005). Under this classic prescription of EBP, preferences for different types of knowledge production vary from sector to sector, some, such as criminology, preferring quantitative behavioral data, and others, such as social policy, preferring qualitative attitudinal data, and others still, such as environmental health, preferring outputs of CBA. However, there is no reason to expect that these preferences are stable and unchanging. In such case, environmental health economists cannot live in an ivory tower of CBA.

Today, the science policy nexus is about more than mutual benefit. During the Second World War, both the harder and softer sciences made great contributions to victory in terms of technologies and transitional administration. Similar strides were expected in the post-war era to the benefit of civilian life. In the 1970s, social science seemed "an endless-frontier" of abundant resources, complete autonomy, plentiful resources, and ready access to decision-making. However, the authority of science has abated somewhat against complexities of an increasingly interconnected and interdependent world. Autonomous science seemed unable to live up to the potential it seemed to claim for itself during the war. In the 1980s and 1990s, government revised the relationship by tightening its conditions for financial support and scientific autonomy. Today, the nexus is grounded on a web of interconnection that provides for contracting and organizational arrangements, research milestones and key deliverables, dissemination procedures, and linkages for KU. Across the web, scientific input into policy involves contingencies and changeable dynamics. Health and environmental policy is no different to any other sector. Policymakers in the sector inhabit a virtual cafeteria approaches to issues and expect to be able to choose from a menu of what kinds of research devices are most suitable for use against different types of issues (Hoppe, 2005).

In such a case, CBA does not occupy a privileged and authoritative position. Its careful practice is no guarantee of its continued relevance. However, the logic of "politics-on-top, experts-on-tap" is also unsuitable to the web of interconnection underlying the contemporary science—politics nexus. Politics does not unilaterally hurl research questions at environmental health economists. Arguably, health economists, such as other social scientists, and perhaps even a little even more so, are motivated by pride in their work, by the desire for influence and by dreams of glory and public heroism. This is not an undesirable state of affairs. It is to be expected. But the implication is that social science ordinarily targets policy-makers. Entrepreneurial health economists stalk the corridors of power. They are smart salespeople. Where policy-makers press them for usable knowledge and timely production, health economists lecture them for asking the wrong questions, while breaking open suit cases filled with better methods and more appropriate ideas (Hoppe, 2005). In the field of health and environmental policy, there are alternatives to CBA analysis for the simple reason that social scientists and policy-makers have a relationship. Transactions from one party to the other about managing instances of transgression and cooperation. In order to manage interactions, both parties need to be familiar with "alternative means of cooperation"; these can include devices such as cost-effective analysis, cost—utility analysis (CUA), robust decision-making (RDM), and multicriteria decision-making analysis.

9.2.1 Cost-effectiveness analysis

The key difference between the various methodologies relevant to environmental health economists are the means by which they measure and value benefits. Cost-effectiveness analysis (CEA) is a form of economic analysis that compares the relative costs and outcomes (or effects) of different courses of action. As we have seen, CBA measures benefits by both the quantity and quality of life years. Its measure may also include other aspects of health relevant to the environmental issue at hand. Typically, its unit of measure, or the means by which it values benefits, is the WTP or human capital. Alternatively, CEA measures benefit either by quantity or quality of life years, with its unit of measurement being either health life years equivalent or quality adjusted life years (QALYs) gained. As such, CEA is a rather simple measure that produces a single unidimensional outcome. Where CBA assigns a monetary value to the measure of effect, CEA is often used in the field of health services, where it may be inappropriate to monetize health effects.

The UK National Health Service (NHS) offers universal health care free at the point of access for the entire UK population. In England and Wales the National Institute for Health and Clinical Excellence (NICE) is responsible for conducting health technology assessments (HTAs), which forms the basis of government recommendations to local health authorities on whether or not new medicines, procedures, and medical devices should be part of the overall basic benefits package. Or in other words, NICE uses HTAs to determine whether or not health technologies are covered under the NHS. HTAs produce cost-effectiveness data, the incremental cost-effectiveness ratio, which defines the marginal health gain for any new technologies in terms of QALYs against the additional costs attributable to the product. This unidimensional measure captures changes in life years and quality of life, which usefully applies across therapeutic areas.

The outcome makes for easy comparison. But, in other contexts, CEA fails to consider important health outcomes organization features that influence decision-making. The German process for HTA is markedly different to those of the United Kingdom and other countries (Klingler et al., 2013). In Germany the health system functions under a social insurance model. Two institutions dominate the HTA process in Germany: the Federal Joint Committee (G-BA) and the Institute for Quality and Efficiency in Health Care (IQWiG). The G-BA is responsible for determining the benefit catalog, while IQWiG helps inform those decisions. Technologies are included on the benefit catalog by the G-BA when additional clinical benefit is demonstrated compared to the standard intervention; cost-effectiveness data plays only a minor role in those decision-making processes. In Germany, it is not only inappropriate to monetarize health impacts of new technologies; it is also inappropriate to deny access to care on the basis of limited gains to life years and QALYs (Klingler et al., 2013; Wright et al., 2017). These divergences are the consequence of a number of factors, some of which are internal to the structure and organization of national health care systems, and others arise from historical and cultural factors associated with the delivery of health care.

In all cases, however, a wide variety of factors will intervene to influence the use and application of particular assessment methodologies and evidence bases and also works against the possibilities for policy learning and transferability in any direct and easy fashion. And so, this is also likely to be the case for the use of CBA in environmental applications. Environmental health economists need to be aware of the potential for divergences. Although CBA may aim to provide some kind of objective measure of the utility of an environmental intervention, we need to be aware that policy-makers respond to multiple stimuli in making interventions, and that national institutions and processes for environmental protection may vary, and that objective "best practice" methods and optimum evidential requirements for CBA are but one element of this wider process. For the future the key challenge for analysts of health and environmental policy may be about developing and adopting an analytical framework capable of identifying and critically analyzing instances of divergence and hybridity regarding the needs of policy-makers within specific contexts and developing relevant methods and measures that enable the formulation of optimal policies in specific contexts and circumstance within a wider view of contributing to improvement of national systems for environmental protection.

9.2.2 Cost—utility analysis

Other measures, such as CUA, also become relevant to the production of knowledge regarding environmental health interventions on the basis of their ability to make contributions under specific circumstance and within diversified contexts. CBA is explicit about addressing whether the benefits of a policy intervention exceed the costs. Consequently, CBA is able to consider a wider range of benefits than a single measure gains to quality of life. For example, CUA might involve the use of patient-specific QALYs in the context of public health care intervention. In the case of environmental health, CUA could conceivably involve the use of community specific QALYS, which, arguably, might be ascertained on the bases of mass-responses to multiattribute utility instruments such as the EuroQol (EQ)-5D (Manca et al., 2005). Under certain circumstances, CUA might involve estimations of an entire community's self-reported health states valued through the aggregation of survey responses. CUA might equally measure more aspects of benefit than the unidimensional QALY. Indeed, CUA enables health-economists to consider potential benefits beyond those involving improvement in health-related quality of life. Estimates might involve vignettes of collective health states under EQ-5D describing the community scenarios regarding environmental policy interventions (MacFarland, 2017). It does not necessarily monetarize these benefits, but it does incorporate a wider range of benefits under the outcome measure it process. As such, CUA is usually more difficult to conduct than CEA. It also involves greater potential for error, and it also takes more time. But, it does not measure of potential benefits in terms of even more complex and time-consuming devices, such as WTP, through which monetary values are assigned to benefits. In this way, CBA retains its position as the most complex, expensive, and conjectural of the three benefit measures.

9.2.3 Robust decision-making

CBA, CUA, and CEA are economic measures of costs and benefits, which differ largely in terms of the way they calculate and value benefits. By contrast, RDM is a decision-making support device. Rather than economic theory and methods, RDM is embedded in stakeholder engagements. Its supports policy interventions under conditions of profound uncertainty. RDM is useful under circumstances in which the parties, relevant to a proposed course of action or problem, cannot agree on how to model the situation. Where scientists remain unsure about probability distributions and the input parameters necessary for the situation, RDM involves both qualitative scenario building thought group discussion and quantitative calculations regarding their outputs (Hall et al., 2012). RDM is about collective decision making in often challenging and quarrelsome situations. It assumes that participants and stakeholder have entrenched disagreements about assumptions and values relevant to the proposed intervention.

Recent years have seen a growing interest in the use of robust methods for helping policy-makers identify not necessarily the optimal policy, but the most robust policy. Interest in robust strategies develops from the fallibility of economic forecasts, increasing occurrence of unanticipated events and the need to make decisions in the context of stakeholders with wildly different interpretations of the current states of affairs and expectations for the future. In this kind of world, RDM attempts to capture a range of plausible future states of affairs and their relative probabilities. Unlike the other method outlined above, RDMs expressed purpose is to inform high-level policy processes.

It is designed to challenge stakeholder with visions of the future based on current policy trajectories. It informs decision-making by providing judgments about the robustness of alternative decision proposals. RDM also identifies scenarios that describe vulnerabilities of proposed strategies for decisionmakers. RDM is very different from CBA, CUA, and CEA. It does provide certainty. It offers robustness. It explicitly attempts to operate under conditions of uncertainty by proposing conceivable sets of futures states that might result from choices between alternative decision strategies. RDM has seen use in US water-management planning, energy policy, and counter-terrorism proposals (Hall et al., 2012). RDM does not result in the ranking of alternative decisions. Instead, it offers decision-making support. It summarizes the trade-offs between proposed strategies and their likely outcomes.

9.2.4 Multicriteria decision analysis

Multicriteria decision analysis (MCDA) is also designed to support decision-making rather than produce unidimensional measures of health and monetary benefit. In fact, MCDA has been proven to be particularly useful in making environmental policy interventions given its ability to consolidate technical measures and information with stakeholder values and conflicting expectations regarding outcomes. MCDA is suited to contexts in which trade-offs are required between environmental and economic, and socio-political and stakeholder views. In practice the methods and process of MCDA have varied according to different policy questions and environmental contexts. However, MCDA typically receives inputs across several dimensions associated with alternatives strategies and expected outcomes, which it weights and scores on the basis of trade-offs across these dimensions. The basic idea is to calculate the total value-score of an alternative weighted across several criteria relevant to the issue at hand (Huang and Keisler, 2011).

Unlike RDA, MCDA is about optimal rather than RDM. MCDA offers a systematic methodology for combing inputs across different dimensions with cost/benefit information and stakeholder views. On this basis, MCDA is capable of ranking different policy interventions. MCDA discovers and quantifies stakeholder views regarding different courses of actions. It does the same for decision-makers. As such, MCDA is a deep contextual approach to optimizing policy interventions. Depending on the relevant questions, MCDA can involve different inputs and process for their discovery and interpretation. It can also utilize different algorithms for their aggregation and ranking. However, MCDA is about formalizing optimal policy interventions. It is about using quantifiable outcomes to influence decision-making across a variety of policy sectors.

As such, MCDA has been proven to be useful in health and environmental policy. Typically, environmental policy interventions involve inputs from the natural and social sciences, and also from ethics and political sciences. Environmental decision-making demands experimental tests, computational models, and tools to assess human health and ecological risks associated with environmental stressors and the impact of remedial and abatement strategies on risk reduction. Applying these tools is difficult. There are risks of uncertainty involved. The range of inputs is multidisciplinary. As such, the same phenomena is often interpreted in different and contradictory ways. Most of all, stakeholders may have vested interests in particular outcomes. They can use inherent uncertainty to direct decision-making toward self-interested ends. In this context, MCDA offers a systematic process, a useful cypher, through which all these competing and contradictory inputs can be formalized, weighted, and prioritized under a single measure and become subject to expert judgment. For these reasons, however, MCDA can be time-consuming, labor intensive, and indeed expensive to operationalize (Huang et al., 2011).

9.3 Conclusion

Science and scientific devices, such as CBA and the other tools and measures outlined above, all involve an implicit effort to rationalize policymaking. In the field of political science, however, such classic attempts at the "rationalization" of policy-making are hardly a new thing. Equally, the idea that policymakers can improve their decision-making via means of scientific knowledge does not speak for itself. A long-standing criticism of the EBP movement holds that the principles of EBM are not transferable to policy situations. Because, often enough, stakeholders across other policy sectors will not accept the outcomes of policy-research. Further, stakeholders will attempt to use research-outputs in strategic ways, as ammunition rather than as a self-evident basis for delivering optimal interventions. Increasingly, the use of rationalizing influences in policy is subject to negotiations between decision-makers and stakeholders. Some of these actors exist in spheres outside the state. Some of them control critical resources. In addition, decision-makers also needed to consider the interests of citizens above the rigors of scientific devices, such as CBA. Indeed, research that fails to reflect the values or interests of stakeholders runs a serious risk of being contested or ignored. And even science itself is not value free. Scientists embody certain values. Across the policy cycle, these values will necessarily compete with other values. Ultimately, science may even lose its authority.

For enthusiasts, however, all policy problems are like a puzzle. And the challenge of policy-making is to solve the puzzle. EBP is a statement about the contemporary need for technical and instrumental rationality in policy-making (Elliott and Popay, 2000). Under this frame, research evidence serves to fill identifiable knowledge gaps within the puzzle of policy. Sometimes, the necessary "filling work" solves the problem. Other times, more gaps are discovered, and additional filling is required. And when sufficient work is completed, the policy problem is solved. In the context of health and environmental policy, CBA is one among several means for carrying out this filling-work. Indeed, the alternatives to CBA outlined above are equal constituents of a science-policy nexus. At the nexus the filling work takes shape. Environmental health economists and policy-makers are able to settle on any one or combination of them for the production of research data in accord with the practical needs of the moment, using them to fill gaps and build the regularity of interactions on which their long-term relationship might profitably unfold.

Beyond the research knowledge that devices, such as CBA, produce, health economists and policy makers also build their relationship by other means. As environmental policy interventions make their way through the policy cycle, stages such as agenda setting, formulation, adoption, implementation and evaluation, environmental health economists become engaged and participate in nuanced and entrepreneurial ways. Health economists engage at different stages of the policy process, providing research data that assists decision makers in the selection of instruments once the policy is formulated. They bring additional items to the political agendas by announcing new findings, providing new information, noting long standing policy problems, and emphasizing a scientific consensus on key policy issues (Stoutenborough et al., 2015).

Ultimately, the relationship between science and policy is critically important to the future. And despite the challenges that self-interested and intransigent stakeholders bring, policy-makers need to take care of how scientists, people such as health and environmental economists, perceive the state of their relationship with policy-makers. Policy-makers need to assure scientists of their influence. Indeed, they need scientists to enjoy a sense of hopefulness about the future. They must carefully guard against the contagion of cynicism. Because policy problems need solutions and policy-makers need scientists to help formulate and deliver them, at some point, and in some cases, scientists, health economists and devices, such as CBA, need to be permitted the last word. Because if experts lose confidence in their ability to influence policy makers, they might stop trying to influence them. In such case, important knowledge gaps will go unfilled. And in the context of a century in which science is important to policy, its withdrawal from policy-making circles might even invite catastrophe. If policy-makers fail to cultivate the intellectual and technical patronage of scientists, they run the risk of scientists retreating from engagement with the policy process altogether.

References

Considine, M., Lewis, J.M., 1999. Governance at ground-level: the frontline bureaucrat in the age of markets and networks. Public Adm. Rev. 59 (6), 467—480.

Davies, P., 2004. Is evidence-based policy possible? In: The Jerry Lee Lecture. Campbell Collaboration Colloquium, Washington, DC.

Elliott, H., Popay, J., 2000. How are policy makers using evidence? Models of research utilisation and local NHS policy making. J. Epidemiol. Community Health 54 (6), 461—468.

Gore, A., 1993. From red tape to results: creating a government that works better & costs less. Report of the National Performance Review. US Government Printing Office, Washington, DC.

Guerriero, C., Cairns, J., 2009. The potential monetary benefits of reclaiming hazardous waste sites in the Campania region: an economic evaluation. Environ. Health 8, 28.

Guerriero, C., Cairns, J., 2011. Cost-benefit analysis of the clean-up of hazardous waste sites. In: Kumar, S. (Ed.), Integrated Waste Management, vol. I. InTech, Rikeja.

Hall, J.W., Robert, J.L., Keller, K., Hackbarth, A., Mijere, C., McInerney, D.J., 2012. Robust climate policies under uncertainty: a comparison of robust decision making and info-gap methods. Risk. Anal. 32 (10), 1657–1672.

Hogwood, B.W., Gunn, L.A., 1984. Policy Analysis for the Real World. New York: Oxford University Press, USA.

Hoppe, R., 2005. Rethinking the science-policy nexus: from knowledge utilization and science technology studies to types of boundary arrangements. Poiesis Praxis 3 (3), 199–215.

Huang, I.B., Keisler, J., Linkov, I., 2011. Multi-criteria decision analysis in environmental sciences: ten years of applications and trends. Sci. Total Environ. 409, 3578–3594.

Klingler, C., Shah, S.M.B., Barron, A.J.G., Wright, J.S.F., 2013. Regulatory space and the contextual mediation of common functional pressures: analyzing the factors that led to the German Efficiency Frontier approach. Health Policy 109 (3), 270–280.

Manca, A., Hawkins, N., Sculpher, M.J., 2005. Estimating mean QALYs in trial-based cost-effectiveness analysis: the importance of controlling for baseline utility. Health Econ. 14, 487–496.

McFarland, A., 2017. A cost utility analysis of the clinical algorithm for nasogastric tube placement confirmation in adult hospital patients. J. Adv. Nurs. 73 (1), 201–216.

Osborne, D., Gaebler, T., 1992. Reinventing Government. Massachusetts: Addison-Wesley.

Pearce, D., Atkinson, G., Mourato, S., 2006. Cost-Benefit Analysis and the Environment: Recent Developments. Organisation for Economic Co-operation and Development, Paris, France

Percy-Smith, J., 2005. What Works in Strategic Partnerships for Children? Barnardo's, Ilford

Saunders, P., Walter, J. A. 2005. Introduction: reconsidering the policy sciences. In P. Saunders, & J. Walter (Eds.), Ideas and Influence. Social Science and Public Policy in Australia (1 ed., pp. 1–20). Sydney NSW Australia: UNSW Press.

Stoutenborough, J., Bromley-Trujilo, R., Vedlitz, A., 2015. How to win friends and influence people: climate scientists' perspectives on their relationship with and influence on government officials. J. Public Policy 25 (2), 269–296.

Wright, J.S.F., Barron, A.J.G., Shah, S., Klingler, C., 2017. Convergence, divergence and hybridity: a regulatory governance perspective on health technology assessment in England and Germany. Global Policy 8 (2), 69–75.

Further reading

Revesz, R.L., 1999. Environmental regulation, cost-benefit analysis and the discounting of human lives. Columbia Law Rev. 99, 941–1017.

Runhaar, H., van Nieuwaal, K., 2010. Understanding the use of science In decision-making on cockle fisheries and gas mining in the Dutch Wadden Sea: putting the science–policy interface in a wider perspective. Environ. Sci. Policy 13, 239–248.

CHAPTER 10

Climate change and ecological public health: an integrated framework

Ariana Zeka[1], Giovanni Leonardi[2] and Paolo Lauriola[3]
[1]Brunel University London, United Kingdom;
[2]London School of Hygiene and Tropical Medicine, United Kingdom;
[3]Italian National Research Council, Institute of Clinical Physiology, Unit of Environmental Epidemiology and Disease Registries, Italy

Contents

Cost-Benefit Analysis of Environmental Health Interventions
DOI: https://doi.org/10.1016/B978-0-12-812885-5.00010-X

10.1 Introduction

The aim of this chapter is to outline why ecological public health approach is a useful framework when trying to understand and measure the public health impacts of complex ecological and climate change, and societal systems transitions. To achieve its aim, the chapter highlights key issues within this framework, and also illustrates with a few examples, to make it more explicit on how this systems approach can assist any economic models of cost—benefits of environmental health interventions.

The chapter has four sections, the first three describe several aspects of the challenge, and the fourth outlines constructive responses and attitudes:

Section 1: "Climate change: the main challenge of the ecological public health approach" provides an overview of the multiple transitions currently ongoing for society, and the reasons an ecological approach to public health provides a perspective required for effective economic analysis of any interventions proposed in environmental health;

Section 2: "Social impacts of climate change, disasters and tipping points" is really another angle on the climate challenge, which includes disasters and expected tipping points as well as slow trends. This is a reason why development of human activities requires economic appreciation of expected future adverse events;

Section 3: "The market and environmental public health" focuses on the largest cultural challenge to society addressing climate change, which is the idea that environmental health is an obstacle to economic development. This section makes a proposal of a new economic approach that addresses environmental health issues in their entirety (including climate change);

Section 4: "Responses to these challenges" focuses on several dimensions of an effective approach to solutions.

The final section provides some preliminary "Conclusions" for an economic analysis of environmental health interventions that do not ignore climate change.

10.2 Section 1: Climate change, the main challenge of the ecological public health approach

"The global scale, interconnectedness, and economic intensity of contemporary human activity are historically unprecedented, as are many of the consequent environmental and social changes. These global changes fundamentally influence patterns of human health, international health care, and public health

activities. They constitute a syndrome, not a set of separate changes that reflects the interrelated pressures, stresses, and tensions arising from an overly large world population, the pervasive, and increasingly systemic environmental impact of many economic activities, urbanization, the spread of consumerism, and the widening gap between rich and poor both within and between countries."

McMichael (2013).

10.2.1 The concept of the "ecological public health" model

10.2.1.1 What is ecological public health versus traditional approach to public health

Repeated calls from world-leading scientists in public health (McMichael, 1999; McMichael and Beaglehole, 2000; Koopman, 1996a,b; Diez-Roux, 2006; Pearce, 1996; Rose 2001; Awerbuch et al., 1996; Susser, 1998; Levins, 1998, 1996) have emphasized the importance of identification and study of *population risk factors* in their social, cultural, and historical context as a critical development for the future of public health science and policy. Although to date epidemiology has successfully identified preventable risks in populations and has been the leading science of public health for providing evidence on the environmental impacts, and also the benefits of environmental interventions on population health, its current methodology has major limitations (Susser and Susser, 1996a, 1996b). In the more traditional view of the science, populations and subsequent health outcomes are often treated as the sums of health of individuals and not as a system of interacting individuals, groups, and society. Public health science and epidemiology more often than not have the tendency of a strong focus on the statistical issues, with a simultaneous lack of distinctive theory that allows understanding of population patterns of disease, which has been described by Krieger (1994) as "method over content." In addition, epidemiologic approaches in use are not designed to explore, understand, and estimate the interrelatedness of multiple and complex risk factors, explore nonlinearity, or understand the nature of change over time of these interactions. Also, in the more reductionist view of the population health sciences, social, political, economic, cultural, and historical contexts as population risk factors are often neglected.

There are several key societal factors such as economic, political, and social (*upstream*), which are the fundamental drivers of population health (Pearce, 1996; Berkman et al., 2000; Marmot and Wilkinson, 2006; Butler and Harley, 2010). These factors are the determinants of the distribution of "intermediary" and more "proximal" risk factors. Factors such as lack of social integration, diminished social capital, poverty, unemployment, crime, increased socioeconomic inequalities, and migration have been described as possible contributors to the observed changes in population health outcomes in many societies/economies. These could be thought of as intermediary linking factors between the larger economic and political reforms (changes of economy and public service, changes in public policy, cuts or the elimination of certain areas of public spending, changes in provision for health care, social disorganization), and direct individual risk factors (smoking, drinking, narcotic use, psychosocial stress, or the increase in environmental pollution). Globalization of economic systems has large impacts on ecosystems on which the humanity survival greatly depends (McMichael, 2013; Kawachi and Wamala, 2007; Rockström et al., 2009; Steffen et al., 2015). Ecological and climate change, "upstream," impact on the "intermediary" food systems, water resources, land change, ecological disease vector changes, which are drivers of more direct, "proximal," risk factors such as availability of and accessibility to food, malnutrition, availability of water, water quality, infectious diseases, and environmental disasters.

McMichael (2013) has written extensively on the concept of interrelatedness of societal and environmental systems and population health, the type of actions that researchers and public health practitioners will need to take for effective benefits of population health. This approach has been echoed and developed further by many leading epidemiologists and public health researchers (Pearce, 2006; Rayner and Lang, 2012). Rayner and Lang (2012) proposed an approach to address the challenge public health researchers and practitioners face in dealing with complex issues of economic, social, environmental, and climate system change. This approach, the ecological public health, considers the human health inseparable from the "health" and working of the environment surrounding us and pays close attention to the change and transitions in those systems that define and determine the human and ecosystem health (Rayner and Lang, 2012).

The ecological public health approach can help to address the challenges faced by public health today, by its aims to integrate complexity, multiple interactions, and change of societal systems. It allows one to pose a question, to explore and understand the possible answers, by the inclusion of variables or factors some of which are measurable, and some not readily measurable. It also makes possible understanding of complex and dynamic population health determinants in a more holistic way, and makes possible understanding which information (current and future) can be informative, what information needs to be better defined and measured, or what statistical methods will better inform public health policy and decision. By doing so, the approach has the ability to understand the ecosystem processes and the societal system as a whole, and the way it determines population health. This adaptable approach is very helpful in exploring complex public health questions in a way that are usable to all. As such, the ecological public health can be a helpful approach to inform economic models of complex environmental interventions. It can also assist in understanding better the co-benefits of such interventions by considering the ecosystem challenge rather than a "siloed" approach to interventions. Levins (1998), in his extensive writings, calls such an approach a "democratization of science" because of its ability to be used by the wider community. Earlier calls from Levins on propositions for population health science ask for cooperative efforts to solve the real-world problems, also by rejecting reductionisms, and favoring complexity, connectedness, dynamism, historicity and contradictoriness of the world, and to insist in "science for the people" (Levins, 1996). It is these concepts that are the fundamental building blocks of the Rayner and Lang's ecological public health vision (Rayner and Lang, 2012).

10.2.2 Societal systems and their transitions

The following sections briefly describe the societal systems and their transitions, as proposed by Rayner and Lang (2012). These system transitions cannot be seen or understood in isolation, and their totality and complexity should not be seen as a challenge but as an opportunity to inform public health actions that contribute to effective improvements of population health.

10.2.2.1 Biological and ecological transitions

Biological transitions are characterized as processes of change of all life forms within and in constant interaction with their environments. Within this transition, all life change occurs with the change of the wider ecosystem. Human population, as any other species in the planet, are in constant contact with their environment: physical, biological, and social. Our existence is highly dependent on the presence of many environmental factors. Consider for example the beneficial human—bacterial coexistence, and the health impacts of reducing this symbiotic existence or human dependency on ecosystem resources, such as water, food, air. Stephen J Gould, in one of his writings, The Full House (Gould, 1996a), viewed the changes in life as variations within complete systems. He presented an integrated view of life's history and made the general argument that humans occupy no preferred status but rather exists as a chance element in the evolutionary process. As such the philosophy of biological existence and change, including that of the human species, should be taken as the "... wonderful life within the full house of our planet's history of organic diversity..." (Gould, 1996a).

In the ecological public health view, human health is shaped by its ecosystem and the changes within. Therefore this approach highlights our dependency and survival on our ecological system. As it is described in several other sections, the human-induced reversible or irreversible impacts on our Nature's health will have transmitted effects on the patterns of health in populations. These patterns will also have an unequal distribution in concurrence with other societal systems in place. For example, evidence has shown that due to warming climates, some infectious diseases may be observable in more temperate climates, although these will likely be also dependent on societal infrastructures and health governance (Altizer et al., 2013). Availability, accessibility, and affordability of foods (see section on resource transition) can impact on occurrence of malnutrition and hunger. Coastal erosion, loss of land, increased water salinity, and loss of freshwater resources can lead to impacts on livelihoods, human security, forced displacement and migration. These risks are particularly amplified in countries with developmental challenges (IPCC, 2014; IPCC AR5, 2014). Climate change related impacts can increase the likelihood of these hazards through changes in air and sea temperatures, ocean acidification, sea level, storms, and increases (or decreases) in precipitation. The frequency, intensity, and duation of extreme weather events, such as coastal flooding and droughts, are also exacerbated by climate change (Intergovernmental Panel on Climate Change IPCC et al., 2014; IPCC AR5, 2014).

10.2.2.2 Demographic changes

The demographic transition is reflected in the changes from high birth and high death rates, to low birth and low death rates. These changes, which are largely observed in developed societies, can be mostly attributed to improvements in the standards of living, investments in human development aspects such as health care, education, and infrastructure. However, differences in birth and death rates still exist between developed and developing economies. Birth rates and death rates are still high in some parts of the world, and life expectancy gap can be as large as/or larger than 20 + years difference between poor and affluent countries, societies, and communities (United Nations Department of Economic and Social Affairs, 2017). The sociodemographic and geopolitical distributions of population profiles and characteristics, also determine this transition. For example, there is an increasing proportion of aging population in most of the high-income countries, in contrast to high fertility rates, and younger populations in some low- and middle-income countries.

This transition, also in concurrence with epidemiologic and health transitions, and overall improvements in public health, technology, has contributed to the stable increase of the global population. At current estimate, the world population of 7.6 billion is expected to reach 8.6 billion in 2030, 9.8 billion in 2050, and 11.2 billion in 2100, according to the most recent United Nations report (United Nations Department of Economic and Social Affairs, 2017). Population growth in combination with economic development has already stressed the ecosystem resources. Its impacts on land use, soil quality, water and food security, loss of biodiversity, and environmental pollution, if unabated, could potentially contribute to a planetary ecosystem not able to sustain human life (Röckstrom et al., 2009; Steffen et al., 2015). The exacerbation of already occurring environmental and ecologic changes could also contribute to further conditions of poverty and disadvantage, circumstances in which fertility rates tend to remain high.

Climate and environmental change, ecosystem resource depletion can impact population movements, within and across countries, another component of demographic transition. Migration and human security, and conflict are attributed to planetary ecosystem changes and are a major concern for human health and development (McMichael, Woodruff and Hales, 2006; McMichael, Barnett and McMichael, 2012; Burrows and Kinney 2016; Watts et al., 2016; Whitmee et al., 2015; McMichael, 2015a). Climate change impacts, in particular those related to basic resource security (such as livelihood, food, water, soil) may lead to up to 1 billion people becoming vulnerable to migration by the end of the century (Watts et al., 2017).

10.2.2.3 Epidemiology and health transition

Rayner and Lang (2012) refer to epidemiologic transition as the observable change in the patterns of the distribution of determinants of the morbidity and mortality in populations. Health transitions are characterized by the change from observable disease pattern to other types of diseases. Due to many national and international efforts, changes in living conditions, healthcare and public health efforts, in combination with human and economic development, there has been a global shift from infectious and diseases linked to malnutrition and poverty, to diseases to noncommunicable and degenerative diseases. However, these patterns are changing as a result of contributions of other transitions: demographic, energy/resource, economic, and cultural.

10.2.2.4 Urban transition

Currently, more than half of the world's population is urban (IPCC AR5, 2014). Cities are very complex social, economic, and ecological hubs of dense population, with increasing demands on energy, food, water, infra structure, and their constant need for land expansion. Besides their constant demands for resources, cities also contribute to shifts in population demographics, and population movements. There are aspects of city life that can contribute to adverse population health due to for example sedentary lifestyle, increased exposure to air pollution, noise, and heat, lack of green space. Cities are also beneficial for people's well-being because they provide innovation, access to goods, and services, and they facilitate social interaction (Rydin et al., 2012).

Cities contribute to about 75% of CO_2 emissions from total energy (IPCC AR5, 2014) and therefore are major contributors to climate change. By 2050, nearly 70% of the global population is projected to live in urban areas (United Nations Department of Economic and Social Affairs, 2017). This transition will require extending and building cities, which will be mainly as a result of rapid urban development in middle and low-income countries (Bai et al., 2018). The rapid building of cities is estimated to contribute about 226 gigatonnes of CO_2 by 2050, about four times the amount emitted from built cities and infrastructure (Bai et al., 2018). Cities are and will be even more so in the future, major contributors to climate and ecological change. But they also offer opportunities for building a sustainable infrastructure and maintaining healthy ecosystems and populations.

10.2.2.5 Resource transition: energy, food, water, and land security

While in the proposed view of Rayner and Lang (2012) energy transition takes a place of its own, we think that in the same context, food, water, and land can also be discussed as vital resources for any society. Population growth puts pressure and increasing demands on resources (energy, food, water), urban transitions, land use, decrease, or even loss in biodiversity (McMichael, 2013; Butler and Mcfarlane, 2018; Mcmichael, Butler, and Dixon, 2015b). The inequitable sufficiency and security of these resources (or otherwise resource availability, accessibility, and utilization) will impact largely on any human development and societal growth (Butler and McMichael, 2010).

Energy is the most important resource for the society and for the well-being of humankind today. It is used in almost all human activities, ranging from the household to businesses and vital societal services. Transition from the current high dependency on cheap forms of energy, such as coal and fossil fuels, also the main contributors to CO_2 and other ambient air pollutants, to less polluting forms of energy (renewable energy), has been very slow, and has occurred mostly in developed countries. Availability of clean and nonpolluting energy and issues of affordability remain a challenge, in particular in middle- and low-income countries. The inequalities of the energy transitions around access and affordability to clean energy in poorer communities and countries have large impacts on the human and ecosystem health and also contribute to energy and environmental inequalities and injustice (Wilkinson et al., 2007).

Globalization of food markets and the high dependency, mostly of developed countries for food sourced from other regions of the world, has impacted on the self-sufficiency and sustainability of food sources in developed and developing communities. The economic power of developed economies to purchase food globally has the likely knock-on effect in poorer countries and communities. Recent examples show that this does not only affects sustainability, affordability, and accessibility to foods, but also the impact on the resources such as water, energy, biodiversity loss, land use, soil degradation, and pollution can contribute to loss of livelihood and drive migration and conflict (Kelley et al., 2015; Butler and Harley, 2010; Butler and Mcfarlane, 2018). Food accessibility and affordability is a serious issue in many parts of the world. Economic circumstances can create vulnerability to food insecurity, such as inflation of food prices, debt, and seasonal unemployment. There is growing evidence of the relationship between food-insecure households and poor health, education, and working capacity. Furthermore, monotonous diets or consuming lower quality foods has been identified as a critical pathway toward decreased health, education, and overall wellbeing (McMichael, Butler, and Dixon, 2015). As a consequence of climate change, the productivity of crops, such as rice, wheat, and cereal, and their nutritional values are expected to decline. In addition, warmer conditions, intensification of climate extremes could cause serious yield losses. These changes alongside other environmental changes in particular loss of soil quality in agricultural intensive parts of the world as a result of modern farming practices are projected to influence food security in many countries (Campbell et al., 2016; Myers et al., 2017).

Environmental pollution, environmental, and climate change will have impacts on these resources (Rockström et al., 2009; Steffen et al., 2015), including impacts on land use availability due to sea-level rise, decreasing soil quality and hydrology, and depleting of freshwater resources. Alterations, for example, in crop yield and fish catch, may have direct implications to socioeconomic factors for example due to reduced agricultural output (Mastrorillo et al., 2016), food security (Warner et al., 2010), and urbanization rates (Barrios et al., 2006).

10.2.2.6 Economic transition

Economic models of constant growth based on cheap fossil fuels, free market, deregulation, reduced state control, and restrictions of state governance of economic growth, led by neo-liberal thinktankers, have contributed to the principles of efficiency versus sufficiency and sustainability (Max-Neef, 2010; Ackerman, 2007; Klein, 2007). The high dependency on resources and uncontrollable exploitation has led to depletion and loss of ecological services humanity depends on.

In recent decades the transition of rapid development and economic growth from high-income countries to middle and low-income countries, together with available technological advancement, relaxed environmental controls, have contributed to the shift of environmental impacts toward less affluent communities. In combination with demographic, ecological, resource, and urban transitions, these shifts have created more opportunities for environmental and health inequalities.

10.2.2.7 Cultural and democratic transition

The cultural transition or change refers to the history of our social organization. Rayner and Lang (2012) refer to this as the change in ideas and material factors that shape the cultural and democratic shifts. Although it is discussed here as a separate transition, its change depends on economic, political, and social shifts. This change holds an enormous capacity—its explosive rapidity and cumulative directionality. Culture is acquired within one generation and also can be transmitted across generations. Consider, for example, musical knowledge, the learning and the passing on the ability of that knowledge, from one generation to another. We have no evidence that human brains have changed biologically since their first appearance as species (Gould, 1996b), thus no evidence of biological transition. However, the human brain capacity to acquire and process information has exponentially grown. This cultural change has also rapid effects in our relations with our ecosystem. While evolutionary processes take millions of years to develop and adapt, human cultural capacity for rapid change had made possible the impact in the natural world within centuries, and much more rapidly in the last century, and in particular in the last five decades.

The rapid globalization, economic, social, and technological change, the way we live, eat, communicate reflect our cultural change. Public health preventive actions, including immunization, smoke-free policies, are changes that have beneficially shaped population health. Food, smoking, alcohol, gambling advertising, fear of vaccination are some of the examples of cultural changes with adverse population health impacts. Together with other societal transitions, these cultural changes influence the observed patterns of population health across the globe and have contributed to the observed environment and health inequalities. The cultural transition is also reflected by the fact that more information is being available through different media, and in particular social media, and also through changes in school educations. These have the power to contribute to the awareness on the ecosystem and climate change impacts.

Democratic transition is depicted as forms of governance, including the rules of governing, the nature and management of institutions, for example forms of health institutions, rights, and laws. This transition can occur when one system of governance changes to another form. It is the shift from an autocracy/authoritarian mode of ruling to a democratic popular influence in politics and policies. Through history these examples have demonstrated in different forms (e.g., transition from communism to more democratic forms of governing). However, these transitions are very complex, and evidence has shown that they do largely influence population health patterns, due to their shock on the societal system construct (e.g., economy, environment, provisions for health care, employment, housing, and education). Recent changes of populist politics in the United States and Europe could also be seen as a democratic transition;

however, their support for ecological sustainability and actions to mitigate climate change impacts on population and ecosystem health are dubious. Also, their rhetoric on migration, without understanding the roots of this phenomenon, has serious potential of damaging the very fabric of our diverse communities, and efforts for equitable societies.

10.2.3 Why is the ecological public health approach the way to address climate change?

The multifaceted nature of climate change and therefore its impacts in the ecosystem and on population health are very important to understand. Climate change can be described by changes in climate variability, the fast-onset climate change (including a change in magnitude and frequency of extreme weather events, droughts, floods, and heatwaves), and the slow-onset climate change (including long term changes in average temperature, rainfall, and chronic droughts or flooding) (IPCC AR5, 2014). The wide temporality, the variability of severity, and the geographic spread of climate impacts, in combination with the variation of the different societal and environmental systems (infrastructure, food, water, land), also affected by climate change need to be considered. Climate change impacts can also be manifested through biodiversity loss, rapidly vanishing glaciers, and increased frequency of extreme events (rain, heat, cold weather, floods, and desertification).

Climate change impacts can be described as physical, biological/ecological, and anthropogenic impacts (McMichael, 2015b). As such climate change should be recognized as a risk multiplier for all other systems and a threat to human health globally. The population health consequences of climate change events can be classified as primary, secondary, and tertiary (Butler and Harley, 2010). Primary effects include, for example, the acute and chronic stress of heatwaves and trauma from increased wildfires and flooding. Secondary or ecological climate aspects may include changes in land cover, flora, and fauna habitats, including disease vectors and pollinators, such as an altered distribution of arthropod vectors, intermediate hosts, and pathogens that will produce changes in the epidemiology of many infectious diseases. Tertiary or anthropogenic aspects include subsequent changes to anthropogenic systems such as crop yield and fish or game catch. Accelerating sea level rise will likely to cause crop and land loss, which in combination with lack of economic, political, and infrastructural preparedness could lead to forced population displacement, risk human security and conflict (IPCC, 2014). Sociopolitical factors impact on environmental change can occur concurrently with impacts of climate change. Changes in land use, urbanization, overexploitation of natural resources, environmental pollution, and geophysical natural hazards are key determinants for ecosystem health , with direct and indirect impacts on population health. These environmental changes often have strong feedback loops, for example, through demographic transition such as urbanization, there are important repercussions on environmental degradation, air and water pollution, energy consumption, and greenhouse gas emissions (Rafiq, Nielsen, and Smyth, 2017).

Taking into account the interlinkage of the impacts of climate change on societal systems and vice versa, the complexity, temporality, and spatiality of these relations, quantifying the climate change impacts in such situations remains a challenge. Additional consideration is needed to assist the recognition of dynamic interactions between the physical, ecological, and anthropogenic aspects of climate change and the level of uncertainty and difficulty to measure and quantify these linkages.

The recent Lancet Countdown report highlights that due to the role of climate change in undermining governance of health and public health progress over the last five decades, climate change presented "the greatest global health opportunity of the 21st century" (Watts et al., 2017). Therefore the interlinking of climate change, environmental change, and human health should form the scientific progress in public health for current and future generations of researchers (Butler, McMichael, 2010; Whitmee et al., 2015).

In summary, climate and ecological change represent the most important challenge for humanity for the present and future, and the impacts are interrelated in all societal systems transitions briefly described here. Ecological public health provides a framework for considering a holistic approach from public health science to public health actions, that takes into account climate and ecological change, and societal systems transitions. It, therefore can assist any economic models that aim to effectively measure public health benefits of environmental interventions.

10.3 Section 2: Social impacts of climate change, disasters, and tipping points

10.3.1 Climate change and its social impacts

Climate change manifests itself as discrete events as well as long-term trends in geophysical indicators. Such discrete events have been termed "disasters" as their social impact is to act as tipping points for human communities, leading for example to displacement. This section illustrates how the increased frequency and severity of events attributable to climate change challenges the task of planning, including economic analysis aimed at maximizing benefit to public health of addressing environmental dimensions of a human activity.

Climate change is likely to have serious and significant impacts on human population health. The mechanisms by which climate change may affect health are becoming better understood. Current quantitative methods of estimating future health impacts rely on disease-specific models that primarily describe relationships between mean values of weather variables and health outcomes and do not address the impacts of extreme events or weather disasters. Extreme events have the potential to disrupt community function, which is of concern for decision makers. Estimating the magnitude and extent of impacts from low probability high impact events is challenging because there is often no analog that can provide relevant evidence and that take into account the complexity of factors determining future vulnerability and health impacts (the social determinants of health) (Kovats et al., 2011).

The popular discourse about climate change tipping points is usually focused on the irreversible changes in the climate system or related geophysical indicators. Tipping points in social systems are equally important. Tipping points are more clearly understood at the local level when, for example, temporary migration becomes permanent and a community becomes unsustainable. Tipping points in social systems are likely to occur at climate exposures (global mean temperature changes) well below the projected thresholds for tipping points in geophysical systems. This is due to the high level of vulnerability in many social systems. Further, the focus on tipping points can distract attention from significant but incremental increases in the burden of disease/loss of welfare (Kovats et al., 2011).

An ability to robustly attribute specific damages to anthropogenic drivers of increased extreme heat can inform societal responsibilities for the costs of both "loss and damage" and adaptation in developed as well as developing countries (Mera et al., 2015; Thompson and Otto, 2015; Frumhoff et al., 2015).

This has been demonstrated, among other health effects, for those attributable to heat such as mortality during hot summers (Mitchell et al., 2016). Therefore it is relevant to economic analysis of environmental health that temperature-related and other types of disasters are considered when considering climate change dimensions of an activity affecting health.

10.3.2 Monitoring, assessing, and understanding disaster risks

The incidence of natural and technological (i.e., anthropogenic) disasters is steadily increasing all around the world (Lauriola et al., 2018) (Figs. 10.1 and 10.2).

From 1960 to 2018, there were a total of 22,058 disasters worldwide, comprising 13,800 natural, 8245 technological, and 13 complex disasters. Combined, they caused 6,296,593 deaths, 8,649,396 injuries, and affected almost 8 billion humans (Data source: EM-DAT The International Disaster Database, last update April 16, 2018, definitions are shown in the same link). Fig. 10.3 presents the disaster incidents by subgroups (natural) and subtypes (technological). However, while the stakeholders and methods for response are similar for both natural and technological disasters, this is not necessarily the case for prevention and preparedness. Preventing the determinants of natural disasters, such as global climate change, requires interdisciplinary policies and interventions, moving beyond traditional public health and emergency services.

The impact of a disaster is a function of hazard and vulnerability; from a climate change perspective, vulnerability is sometimes defined as a function of exposure, sensitivity, and adaptive capacity (IPCC AR5, 2014).

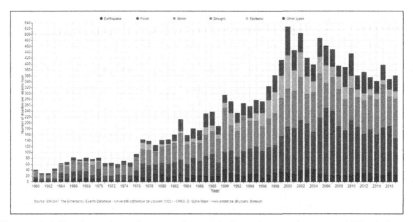

Figure 10.1 Total number of reported natural disaster types between 1960 and 2017 in the world (Last Database update: April 16, 2018).

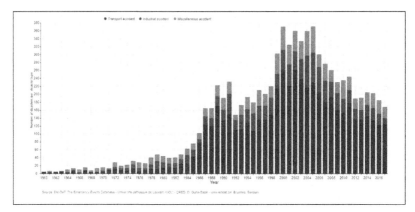

Figure 10.2 Total number of reported technological disaster types between 1960 and 2017 in the world (Last Database update: April 16, 2018).

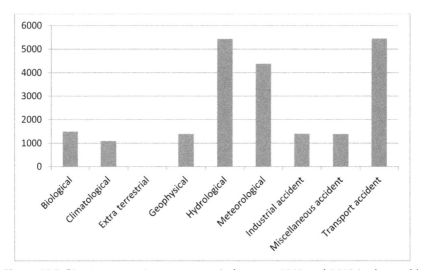

Figure 10.3 Disaster categories occurrence in between 1960 and 2018 in the world. *Data Source: EM-DAT, last update April 16, 2018.*

According to Watts et al. (2017), "owing to impressive poverty reduction and health adaptation efforts, this increase in weather-related disasters has not yet been accompanied by any discernible trend in number of deaths or in number of people affected by disasters. One plausible conclusion is that this represents an increase in health service provision and risk reduction." Despite this, the health impact of disasters (natural and technological) is foreseen to increase in the next few decades, including in high-income countries, proving that no countries are immune.

Several factors contribute to rising impact of disasters through increased individual and collective vulnerability, including

- increased population density;
- increased settlement in high-risks areas;
- increased technological hazards and dependency;
- increased terrorism;
- aging populations in industrialized countries;
- emerging infectious diseases; and
- international travel.

We must therefore consider that disasters can push people into poverty in such a way that disaster risk management can be considered a poverty reduction policy. As poverty reduction policies make people less vulnerable, they can be considered part of the disaster risk management toolbox. Indeed, if the frequency and severity of natural disasters increase, the cost of catastrophic loss will soar, with governments, corporations, aid organizations and tax payers being left to bear the costs. A brief summary of the estimation of cost is provided by RE-Swiss (Table 10.1).

As such integrating health and environmental risks in an overarching model may lead to a reduction of societal costs. These intrinsic features could help better overcome the main difficulties encountered in disaster events: lack of integration among institutions disciplines and professionals before, during, and after the event. (Fig. 10.4).

Unlike the spread of diseases, patterns and future likeliness of extreme events is less understood despite that extreme events have the potential to

Table 10.1 Economic losses, in USD billion and as a % of global GDP, 2017[a] (Swiss-RE, 2018).

Regions	in USD bn	in % of GDP
North America	244	1.17
Latin America and Caribbean	32	0.59
Europe	24	0.12
Africa	3	0.14
Asia	31	0.11
Oceania/Australia	3	0.22
Total	337	
World total		0.44
10-Year average[b]	190	0.25

[a]Rounded numbers.
[b]Inflation adjusted.

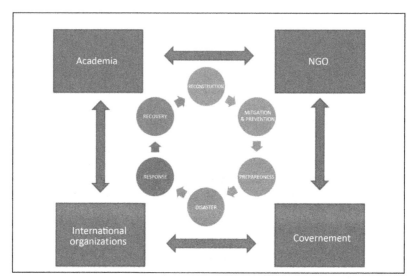

Figure 10.4 Disasters and actions integration.

disrupt community and economic functions of a society, which is of concern for decision makers. Estimating the magnitude and extent of impacts from low probability, high impact events is challenging because there is often no analog that can provide relevant evidence and that take into account the complexity of factors determining future vulnerability and health impacts. In the past, environmental health problems have been successfully addressed by controlling a single source of pollutant or exposure. Today's problems are often more complex. An integrated approach is needed to assess and monitor the relationships between environmental factors and human health in a broader spatial, socioeconomic, and cultural context.

10.3.3 Social tipping points

Studies of social impacts of climate change suggest that key thresholds (or tipping points) for human and social systems are likely at global mean temperatures well below those estimated for the biophysical systems (Kovats et al., 2011). There are several definitions of tipping points in the literature. A tipping point in the climate system can be defined as threshold that could abruptly and perhaps almost irreversibly switch a system to a different (climate) regime (Frame and Allen, 2008). The current evidence from climate science is that this is unlikely to happen this century.

Tipping points can also be described in relation to the irreversibility of impacts, for example, when a switch from temporary to permanent migration leads to the collapse of a particularly community. Because such terms as "tipping point" and thresholds are not well defined, it leads to confusion. Further, there are ambiguities and interdisciplinary differences in definitions for specific terms such as "catastrophe" and "dangerous." Abrupt changes in the health of population are possible when "tipping points" are encountered. Examples from recent history include those associated with socioeconomic collapse (e.g., postcommunist Russia). Abrupt changes in adaptive capacity are also possible and important. A major climate extreme event could lead to abrupt changes in the health status of a population. Another example is the severe drought and heatwave in Russia in 2010 which caused the price of wheat to increase sharply resulting in food riots in North Africa. The interaction between the severity of the event and the capacity of the population to deal with it is very important (Kovats et al., 2011).

10.3.4 A focus on community resilience

Community and disaster resilience are, in practice, largely synonymous terms. Both are inclusive and holistic concepts, capable of incorporating most other descriptions of resilience. The notion of community resilience developed, in part, from the recognition that many of the protective factors that enhance the psychological resilience of key groups of individuals facing adversity, such as vulnerable adolescents, operate at the community level; yet the concept can be readily extended to include elements from different disciplines concerned with managing crises. These might include the fault tolerance of power, water, and communications networks; the survivability of buildings, bridges, and other physical infrastructure; organizational preparedness and good governance; and less tangible but important factors such as public trust and social cohesiveness. These components contribute to a desirable (normative) ideal of "community resilience" to potential disasters. Social—ecological resilience overlaps with the previous concepts but places human society firmly in the context of its wider habitat. It reflects the buffering capacity of the physical and natural environment, combined with the adaptive capacity of the people within it. Resilience is the degree to which a social/ecological system can sustain itself in the face of disturbance before crossing a critical threshold, leading to failure and loss of structure and identity. Originally derived from empirical observations and mathematical modeling of natural ecosystems, it conveys the properties of both resistance and adaptation to those external forces acting to change the status quo. It does not include the process of recovery from a disaster and is neutral in relation to the desirability of a society's current functional state. These concepts can be applied in many diverse settings. Inclusive notions of resilience provide a framework for planning any activity within a framework of disaster risk reduction (DRR) and including consideration of the wider physical, psychosocial, and economic factors that help populations resist and adapt to both acute dangers—such as extreme weather events or natural hazards—and to more gradual "rising tide" public health threats, such as emerging infectious diseases or other aspects of climate change (Castleden et al., 2011). This is particularly evident when examining the need for planning of water-related activities, both for economic activities related to water management and water use, such as in agriculture and forestry, energy, and industrial production.

10.3.5 Training for disaster risk reduction

An approach that aims to include these considerations means that economic analysis has the potential to design development to avoid disasters and their social and health impacts. This is the intended benefit of a multidisciplinary course on prevention of disasters organized in Modena (EmTASK) (Italy) following a reflection on the pervasive social impacts of multiple local disasters in the region (heatwaves, floods, windstorms, vector-borne disease new to the area, earthquakes). Whether or not an individual event may be attributed to climate change, the impression has been that a majority of them could be attributed to either climate or other changes with a cumulative effect on local communities. The multidisciplinary approach to training of public officials and others in economic analysis, as well as legal, scientific, engineering, and public health aspects, represents a positive step to resilience of that society in the face of future disasters.

10.3.6 Sharing such information and on how it is created

Society, and in particular public agencies and economists working for them, have a responsibility to prevent, prepare, and respond to incidents causing widespread population exposure to extreme events including disasters. Progress in DRR research has shown that it is often not the hazard that determines a disaster, but the vulnerability, exposure, and ability of the population to anticipate, respond to, and recover from its effects. A shift from pure hazard response to the identification, assessment, and ranking of vulnerabilities and risks (including their unequal distribution in populations) became critical. The "Sendai framework for DRR 2015—30" highlights concerns on human health and well-being that are common to DRR, climate change, and sustainable development.

In considering public health activities aimed at prevention of future natural disasters, public health agencies have access to a range of conceptual and practical tools. These will range from a focus on the hazard elements of a disaster, to the vulnerability of the population or the infrastructure. Therefore the prevention of accidents represents an agenda that overlaps with DRR. The capacity of a public health service to contribute to DRR will relate to its vision of a population aware of its vulnerabilities in terms of groups of people and also infrastructure available. In other words, activities on prevention of disasters overlap to a large extent with the mainstream work of public health agencies but require a wider range of partnerships with decision makers, scientific and technical institutes, that would join forces for addressing people and infrastructure vulnerabilities as identified on an ongoing basis. This new challenge may involve the capacity of public health agencies to work with engineers, geologists, architects, economists, legal experts, as well as broader cultural experts such as linguists, historians, and others engaged in accounting for the identity of a community, with a common purpose of addressing any vulnerabilities in a realistic time frame in order to avoid the natural tendency to escape and crushing what has been established in the age. Prevention of disasters, in this sense, overlaps with societal development as informed about long-term requirements for agricultural and forestry infrastructure, industrial development, transport, built environment, and other routine aspects of human societies, with the added dimensions posed by pressures attributable to environmental change.

10.4 Section 3: The market and environmental public health

This section aims at introducing a comprehensive setting in which any cost-benefit analysis (CBAs) dealing with environmental—health issues should be developed.

10.4.1 Is environmental public health an obstacle to economics?

Starting from Edwin Chadwick (1800−80), the British public health reformer, coming to the World Health Organization's Commission on Macroeconomics and Health, chaired by the US economist Jeffrey Sachs in 2002, it has been repeatedly claimed that investments in public health aid socioeconomic development. All of these statements were recommended just from a strict utilitarian viewpoint. The WHO Commission stated "We believe that the additional investment in health − requiring of donors roughly one-tenth of one percent of their national income − would be repaid many times over of lives saved each year, enhanced economic development, and strengthening global security" (Commission on Macroeconomics and Health, 2001).

Nevertheless, environmental public health is frequently taken as a killjoy, as something which obstacles the private investments or at least, doesn't allow to lead visible output, useful to politicians to be associated to their short-term mandate.

This section is aimed to show in a clear but scientific manner how this approach is mainly due to the narrow-mindedness, which is a typical feature of our modern societies too quick and shallow attitudes, mainly in the field of communication.

Earlier words by Wilde (1891), that "progress is the realisation of Utopia", were reframed by Rayner and Lang (2013) in "progress is the realization of public health," where public health (in particular the environmental one), is not just a utopia (as Oscar Wilde said) but a very practical and real issue.

The International Network on Public Health and Environmental Tracking INPHET (2014) recent statement "At a time of growing recognition of these impacts, of financial crises and of globalization that demands greater European competitiveness, we thus believe that better tracking of the environment and its effects can help achieve the two goals of healthier populations and healthier economies", concurs with the view by Rayner and Lang (2012).

Coming to the core of this section, it is necessary to clarify some central questions: "What is development? Can economic growth be decoupled from environmental or health damage? Is there a limit to the advancement of general well-being within an endless economic development? Can health and the environment be internalized into dominant market economics" (Rayner and Lang, 2012).

10.4.2 The crisis of capitalism

Ahead of the greatest global economic and financial crisis, Ruffolo (2008), an influential Italian economist who worked for the Italian Ministry of the Environment (1987–92), wrote "Capitalism is close the end in the next centuries." In his book he stated that capitalism has at least three intrinsic limits due to its growth and sustainability: physical/ecological, social, and financial (Ruffolo, 2008). He did not know that the last contradiction (to accumulate monetary resources which were not real) would have triggered the social and economic crisis which we are still facing a decade later.

In Jacobs and Mazzucato (2016) edited book "Rethinking Capitalism, Economics and Policy for Sustainable and Inclusive Growth" the authors refer to an "innocent but pointed question" put in November 2008, at the peak of the global financial crash[1] by the 82-year-old British Queen at the London School of Economics: "Why did nobody notice it?" (Pierce, 2008).

These two economists in collaboration with many other contributors argue against the dominant orthodox neo-liberal economic theory according to Adam Smith (1723–90), David Ricardo (1772–1823), and their followers. Milton Freedman, the Head of Chicago School of Economics, developed the neo-liberal free market trend in economics, also followed by the "Chicago School Boys", amongst whom was Jeffrey Sachs (Klein, 2007), which is the basis of the current preeminent approach of most economic choices in the western and most eastern world.

The basis of their criticism is the need to integrate experience and theory: "Capitalist economies are not theoretical abstractions, but complex and dynamic systems, embedded in specific societies, as well as in natural environment governed by biophysical laws. They are forms of multiple relationships between real and heterogeneous economic actors whose behavior is not that of idealized 'representative agents', but arises from their particular characteristics and choices in different circumstances. These relationships give rise not to equilibrium, but to dynamic patterns of growth and change. The macroeconomic outcomes they generate are more than simply the sum of theirs microeconomic parts. Their problems are not the failure of markets which "normally" succeeded, but arise from fundamental characteristics and structures. So to understand how they work, and to explain how policy can help them work better, we need a much richer approach" (Jacobs and Mazzucato, 2016).

---

[1] Lehman Brothers Holdings Inc bankruptcy happened on September 15, 2008.

This is the reason why the overall productivity slowdown, also named "secular stagnation" has been insufficiently explained by "orthodox theorists," while it should be seen as a transition phase toward a "global sustainable golden age" (Peretz, 2016) (see later). A particular importance should be accounted to innovation first and foremost taking into account the concerns due to climate change. As Dietz and Stern (2015) have underlined, climatic change is likely to undermine the core economic assets (in particular in infrastructure and natural capital) that drive growth and productivity. The economic costs are therefore likely to get higher and higher (Zenghelis, 2016a). All these considerations are particularly serious while considering that CO_2 is not avoidable as in the case of other pollutants (i.e., SO_x), unless energy sources are changed.

10.4.3 Innovation

David Warsh in his book "Knowledge of the wealth of nations", complained that the new economic categories: persons, ideas, things—should replace the older ones: land, labor, and capital— did not contaminate enough the economic literature (Warsh, 2006).

"Accelerating the rate of innovation is crucial to long-term growth and for meeting some of the great challenges — such as climate changes, natural resource scarcity and improved healthcare — which societies today face" (Mazzuccato, 2016). As such a new relationship must be envisaged between public and private sector in this field within a new framework where innovation is as follows:

- *Collective*, based on public—private resources integration and where the application of the skills and efforts of many actors and individualities generate organizational learning that results in competitive products (see below).
- *Uncertain*, the outcomes of which are to some extent not completely predictable, and not preordained, and it is due to technology, market, and competition.
- *Path dependent and cumulative*, which means that the ways in which existing infrastructure and ideas interact to set the course for future change. For instance, London's city plan, also including its modern shape and extension, is partially determined by Roman planning implemented 2000 years ago (Zenghelis, 2016b).

In general, business invests *if and only if* it has "enough evidence" for future returns, which is its legitimate and understandable approach.

On the other hand, coming back to the "example" of climate change, it must be strongly pointed out that it is a collective concern, a "tragedy of the commons." To replace energy sources, transport, agriculture, urban planning, behaviors, it will be necessary for a concerted action to face resistance in particular those arising from short-term economy (financialization), while our major duty and effort should be in favor of future generations (Franciscus, 2015).

As such, the role of the state must be far stronger and broader over providing resources to private innovation, to encourage what "was aleardy in their minds." It should be a "mission-orientation" which in general means to create new market landscapes. In many cases, this will need to overcome early high costs, which are likely to breed political resistance first and foremost though the citizens awareness and advocacy.

In essence, it means what Carlota Peretz (2016) stated while speaking about "a shift in consumer demand" through a growth based more on services and intangibles. It means the replacement of "products" with "services" through the called "circular economy," which means a development of all those services included in the "shared economy" approach in which information communications technology (ICT) allows citizens to share goods and services (car cub, households tools, etc.). ICT is a crucial innovation tool throughout the extraction of natural resources to transformation, distribution, logistic and reuse.

10.4.4 Productivity and coproduction

According to Lazonik "It is organizations - including household families, business enterprises, and government agencies - and market that invest in the productive capabilities embodied in physical and human capital that generate productivity." Developed markets in labor, capital, and products are the result, not the cause, of the growth of innovative enterprise. Their goals are to produce competitive goods and services. A business that generates higher quality, lower cost products over a certain period is an innovative enterprise, and costs are the result of the innovative strategy (Lazonik, 2016).

In the presence of innovation, just organizations (and not markets) invest in the collective and cumulative learning that enables a firm to confront, and possibly overcome, the uncertainty bound to innovation.

As a result enterprises are social organization, where higher quality and low-cost products are generated by sharing the value gains with leading groups of workers, whose contribution of skill and effort are essential to improve and increase of productivity. Companies in Germany, Scandinavia, and Japan, for example, are structured to involve different stakeholders, including their employees, aiming at long-term production where investments are first and foremost allocated in the enterprises.

The Nobel Prize winner Stiglitz (2016) in his chapter on "Inequality and Economic Growth" shows that inequality is rising and the huge growth of top incomes "... has coincided with an economic slowdown." In the past 25−30 years, Gini index—the common index to measure inequality—has increased by about 29% in the United States, 17% in Germany, 14% in the United Kingdom, 12% in Italy, 11% in Japan, and 9% in Canada. There are many attempts to explain such an unquestionable tendency. Inequality can be due to "exploitation, discrimination, and monopoly of power," and also strongly conditioned by "many institutional and political issues" such as "industrial relations, labor market institutions, welfare, and tax systems."

The key issue is rent-seeking which in general destroy wealth. "A monopolist who overcharges for her or his product takes money from those whom she or he is overcharging and at the same time destroy value. To get her or hid monopoly price, she or he has to restrict production." The crucial point is that rent is increasing (due to the increase in land rents, intellectual property rents, and monopoly power). As such "wealth increases, but this not lead to an increase in the productive capacity of the economy...With more wealth put into these assets, there may be less invested in real productive capital (Stiglitz, 2016)."

The results are as follows:

- Differently to the usual justification that inequality is necessary to induce a savings and investments growth, "there are better ways of inducing savings than increasing inequality. The government can tax the income of the riches, and use the funds to finance either private or public investments; such policies to reduce inequalities in consumption and disposable income, and lead to increased national savings (appropriately measured)";
- Accordingly, it must be underlined that jobs are not created by creative entrepreneurs, but by *demand*, and inequality has negative effects on that, either because it has a negative effects on medium-term growth (as shown by OECD), or because "inequality leads to weak aggregate demand. The reason is easy to understand: those at the bottom spend a larger fraction of their income those at the top. In addition, inequality reduces opportunity which "lower growth in the future."

- Finally "societies with greater inequality are less likely to make public investment which enhances productivity, such as transportation, infrastructure, technology and education."

Bearing all these issues in mind, Jacobs and Mazzuccato claim the role of policy is "not only simply to 'correcting' the failures of the wise free markets. It is rather to help to create and shape markets to achieve the coproduction, and the fair distribution of economic value." As Western capitalism showed important and endogenous drawbacks "a more innovative, sustainable and inclusive system is possible. But it will require fundamental changes in our understanding of how capitalism works, and how public policy can help create and shape a different economic future." It means that also developing countries will take part in this sustainable global golden age (Perez, 2012).

10.4.5 Policy, markets, and citizens

As we said before, the Jacobs and Mazzuccato's book must be taken as a landmark for a new strategy toward an "economic and environmental public heath" more effective approach, either from a theoretical or *in the field* point of views.

Nevertheless, they miss two additional issues:
1. Who are politicians?
2. What is the role of citizens?

On the former one, it is essential to remember and to remind that politicians are not an abstract expression of policy; they represent citizens (obviously in real democracies). Hence, the power *is* and *must be* in charge of citizens!

On the latter one, it must be taken into proper account that a citizen is
- a *voter* and sometimes an advocate;
- a *consumer*, the one who to some extent induce *the demand* (see before); and
- an *employee* (see before).

In conclusion, one of the aims of this chapter and of this book as a whole is to offer tools and arguments to policy taken as a collective agreement[2] and in particular among citizens, toward a *mission-oriented goal* based

---

[2] "A set of ideas or a plan of what to do in particular situations that has been agreed to officially by a group of people, a business organization, a government, or a political party" (Cambridge Dictionary).

on innovation and long-term expectations, mainly but not only in the case of Climate Change.

In point of fact, these tools and arguments must be based on cost—benefits analysis, which is expected to disclose and show how important are the warnings and what are the opportunities in view of a "sustainable global gold age," from both, an individual health and wellbeing and common environmental goods (Ackerman, 2007). What we would like to show is that the market equilibrium among customer and producers is the final goal of *all* human being and not only in favor of those who are more favored, which must be proved by means of quantitative, analytical, and also empirical issues.

Nevertheless as Ackerman writes "Our decisions about [climate] policy are, above all, ethical and political judgments about what we can and should do for each other today, and for the future generations that will follow us"..."The larger goal is to inform the urgent and practical debate about [climate] policy and to explain why the resolution of that debate will not emerge from economic modeling alone" (Ackerman, 2007).

10.5 Section 4: Responses to these challenges

To face complexity we outlined in previous sections, the mainstays that should inform responses are as follows:
- Understanding
- Integration
- Participation

10.5.1 Understanding

An important aspect of today's society is the current dilemma of the role of science and technology in conjunction with the profound crisis of the political class.

More specifically decisions dealing with health implications that aim at attaining goals of planned initiatives (actions) on the basis of knowledge (evidence) have to consider what needs to be known but also what can be known. On that basis, it will be possible to come to decision on what has to be done.

All this depends on the organizational and economic investment, on the willingness to know and face real and present problems but also, and not least, on the economic and political activities that led to the risk.

In general, the questions that are the basis of a process of identifying and preventing environmental and health risks are:
1. *Who* must produce evidence?
2. *What type* of evidence is necessary?
3. *How* will this evidence be produced?
4. *What quality* of evidence is necessary?
5. *How strong* must the association be in order to declare a substance "toxic" (e.g., carcinogenic, teratogen) and reduce exposure?
6. Which values must be attributed to the *Precautionary Principle?*

These issues have been fully treated in detail by David Gee of the European Environmental Agency[3] (Gee, 2012).

Here it is essential to remember that understanding is a complex process that needs discipline and professional integration, clear-cut definition of the limits, and possible errors of each specific environmental health scientific studies (experimental/observational studies).

The statement that the *absence of evidence* is not *evidence of the absence* must be explicitly recognized.

Therefore an evaluation closely linked to the traditional reduction type of approach could misleadingly conclude that certain actions deemed useless have, in fact, served a real purpose in changing the perceptions and behavior at risk for the individual, the community, and the environment.

In addition, it is important to note that the difference between *lifestyles* and *environmental risk factors* is only an operative simplification. In fact, in sociology there are two schools of thought: the first states that structures (environment) are nothing more than the actions of collective individuals, and the second emphasizes the role structures have on the actions of individuals (Thorogodd, 2002).

In reality there is a dynamic interaction among individuals and structures with reciprocal influences on each other.

In conclusion the evaluation and the production of evidence should be placed in a context of multicausality, complexity, uncertainty, and ignorance.

Last but not least, dealing with the relationship between understanding and action the precautionary principle (PP) must be properly taken into

3
- Gee, D, Children's Health, multicausality and the precautionary principle, Paper presented at the UPEM conference in Copenhagen 7–9 June 2004.
- David Gee, Conference on Occupational and Environmental Cancer Prevention University of Stirling, 25 April 2008.

proper account (Lauriola, 2006). PP has a long history in medicine and health care: the main objective of public health is to prevent diseases and promote health, which amounts to the application of the principles of prevention and precautionary (Pearce, 2006).

In general, this approach is considered when the environmental damage has not (yet) been identified or even in the absence of risk.

Admittedly two other fundamental elements are necessary to understand this principle and explain the term "actions" that we mentioned before. First: that the reference to precautionary principle implies a need for greater knowledge; second: that we must rely on technologies that guarantee the greatest safety.

In other words, this does not imply only a diagnostic effort, but it also and especially entails an effort to formulate proposals. This means that PP does not mean "blocking activities," but on the contrary, it is responsible for developing further knowledge and presenting alternative proposals.

10.5.2 Integration

As we had already strongly and widely underlined, complexity is an essential trait of environmental health issue, which can be effectively faced only by an interdisciplinary approach as it has been shown by the IPCC.

But dealing with the issue of integration, there are many other very sensitive features which have to be considered important under any circumstance on both the general and local level. What relationship should there be between the research funded by public institutions and those financed by special interest groups (mobile phone companies, tobacco industry, etc.)? Should only researchers with academic credentials be accepted or should experts with a local territorial knowledge be used? What role should be played by citizens and workers?

We do not believe there is one single answer. Instead, we believe that it would be even worse to think that one exists. Obviously, investigations carried out by public institutions, by definition, should guarantee independence and work toward the exclusive interest of the well-being of the community, but it is also clear that given the multitude of requests and limitation of resources this is not always possible. On the other hand, studies created, conducted, or in any case financed by special interest groups could be useful in order to understand if and how to invest in new business activities. Therefore an integration of these should not be excluded outright, but prior to any undertaking, a clear moral code of conduct should be openly declared or in any case always evaluated. In other words, to declare something independent is not at all an easy and straightforward operation. Precisely for this reason, it is necessary to address the problem of "transparency" which means to declare in advance the real objectives that motivate the study, or determine what the "conflicts of interest" are. This does not mean that it is impossible to conduct this type of research, but it simply means it is necessary to declare in advance the validity of the researcher rather than defend it after the results have already been made public. Sometimes the results could even contradict the interests of those who had initiated the research, and this would obviously reinforce the integrity of the researcher. On this issue, it would be useful to establish a working definition or a standard procedure (predefined statement on conflict of interest by study sponsors) of the term "conflict of interest."

Likewise, know-how developed in a nonacademic environment, but in the field, must be considered an opportunity to enhance knowledge and professional expertise. Therefore initiatives that involve well-reputed research institutes that certify and utilize this knowledge and consequently for various reasons do not end up with the usual "peer review" must be promoted (e.g., information generally not interesting for the scientific community, but nevertheless important knowledge that must be complied quickly in order to meet the needs of the local administration and population).

The contribution of citizens and workers with their "lay" and "local" knowledge (defined as a homogeneous group in the past), besides being an early warning sign on the part of the victims (be careful of distorting selections such as: "pensioner party fallacy," "healthy worker" effects), provides a real analysis of conditions (life/work), and exposure and can present solutions on how to reduce them. This also allows for the identification of more efficient alternatives (in the field) and often represents an essential support in developing local and general knowledge (see asbestos case).

We can all agree that knowledge is a common benefit to which everyone must be willing to contribute but always in such a way that is transparent, humble, and respectful of others.

But the need of integration, which is so clear in the field of research if we account the complexity of reality, becomes even more relevant while facing the need to integrate the role of science and policy in view of an evidence-informed policy making.

There is evidence that there is an increasing interest in integration, both within scientists' and politicians' communities (Bultitude et al., 2012), but it is not clear how it can be attained.

Recently, some researchers investigated this issue and summarized 14 strategies or approach to attain an effective integration of science and policy (Choi et al., 2016). As a whole, this process is not unique or linear; it largely depends on where, when, and most importantly why it is carried out (see Section 10.3). Nevertheless, it is essential to point out that this issue is crucial to face effectively either in terms of understanding or of action.

10.5.3 Participation

The environment in which we live and work affects both our health and our economic productivity, among other impacts. At a time of growing recognition of these impacts, of financial crises, and of globalization that demands greater European competitiveness, we thus believe that better tracking of the environment and its effects can help achieve the two goals of healthier populations and healthier economies. Indeed, improving the environment and reducing its impact on health should be viewed as an opportunity to boost competitiveness and, by extension economy, since health and sustainability are pillars of wellbeing and productivity, especially in a time of socioeconomic and even cultural crisis (INPHET, 2014).

The classical economics of Adam Smith (1723–90), David Ricardo (1772–1823), and their followers focus on physical resources in defining its factors of production and discuss the distribution of cost and value among these factors. Adam Smith and David Ricardo referred to the "component parts of price" (Smith, 1776) as the costs of using the following:

- Land or natural resource—naturally-occurring goods such as water, air, soil, minerals, flora, and fauna that are used in the creation of products.
- Labor—human effort used in production which also includes technical and marketing expertise. Labor can also be classified as the physical and mental contribution of an employee to the production of the good(s).
- The capital stock—human-made goods which are used in the production of other goods. These include machinery, tools, and buildings.

The classical economists also employed the word "capital" in reference to money. Money, however, was not considered to be a factor of production in the sense of capital stock since it is not used to directly produce any good.

The French sociologist Pierre Bordieu (1930−2002) identified three different dimensions of capital: economic, cultural, and social (Beasley-Murray, 2000).

In particular the concept of social capital became fashionable only relatively recently. Lynda Hanifan (1879−1932) is credited with introducing the concept of social capital "those tangible assets [that] count for most in the daily lives of people: namely goodwill, fellowship, sympathy, and social intercourse among the individuals and families who make up a social unit" (Hanifan, 1916).

It is defined by the OECD (2007) as "networks together with shared norms, values and understandings that facilitate co-operation within or among groups."

There's much debate over the various forms that social capital takes, but one fairly straightforward approach divides it into three main categories:

- Bonds: Links to people based on a sense of common identity (people like us)—such as family, close friends, and people who share our culture or ethnicity.
- Bridges: Links that stretch beyond a shared sense of identity, for example, to distant friends, colleagues, and associates.
- Linkages: Links to people or groups further up or lower down the social ladder.

In this context, social cohesion means that those who feel to be part of a community are naturally induced to invest in that area either in economical terms or cultural ones, and, last but not least, a peaceful and innovative community could be a better opportunity for investments from outside that area (e.g. foreign funds).

All these arguments lead to the core of the problem, which is to internalize all the externalized or unaccounted costs. In this approach, ecosystems are judged to be "natural capital." The strategy is to encourage ways to add economic value to environmental health resources to be integrated with policies and decisions frameworks for resource production and consumption.

To sum up "the state of public health, the concrete expression of health within families, communities and indeed whole societies, informs the collective sense of human dignity and achieved quality of life. In part the discussion of democracy is also a statement about what it is to be human, what obligations people have to others, how collective decisions are made and what role individuals, from those on high to the humble, have in setting the direction for society. The health of the people and subtle as well as voting democratization of society and economy are entwined" (ecological public health) (Rayner and Lang, 2012).

10.6 Conclusions

Climate and environmental change are the biggest challenge for humanity and its survival. It is, therefore, essential to understand more comprehensively and effectively what the effects on the environment and the health are. The ecological (ecosystem) public health approach, also seen as democratization of public health sciences, highlights the need to consider several key societal systems when assessing climate and environmental change impacts on population health. The interlinkages and the dynamicity of these systems in defining population health are key when informing research and evidence-based decision making.

This way of thinking also means that epidemiology, the pillar for public health science, works within this ecological public health framework, and must work side by side with environmental, ecological economists in developing approaches that address complex cost—benefit challenges in environment and health. The ecological public health approach also encourages a transdisciplinary collaborations to address complexity that should include scientists and practitioners from social sciences, demography, energy, water, food systems and policies, economists, urban planners, climate and biodiversity scientists, just to name a few. These types of collaborations will improve understanding, measurement, and quantification of population health impacts of complex ecological and climate change. This approach is also useful to face effectively the real contradictions and drawbacks of our modern societies, most importantly justice and equity, and has consideration of vulnerability, adaptation (maladaptation), mitigation, and resilience (Kelman et al., 2015).

Our suggestion is that when we are aiming at developing and implementing cost—benefit analyses, it is essential to work within the proposed framework of ecological public health. This approach makes possible to understand and assess the role of social, economic, demographic, and environmental determinants within the complex systems framework, taking also into account the systems temporality, spatiality, and dynamicity. Only this way one can improve evidence-based decisions-making and preventive actions for public health policy, and potentially contribute to cobenefits of interventions.

Why are current economic models not taking into account this challenge? This is likely due to the skepticism about the impacts of climate change by the classic economists. Also, there is still difficulty in considering complexity and uncertainty of the impacts of climate change in current economic models (Ackerman, 2007). The prioritization of ecosystem and human health are still lacking from current economic intervention models (Dietz and Stern, 2015). Adapted economic models that take into account climate and ecological change impacts on societies, and also models that incorporate sustainability, planetary insurance and discounting concepts to address climate change are proposed (Ackerman, 2007). Consideration of environmental and social justice, and economic models that inform policy for sustainable and inclusive growth would also be informative for any progress in reducing the overall environmental and climate change impacts on ecosystem and human health (Ackerman, 2007; Jacobs and Mazzucato, 2016).

At present, economic analysis is a key dimension of the planning of all organized human activity. The challenges posed by the combined effects on society of the multiple transitions described in section 1 of this chapter, make effective planning more difficult or ineffective, including its economic aspects. The assumption of a steady progress and a regular annual cycle of planning leading to more effective management or resources has become unrealistic, when in fact an increasing frequency of adverse events, or disasters, has become the norm. Rather than achieving their goal of a stable and prosperous society, human activities planned with this assumption reduce the resilience of society. Therefore explicit consideration of the role played by events emerging as manifestation of combined long-term trends needs to move center stage in planning of all human activities that could affect health. These include activities in all policy sectors, so this is also a new task for economic analysis of environmental factors affecting health.

To illustrate the practical possibilities of an economic approach that addresses the considerations in this chapter, it seems appropriate to make an effort to explore the usefulness of the ecological public health approach to cost–benefit analyses of environmental intervention on a specific topic. We chose disasters as a broad topic encompassing mortality, injuries, and other adverse health effects directly or indirectly caused by climate change. Disasters make an illustration of the possibility that an ecological/environmental approach would assist in framing how preventive actions and economic analyses informing these can be guided. This is represented in Table 10.2, which is an adaptation of the concept proposed by Rayner and Lang (2012).

In considering possible benefits to health from prevention of future natural disasters the ecological public health framework can be summarized in four possible dimensions of existence that require altering: material, biological, cultural, and social worlds. The agents that have a role in designing and effecting this change can be summarized in three groups: (1) governments and public health agencies, (2) markets, and (3) the public. This way, the identification of interventions by specific actors can be mapped against all dimensions of human existence, and the costs and benefits of each intervention can be assessed appropriately, within a context of overall capacity to address an apparently unmanageable challenge. Table 10.2 provides a possible selection of interventions as categorized.

For example, focusing on the role of governments and public health agencies, it is recognized that these have access to a range of conceptual and practical tools. These will range from a focus on the hazard elements of a disaster, to the vulnerability of the population, or the infrastructure and resources of a community. When indirect health impacts are included, agriculture and forestry represent a sector of human activity that comes within scope, in view of the adverse health impacts on nutrition and welfare that could derive from flooding and other extreme events damaging crops and forests. Therefore overall the prevention of accidents represents an agenda that overlaps with disaster risk reduction. The capacity of a public health service to contribute to disaster risk reduction will relate to its vision of a population aware of its vulnerabilities in terms of groups of people and also infrastructure and resources available. Activities on prevention of disasters overlap to a large extent with the mainstream work of public agencies including public health institutions but require a wider range of partnerships with decision makers, scientific and technical institutes, that would join forces for addressing people, infrastructure, and resource vulnerabilities as identified on an ongoing basis. This new challenge may involve the capacity of public health agencies to work with engineers, geologists, architects, economists, legal experts, as well as broader cultural experts such as linguists, historians, and others engaged in accounting for the identity of a community. This is done with a common

Table 10.2 How the ecological public health approach can be used for economic cost—benefit analyses of environmental interventions: case study—disaster-related mortality and injuries.

		Altering the four dimensions of existence to minimize disaster risk			
		Material	**Biological**	**Cultural**	**Social**
Focus of action	Making governments work for health by:	Ensuring all citizens have a requisite level of access to safe housing, schools, and services	Define parameters for infrastructure developments inclusive of expected future risk of extreme events	Setting incentives for agricultural and forestry production resilient to damage by flooding and other extreme but predictable events	Setting clear, long-term cultural goals
		Setting minimum income standards that supports access to safe housing and services	Develop quality standards for insurance that modulate premium according to local disaster risk	Focusing subsidies to promote crops and forest ecosystems resilient to climate change in specific regions	Help educate "ecologically sustainable infrastructure development" to build a safer future
				Setting and paying for high standards of public-sector agricultural and forestry development procurement and other fiscal measures to manage demand	Supporting the strengthening of social rituals when people bond through community events for better reconstructions after disasters
	Using public				
	Making markets work for health by:	Making procurement contracts for infrastructure reflect parameters inclusive of future risk of extreme events	Change price signals of agricultural and forestry products to favor resilient crops and ecosystems	Supporting explicitly ecological information for purchasers in the public sector (local authorities/communities)	Promoting forward-looking design for building developments, that include services accessible to low-income social groups

(Continued)

Table 10.2 (Continued)

	Altering the four dimensions of existence to minimize disaster risk			
	Material	Biological	Cultural	Social
	Reducing reliance on fossil fuels to encourage continuity of agricultural and forestry production during energy transition to renewables	Promoting the use of sustainable agricultural and forestry practices	Promoting more flexible and diverse partnerships with consortia of builders and agricultural and forestry	Align companies' success with consumer safety in the face of expected extremes of weather Promoting only self-regulation that works for community safety Accepting restrictions on
Making the public live healthily by:	Increased adaptation capacity (community networks, system for resource sharing, system for emergency evacuation)	Altering the composition of their expenditure toward housing and leisure choices resilient to extreme events	Consider cultural heritage in the evaluation of priorities for reconstruction after disasters	Engage in planning development for own neighborhood
Using community meetings for planning debates as an affirmatve social engagement				

purpose of addressing any vulnerabilities in a realistic time frame in order to avoid the natural tendency to escape and crushing what has been established in the ages. Prevention of disasters, in this sense, overlaps with societal development as informed about long-term requirements for agricultural and forestry sectors, industrial development, transport, built environment, and other routine aspects of human societies, with the added dimensions posed by pressures attributable to environmental change.

A similar discussion could be developed focusing on the role of markets and of members of the public. Overall, from each cell in Table 10.2, an integrated and informed economic evaluation could be designed in a way that is expected to identify key dimensions of benefit to public health in the face of challenges posed by climate change.

References

Ackerman, F., 2007. Can we afford the future? The economics of a warming world. The New Economics. Zed Books.

Altizer, S., Ostfeld, R.S., Johnson, P.T.J., Kutz, S., Drew Harvell, C., 2013. Climate change and infectious diseases: from evidence to a predictive framework. Science 341 (6145), 514−519. Available from: https://doi.org/10.1126/science.1239401.

Awerbuch, T.E., Brinkman, U., Eckardt, I., et al., 1996. Globalization, development, and the spread of disease. In: Mander, J., Goldsmith, E. (Eds.), The Case Against the Global Economy. Sierra Club Books, San Francisco, CA.

Bai, X., Dawson, R.J., Ürge-Vorsatz, D., Delgado, G.C., et al., 2018. Six research priorities for cities and climate change. Nature 555, 23−25.

Barrios, S., Bertinelli, L., Strobl, E., 2006. Climatic change and rural-urban migration: The case of sub-Saharan Africa. J Urban Econ 60 (3), 357−371.

Beasley-Murray, J., 2000. Value and Capital in Bourdieu and Marx. In: Brown, N., Szeman, I. (Eds.), Pierre Bordieu: Field-Work in Culture. Rowman & Littlrfield, Lahman, MD, pp. 100−119.

Berkman, L.F., Glass, T., Brissette, I., et al., 2000. From social integration to health: Durkheim in the new millennium. Soc. Sci. Med. 51, 843−857.

Bultitude, K., Rodari, P., Weitkamp, E., 2012. Bridging the gap between science and policy: the importance of mutual respect, trust and the role of mediators. JCOM 11 (3), 1−4. September.

Burrows, K., Kinney, P.L., 2016. Exploring the Climate Change, Migration and Conflict Nexus. Int J Environ Res Public Heal J 13 (443), 1−17.

Butler, C., Mcfarlane, R.A., 2018. Climate Change, Food Security, and Population Health in the Anthropocene. Encyclopedia of Anthropocene 2, 453−459. Available from: https://doi.org/10.1016/B978-0-12-809665-9.09745-7.

Butler, C.D., Harley, D., 2010. Primary, secondary and tertiary effects of eco-climatic change: The medical response. Postgraduate Medical Journal 86 (1014), 230−234. Available from: https://doi.org/10.1136/pgmj.2009.082727.

Butler, C.D., McMichael, A.J., 2010. Population health: where demography, environment and equity converge. J Public Health (Oxf) 32, 157−158.

Campbell, B.M., Vermeulen, S.J., Aggarwal, P.K., Corner-Dolloff, C., Girvetza, E.A., Loboguerreroa, R., et al., 2016. Reducing risks to food security from climate change. Global Food Security 11, 34−43.

Castleden, M., McKee, M., Murray, V., Leonardi, G., 2011. Resilience thinking in health protection. J. Public Health 33 (3), 369−377. Apr 6.

Choi, B.C.K., Li, L., Lu, Y., Zhang, L.R., Zhu, Y., Pak, A.W.P., et al., 2016. Little Bridging the gap between science and policy: an international survey of scientists and policy makers in China and Canada. Implement. Sci. 11, 16.

Commission on Macroeconomics and Health, 2001. Macroeconomics and Health: Investing in Health for Economic Development. Harvard University/Center for International Development/World Health Organization, Geneva, p. 8.

Dietz S., Stern N., 2015. Endogenous growth, convexity of damage and climate risk: how Norhaus' frame work supports deep cuts in carbon emission. Econ. J. 125 (583), 574−620 D. Zenghelis in ibid pag 173.

Diez-Roux, A.V., 2006. Integrating social and biological factors in health research: a systems view. Ann. Epidemiol. 17, 569−574.

EmTASK. <http://www.emergenze.unimore.it/site/home.html>.

Frame, D., Allen, M., 2008. Climate change and global risk. In: Bostrom, N., Ćirković, M.M. (Eds.), Global Catastrophic Risks. Oxford University Press, Oxford, ISBN: 9780198570509, 0198570503.

Franciscus, 2015. Lettera Enciclica Laudato Si' Del Santo Padre Francesco Sulla Cura Della Casa Comune La giustizia tra le generazioni, pp. 122−125

Frumhoff, P.C., Heede, R., Oreskes, N., 2015. The climate responsibilities of industrial carbon producers. Clim. Change 132, 157−171.

Gee, D., 2012. Late Lessons from Early Warnings and EMF. <http://www.bioinitiative.org/report/docs/section_16.pdf>.

Gould, S.J., 1996a. The Full House: The spread of Excellence from Pluto to Darwin. Random House, New York.

Gould, S.J., 1996b. The Mismeasure of Man. W. W. Nortona & Co, New York and London.

Hanifan, L.J., 1916. The rural school community center. Ann. Am. Acad. Polit. Soc. Sci. 67, 130−138.

INPHET, 2014. Why Environmental and Public Health Tracking: The Modena Position Paper for the Italian Presidency of the EU Council "for a Better Environment and Health." <http://inphet.org/...>.

Intergovernmental Panel on Climate Change 5th Assessment Report (IPCC AR5) (2014). Climate Change 2014, Impacts, Adaptation, and Vulnerability In: Field, C.B., V.R. Barros, D.J. Dokken, K.J. Mach, M.D. Mastrandrea, T.E. Bilir, et al. (Eds.). Geneva, Switzerland, 2014.

Intergovernmental Panel on Climate Change (IPCC), 2014. Climate change 2014: synthesis report. In: Pachauri, R.K., Meyer, L.A. (Eds.), Contribution of working groups I, II and III to the Fifth Assessment Report Of The Intergovernmental Panel On Climate Change. Core Writing Team. Intergovernmental Panel on Climate Change, Geneva, Switzerland.

Jacobs, M., Mazzucato, M., 2016. Rethinking Capitalism, Economics and Policy for Sustainable and Inclusive Growth. Wiley Blackwell.

Kawachi, I., Wamala, S., 2007. Globalization and Health. Oxford University Press, Oxford, UK.

Kelley, C.P., et al., 2015. Climate change in the Fertile Crescent and implications of the recent Syrian drought. Proc. Natl. Acad. Sci. U.S.A. 112 (13), 3241−3246. Available from: https://doi.org/10.1073/pnas.1421533112.

Kelman, I., Gaillard, J.C., Mercer, J., 2015. Climate change's role in disaster risk reduction's future: beyond vulnerability and resilience. Int. J. Disaster Risk Sci. 6, 21−27. Available from: https://doi.org/10.1007/s13753-015-0038-5.

Klein, N., 2007. The Shock Doctrine: the rise of Disaster Capitalism. Pinguin Books. Great Britain.

Koopman, J.S., 1996a. Comment: Emerging objectives and methods in epidemiology. Am. J. Public Health 86, 630−632.

Koopman, J.S., 1996b. Individual causal models and population system models in epidemiology. Am. J. Public Health 89, 1170−1174.

Kovats, S., Ebi, K., Annunziata, G., Bagaria, J., Banatvala, N., Baschieri, A., et al., 2011. Health Impacts of Catastrophic Climate Change: Expert Workshop. Avoid Dangerous Climate Change (AVOID). Technical Report. Met Office Hadley Centre for Climate Prediction and Research, Exeter, UK. <http://researchonline.lshtm.ac.uk/id/eprint/2551557>.

Krieger, N., 1994. Epidemiology and the web of causation: has anyone seen the spider? Soc. Sci. Med. 39, 887−903.

Lauriola, P., Leonardi, G., Righi, E., Bayleyegn, T., Schnall, A., Malilay, J., et al., 2018. Natural Disaster − Environmental Health Preparedness In: Encyclopedia of Environmental Health, Elsevier Ed Reference module DOI: 10.1016/B978-0-12-409548-9.11140-6.

Lauriola, P., 2006. Perché proprio a me?» Come si costruiscono scelte condivise. SNOP 69, 35−39.

Lazonik, W., 2016. Rethinking Capitalism, Economics and Policy for Sustainable and Inclusive Growth. Wiley Blackwell, pag76.

Levins, R., 1998. Qualitative mathematics for understanding, prediction and intervention in complex ecosystems. In: Rappaport, D., Costanza, R., Epstein, P., Levins, R. (Eds.), Ecosystem Health: Principles and Practice. Oxford University Press, Oxford, UK.

Levins, R., 1996. Ten propositions for science and antiscience. In: Ross, A. (Ed.), Science Wars. Duke University Press.

Marmot, M., Wilkinson, R., 2006. Social Determinants of Health, second ed. Oxford University Press, Oxford, UK.

Mastrorillo, M., Licker, R., Bohra-Mishra, P., Fagiolo, G.,D., Estes, L., Oppenheimer, M., 2016. The influence of climate variability on internal migration flows in South Africa, Glob Environ Chang [Internet], 39. Elsevier Ltd, pp. 155−169. Available from. Available from: http://dx.doi.org/10.1016/j.gloenvcha.2016.04.014.

Max-Neef, Manfred, 2010. The World on a collision course and the need for a new economy. Contribution to the 2009 Royal Colloquium. AMBIO 39, 200−210. Available from: https://doi.org/10.1007/s13280-010-0028-1.

Mazzuccato, M., 2016. Rethinking Capitalism, Ecomics and Policy for Sustainable and Inclusive Growth. Wiley Blackwell, p. 99.

McMichael, A.J., 1999. Prisoners of the proximate. Loosening the constraints on epidemiology In the age of change. Am. J. Epidemiol. 149, 887−897.

McMichael, A.J., Beaglehole, R., 2000. The changing global context of public health. Lancet 356, 495−499.

McMichael, A.J., Woodruff, R.E., Hales, S., 2006. Climate change and human health: present and future risks. Lancet 367 (9513), 859−869. Available from: https://doi.org/10.1016/S0140-6736(06)68079-3.

McMichael, C., Barnett, J., McMichael, A.J., 2012. An ill wind? Climate change, migration, and health. Environ. Health Persp. 120 (5), 646−654.

McMichael, A.J., 2013. Globalisation, climate change and human health. N. Engl. J. Med. 2013 (368), 1335−1343.

McMichael, C., 2015a. Climate change-related migration and infectious disease. Virulence 6 (6), 548—553. Available from: https://doi.org/10.1080/21505594.2015.1021539.

McMichael, A.J., Butler, C.D., Dixon, J., 2015b. Climate change , food systems and population health risks in their eco-social context', Public Health. 129 (10), 1361—1368. doi: 10.1016/j.puhe.2014.11.013.

Mera, R., et al., 2015. Climate change, climate justice and the application of probabilistic event attribution to summer heat extremes in the California Central Valley. Clim. Change 133, 427—438.

Mitchell, D., Heaviside, C., Vardoulakis, S., Huntingford, C., Masato, G., Guillod, B.P., et al., 2016. Attributing human mortality during extreme heat waves to anthropogenic climate change. Environ. Res. Lett. 11 (7), 074006.

Myers, S.S., Smith, M.R., Guth, S., Golden, C.D., Vaitla, B., Mueller, N.D., et al., 2017. Climate change and global food systems: Potential impacts on food security and undernutrition. Annu. Rev. Public Health 38, 259—277.

OECD, 2007. Human Capital: How What You Know Shapes Your Life.

Pearce, N., 1996. Traditional epidemiology, modern epidemiology, and public health. Am. J. Public Health 86, 678—683.

Pearce, N., 2006. Public health and the precautionary principle. In: Martuzzi, M., Ticker, J.A. (Eds.), The Precautionary Principle: Protecting Public Health, The Environment and The Future of Our Children. WHO-Europe, Rome, Italy.

Peretz, C., 2016. Rethinking Capitalism, Economics and Policy for Sustainable and Inclusive Growth. Wiley Blackwell, pp. 202—203.

Perez, C., 2012. Why IT and the Green Economy are The Real Answer to the Financial Crisis. Green Alliance Blog

Pierce, A., 2008. The Telegraph. <http://www.telegraph.co.uk/news/uknews/theroyalfamily/3386353/The-Queen-asks-why-no-one-saw-the-credit-crunch-coming.html>.

Rafiq, S., Nielsen, I., Smyth, R., 2017. Effect of internal migration on the environment in China. Energy Econ. 64, 31—44.

Rayner, G., Lang, T., 2012. Ecological Public Health: Reshaping the Conditions for Good Health. Taylor & Francis Ltd, London, UK.

Rydin, Y., Bleahu, A., Davies, M., Dávila, J.D., Friel, S., De. Grandis, G., et al., 2012. Shaping cities for health: complexity and the planning of urban environments in the 21st century. Lancet 379, 2079—2108. Available from: https://doi.org/10.1016/S01406736(12)60435-8. Published Online May 30, 2012.

Rockström, J., Steffen, W., Noone, K., Persson, A., Chapin III, F.S., Lambin, E.F., et al., 2009. A safe operating space for humanity. Nature 461, 472—475. Available from: https://doi.org/10.1038/461472a.

Rose, S., 2001. The poverty of reductionism. In: Singh, R.S., Krimbas, C.R., Paul, D.B., Beatty, J. (Eds.), Thinking About Evolution. Historical, Philosophical, and Political Perspective. Cambridge University Press, Cambridge, UK.

Ruffolo, G., 2008 Il capitalismo ha i secoli contati, Ed Gli Struzzi Einaudi.

Smith, A., 1776. The Wealth of Nations. *Wealth of Nations*, Library of Economics and Liberty.

Steffen, W., Richardson, K., Rockström, J., Cornell, S.E., Fetzer, I., Bennett, E.M., et al., 2015. Planetary boundaries: guiding human development on a changing planet. Science 347 (6223), 1259855. Available from: https://doi.org/10.1126/science.1259855.

Stiglitz, J.E., 2016. Inequality and Economic Growth. In: Jacobs, M., Mazzucato, M. (Eds.), *Rethinking Capitalism*: Economics and Policy for Sustainable and Inclusive Growth. Wiley-Blackwell, pp. 134—151.

Susser, M., Susser, E., 1996a. Choosing a future for epidemiology: I. Eras and paradigms. Am. J. Public Health 86, 668—673.

Susser, M., Susser, E., 1996b. Choosing a future for epidemiology: II. From black box to Chinese boxes and eco-epidemiology. Am. J. Public Health 86, 674−677.

Susser, M., 1998. Does risk factor epidemiology put epidemiology at risk? Peering into the future. J. Epidemiol. Community Health 52, 608−611.

Swiss-RE, 2018. Sigma Natural Catastrophes and Man-Made Disasters in 2017: A Year of Record-Breaking Losses No 1/2018

Thompson, A., Otto, F.E., 2015. Ethical and normative implications of weather event attribution for policy discussions concerning loss and damage. Clim. Change 133, 439−451.

Thorogodd, N., 2002. What is the relevance of sociology for health promotion. In: Bunton, R., masc Donald, G. (Eds.), Health Promotion, Disciplines, Diversity and Developments, second ed. Routledge.

Warner, K., Hamza, M., Oliver-Smith, A., Renaud, F., Julca, A., 2010. Climate change, environmental degradation and migration. Nat Hazards 55 (3), 689−715.

Warsh, D., 2006. Knowledge and he wealth of nations Norton.

Watts, N., Amann, M., Ayeb-Karlsson, S., et al., 2017. The lancet countdown on health and climate change: from 25 years of inaction to a global transformation for public health. Lancet 391 (10120), 3−49October 2017. Available from: https://doi.org/10.1016/S0140-6736(17)32464-9.

Watts, N., et al., 2016. The lancet countdown: tracking progress on health and climate change. Lancet 6736 (16), 1−14. Available from: https://doi.org/10.1016/S0140-6736(16)32124-9.

Whitmee, S., et al., 2015. Safeguarding human health in the Anthropocene epoch: report of the Rockefeller Foundation-Lancet Commission on planetary health. Lancet 386 (10007), 1973−2028Elsevier Ltd. Available from: https://doi.org/10.1016/S0140-6736(15)60901-1.

Wilde, O., 1891. The Soul of Man Under Socialism

Wilkinson, P., et al., 2007. A global perspective on energy: health effects and injustices. Lancet 370, 965−978.

United Nations Department of Economic and Social Affairs, May 2017. World Population Prospects. The 2017 Revision. United Nations Department of Economic and Social Affairs, New York. <https://www.un.org/development/desa/publications/world-population-prospects-the-2017-revision.html>.

Zenghelis, D., 2016a. *Rethinking Capitalism, Economics and Policy for Sustainable and Inclusive Growth*. Wiley Blackwell, p. 173.

Zenghelis, D., 2016b. *Rethinking Capitalism, Economics and Policy for Sustainable and Inclusive Growth*. Wiley Blackwell, p. 178.

CHAPTER 11

Case study: a realistic contaminated site remediation and different scenarios of intervention

Carla Guerriero[1,2], Stefano Papirio[3], Francesco Pirozzi[3], Andrea Ranzi[4], L.E. Loria Rebolledo[5] and Verity Watson[5]

[1]Department of Economics and Statistics, University of Naples Federico II, Naples, Italy
[2]Centre for Studies in Economics and Finance (CSEF), Naples, Italy
[3]Department of Civil, Architectural and Environmental Engineering, University of Naples Federico II, Naples, Italy
[4]Center for Environmental Health and Prevention, Regional Agency for Prevention, Environment and Energy of Emilia Romagna, Modena, Italy
[5]Health Economics Research Unit, University of Aberdeen, Aberdeen, United Kingdom

Contents

Cost-Benefit Analysis of Environmental Health Interventions
DOI: https://doi.org/10.1016/B978-0-12-812885-5.00011-1
229

11.1 Introduction

The objective of this chapter is to describe using a step-by-step process how to construct a cost—benefit analysis (CBA) using Excel. The case study described in this chapter is the remediation of an industrial site located in proximity to a small village in Mexico.

11.1.1 Background

The intense industrial activity and improper waste-management policies carried out in the past years require an immediate intervention and an enhanced attention from the scientific community and authorities. This will also attract the interest of worldwide societies and push future generations to bear such a big liability.

Although addressing a significant problem, the remediation of contaminated sites has indeed a short history that dates to the 1980s. This discipline was born to face environmental concerns related to past and present anthropogenic activities, which have led to the contamination of the natural matrixes (i.e., soil, water, and air) as well as detrimental effects to human health. The complexity of contaminated soil remediation is due to (1) the strong interconnection of the factors and parameters involved (e.g., physical, chemical, biological, geological, societal, and economic among others) and (2) the multiphase approach that, moving from site characterization to the selection of the best remediation technology, represents a highly challenging and resource—consuming aspect. The following section describes the scenario of the case study.

11.1.2 Scenario for environmental health interventions

In the present work, the remediation of a contaminated site is proposed as a case study. The use of "realistic conditions" has been preferred to "real conditions" as the former allows to better evaluate the variables and merge the multidisciplinary aspects of this book within the case study. Mexico was selected as a hypothetical setting because its status as a newly industrialized country means that a CBA for the remediation of an industrial site would be likely applied.

The hypothetical case study can be framed in terms of a local government proposal to turn an economically poor-performing industrial site into a green park. The site has a contaminated soil, and it is surrounded at a short distance (a few kilometers) by a populated area. There have been some concerns that the site has had adverse health effects on the local community which has driven actions from the local government. However, the proposal was resisted in the past by some of the resident population because of their employment needs. But now, the site is no longer in operation and the plant is to relocate in a 10-year time span, and the area will be turned into a recreational area. The industrial site in question is an oil refinery plant located in the south of Mexico.

The population exposed to the pollutants is a small town of 50,000 inhabitants (10% are children aged 5−14, 11% are 6−18 years, 73% are adults). Three pollutants released from the site and considered in this study are particulate matter below 10 μm (PM$_{10}$), particulate matter below 2.5 μm (PM$_{2.5}$), and benzene. The average annual values measured for the three pollutants are 30, 22, and 10 μg/m^3 (see Table 11.1). Out of these values, the fraction deriving from the industrial site emissions is 6.4 for PM$_{10}$ and PM $_{2.5}$ and 8.0 μg/m^3 for benzene.

The local government has requested a full health impact assessment and an economic evaluation of two feasible interventions to remediate the site beside the null intervention. The status quo is the "null intervention," which is used for comparative evaluation purposes. Thus, the three possible scenarios evaluated in the present case study are the following:

1. *No intervention* (i.e., null intervention)
2. *In situ intervention*, which consists of a treatment of the soil in the contaminated site
3. *Ex situ intervention* , which consists of a treatment far from the contaminated site after the soil excavation and transport.

The three scenarios are associated with different exposure risks and times, as well as varying tangible and intangible costs. The "no intervention" would result in the longest exposure time because the contaminant would persist until the complete dispersion of the volatile compound, which may take up to 50 years.

11.1.3 Description of soil, migration route, and properties of the contaminant, and contamination extension

The soil of the industrial site is assumed to be a homogeneous mixture of sand and silt with a permeability coefficient of roughly ($k =$ $10^{-4}−10^{-5}$ m/s), which is high enough to allow for an "in situ" intervention. Inhalation through the "air pathway" is considered the sole exposure route in this case study for both particulate matter and benzene (Fig. 11.1). The water table is present at a safe distance (tens of meters) from the lower contamination surface (Fig. 11.2), implying no pollution

Table 11.1 Pollutants concentrations with different interventions.

	Year 0	Industrial related	Year 1	Year 2	Year 2	Year 4	Year 5–50
PM_{10}							
No intervention ($\mu g/m^3$)	30	6	30	30	30	30	30
In situ remediation ($\mu g/m^3$)	22	4	28.8	25.8	24	24	24
Ex situ remediation ($\mu g/m^3$)	10	8	33	33	24	24	24
$PM_{2.5}$							
No intervention ($\mu g/m^3$)	30	6	22	22	22	22	22
In situ remediation ($\mu g/m^3$)	22	4	21.2	19.2	18	18	18
Ex situ remediation ($\mu g/m^3$)	10	8	24	24	18	18	18
Benzene							
No intervention ($\mu g/m^3$)	30	6	10	10	10	10	10
In situ remediation ($\mu g/m^3$)	22	4	8.4	4.4	2	2	2
Ex situ remediation ($\mu g/m^3$)	10	8	14	14	2	2	2

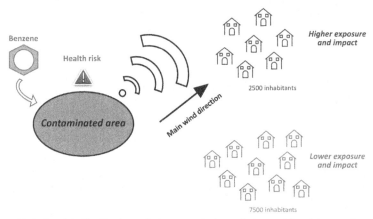

Figure 11.1 Spatial distribution of the population of the residential area impacted by the contamination at the nearby oil-refinery plant. A community of 2500 inhabitants is located on the preferential wind direction and, thus, more exposed to benzene contamination.

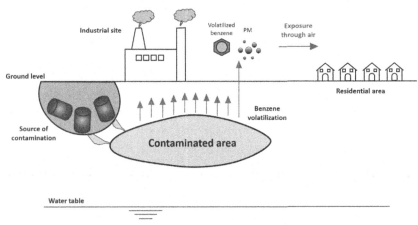

Figure 11.2 Extension of the contamination by benzene in the soil underneath the oil refinery plant. The source of contamination is due to the presence of deteriorated waste containers, which have been buried during the operation of the industrial process. The migration/exposure pathway and the location of the inhabitants of the nearby residential area have also been indicated.

of the groundwater and no migration of benzene through the "water pathway" (i.e., contamination of groundwater, withdrawal of water through wells, and ingestion of water).

Indeed, benzene is a highly volatile compound with a vapor pressure of 94.8 mmHg at 25°C and a boiling point at 80°C. Besides a high volatility, benzene is also characterized by a considerable solubility: 1.79 g/L in water at 20°C. These characteristics make benzene a biodegradable compound, that is, attackable by microorganisms (especially bacteria), that is capable to reduce benzene when favorable conditions for their metabolism are provided. However, benzene is known to be toxic for microbial activity at high concentrations, and its carcinogenic effects on human health have thoroughly been reported.

The dimensions of the contaminated site are approximately 200 m wide × 200 m long × 3 m deep. The contamination is mainly related to leakages from the deterioration of underground tanks and barrels (Fig. 11.2) containing wastes of the oil refinery process. During the years, the waste-containing barrels have been buried at a depth of 5 m, and the contamination has spread to 8 m from the ground level.

11.1.4 Description of the remediation techniques proposed

Due to the benzene characteristics, that is, high volatility and biodegradability in the presence of benzene-consuming microorganisms, the in situ intervention proposed is a "combined soil vapor extraction/bioventing" technique. Soil vapor extraction (SVE) is a remediation process of the nonsaturated soil portion that aspirates an air stream by means of a vacuum pumping system and extraction wells, which are directly planted in the contaminated area (Fig. 11.3). Air must be necessarily aspirated (and not sparged) through the contaminated area, as the removal mechanism of the contaminant is purely physical, based on the solid—gas mass transfer (i.e., volatilization). Therefore, the benzene-containing air stream, which has passed through the contaminated soil, requires proper collection and treatment prior to being released in the atmosphere. The aspirated gas stream can also contain traces of PM_{10} and $PM_{2.5}$, which have to be removed in the air treatment system.

When the removal mechanism of benzene from soil is also biological, that is, due to the degradation of soil microbial communities capable of removing benzene in the presence of higher concentrations of oxygen (provided by the air flow through the soil), the remediation technique is known as "bioventing" (Fig. 11.3A). Different from SVE, air might be alternatively pumped from the ventilation wells into the contaminated air in bioventing applications. However, this implies that the sole removal mechanism is biological, and the bio-treatment efficiency is high enough

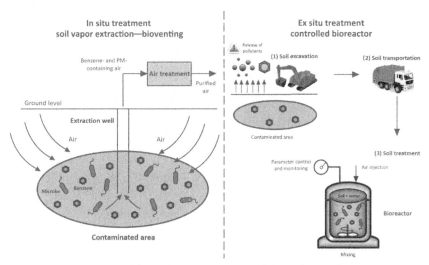

Figure 11.3 Schematic and simple representation of the soil-remediation techniques considered in this case study. A soil vapor extraction/bioventing and the use of a "controlled engineered bioreactor" have been proposed as in situ and ex situ treatment interventions.

to safely release the air stream from the soil to the atmosphere. As it is extremely challenging to separate the physical removal mechanism from the biological, this justifies why a combined removal approach has been proposed.

The volatilization and biodegradation of benzene from a soil can be enhanced by using the above-described processes (i.e., SVE and bioventing) in a controlled bioreactor (Fig. 11.3B), properly engineered to increase the removal efficiency or drastically reduce the treatment times. Besides a preliminary sieving of the soil, which eliminates the noncontaminated fractions, the advantages of this ex situ treatment solution compared to the in situ intervention are as follows:

- Better control of the optimal values of operational parameters, including pH, temperature, oxygen, nutrient concentrations, and water content
- Minimization of uncontrolled benzene-containing emissions
- Enhanced contact between soil and microorganisms as well as soil and air, promoting biodegradation and volatilization, respectively

- Presence of an energetic mixing that disregards the effect of soil permeability. The air flow-rate is not limited by the soil permeability and only depends on the amount of air pumped into the reactor
- Possibility of using previously benzene-enriched microbial communities to further stimulate degradation

However, as already said in the previous section, the soil must be excavated and transported to the treatment plant, which increases operational costs. Furthermore, the excavation of soil results in a release of a higher amount of PM_{10} and $PM_{2.5}$ (Table 11.1), which can adsorb benzene onto its surface and increase the environmental risk when inhaled by the inhabitants.

The effect on the industrial-related pollutants is different according to the type of remediation. With the in situ remediation, the amount of the three pollutants due to the industrial site is expected to decrease by 20% in the first year, 50% (of the initial value) in the second year, and the remaining 30% in the third year. With ex situ remediation, an increase in industrial related pollutants emissions by 50% occurs in the first 2 years during soil excavation, while the pollutants due to industrial site emissions are completely removed from the site in the third year. Table 11.1 provides a description of the pollutant emissions for the three interventions considered.

11.2 Objectives

The objective of this case study is to quantify, from a societal perspective, the costs and the benefits associated with the three different remediation alternatives using the CBA approach. The analytical framework used to estimate the monetary benefit and costs arising from the remediation of the industrial site is the approach described in Fig. 11.4 (see Chapter 2: Environmental health interventions for the treatment of waters, solids, and soils, for further details).

The remaining part of this chapter shows how to solve the case study. Each section is dedicated to illustrating the seven-steps described in Fig. 11.4. Within each section, the first part explains the methodology behind the analysis (as illustrated in detail in the previous chapters) and a step-by-step guide to construct the analysis model with Excel. Basic familiarity with Excel is assumed. The files for the analysis are available for download at the following link: https://www.elsevier.com/books/cost-benefit-analysis-of-environmental-health-interventions/guerriero/978-0-12-812885-5.

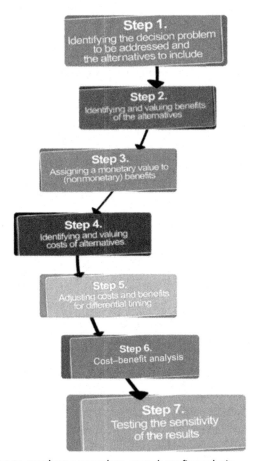

Figure 11.4 Steps to conduct a complete cost—benefit analysis.

11.3 Methodology

11.3.1 Step 1: Defining the analysis

11.3.1.1 Step 1 methodology

As described in detail in Chapter 2, Environmental health interventions for the treatment of waters, solids, and soils, the first step of CBA involves making general choices concerning the decision problem and the underlying assumptions of the study. As recommended by CBA guidelines, the perspective adopted for the case study analysis is a societal one. Essential for the CBA is to determine the time horizon over which estimating costs and benefits. There is uncertainty regarding the length of time over which a clean-up intervention will display their benefit. The permanence of clean-up depends on two elements: the intrinsic composition of the contaminated site and the adopted remediation technology. In this case study both alternatives—ex situ and in situ remediation—remove the pollutants permanently; however, in the baseline scenario, the period over which policy benefits arise is assumed to be 50 years. Two one-way sensitivity analyses are conducted for a shorter, 30 years, and a longer, 100 years, time horizon. Future costs and benefits are discounted using a constant 4% discount rate as recommended by the European Commission (EC, 2014). Extensive one-way sensitivity analyses and a probabilistic sensitivity analysis (PSA) will be performed to evaluate the robustness of the results to these model assumptions. All the values in the analysis are expressed in 2014 US$.

11.3.1.2 Excel exercise 1

Use the data provided in the text to populate the *Step 1* worksheet. The cells to be completed are green. Using the figure provided in the text, fill in the cell C3 with the size of the target population (50,000 inhabitants). Automatically the worksheet will estimate the number of children aged 5−14 years ($=C3 \times 0.10$), the number of children aged 6−18 years ($=C3 \times 0.11$), and the adults' population ($=C3 \times 0.73$).

For Year 0, the numbers corresponding to the pollution due to the industrial site (see text above) have already been included. In the no-intervention scenario, they remain the same for the entire time horizon. The final part of the exercise consists of filling in the cells D19:I19 (all the green cells) with the data provided in Table 11.1. Table 11.1 provides the industrial pollution in the two interventions scenario. As mentioned above, "With the in-situ remediation, the amount of the three pollutants is expected to decrease by 20% in the first year, 50% (of the initial value) in the second year and the remaining 30% in the third year. With ex situ remediation, an increase in pollutants emissions by 50% occurs in the first two years during soil excavation, while the pollutants due to industrial site emissions are completely removed from the site in the third year." Using this information, the industrial pollution for each year and pollutant can easily be estimated. To provide an example, the analysis has already been performed for PM_{10}.

11.3.2 Step 2: Quantifying the health benefits

11.3.2.1 Step 2 methodology

After reviewing the epidemiological evidence on the health effects of PM_{10}, $PM_{2.5}$, and benzene, we decided to include in the case study five different health outcomes. Three are long-term outcomes: reduction in adult all-cause mortality, lung cancer, and adult leukemia. The other two are short-term effects: asthma attacks in children and child bronchitis. As mentioned in Chapter 3, when assessing short-term impacts of air pollutants, baseline health-outcome data should be calculated using the same years of air pollution data. When assessing long-term impacts of air pollutants, baseline health outcome data can be estimated using all available years, implicitly considering that the estimated chronic exposure from the available years is representative of the cumulative average population exposure. The data on concentration response functions (CRFs) for each of the health outcomes considered are reported in Table 11.2.

As mentioned in Chapter 3, to quantify the potential health benefits associated with each intervention, it is essential to select the health outcomes and collect population specific health data (e.g., mortality rate and prevalence of asthma). The mortality rate for the target population considered is 10.3 per 1000 inhabitants, while the observed prevalence of childhood asthma and bronchitis are 3.5% and 7%, respectively. The incidence of lung cancer in the adult population is 8 cases per 1000 inhabitants. Adult leukemia incidence is 0.2%.

The formulas used in the case study to estimate the number of cases associated with the industrial pollution exposure (AC) is the following

Table 11.2 Health outcomes and concentration response functions.

Pollutant	Health outcome	CRF (CIs)	Reference
PM_{10}	Children bronchitis (6−18 years)	RR: 1.08 (0.98−1.19)	World Health Organization Expert Meeting (2013)
$PM_{2.5}$	Adult mortality	RR: 1.07 (1.04−1.09)	World Health Organization Expert Meeting (2014)
PM_{10}	Children asthma (5−14 years)	RR: 1.028 (1.006−1.051)	World Health Organization Expert Meeting (2013)
$PM_{2.5}$	Adult lung cancer	RR: 1.09 (1.04−1.14)	Hänninen et al. (2014),
Benzene	Adult leukemia	UR: 6.00×10^{-6} (2.20×10^{-6}, 7.80×10^{-6})	Hänninen et al. (2014)

CIs, Confidence intervals; *CRF*, concentration response function; *RR*, relative risk; *UR*, unit risk.

(see Chapter 3: Health impact assessment: quantifying the health benefits and costs):

$$AC = \gamma - \gamma_0 = \gamma - \gamma/e^{\beta*(\Delta x)} \tag{11.1}$$

where γ is the annual observed outcomes in the target population, and γ_0 is the number of outcomes observed without industrial related pollution. Δ_y is the decrease in the health outcome associated with a decrease in pollutant concentrations; Δ_x is the decrease in the pollutant concentration in a given scenario, while β is the coefficient of the CRF.

For adult leukemia only, the formula to estimate the number of attributable cases is

$$AC = C_{air} x\ UR \tag{11.2}$$

where UR is the additional risk of leukemia throughout the lifespan of the target population whose components are exposed continuously throughout life to a concentration of 1 $\mu g/m^3$ of the substance; C_{air} is the atmospheric concentration of benzene.

11.3.2.2 Excel exercise 2

Open the Excel worksheet *Step 2* and enter the input values in the green cells. The CRF values (95% CIs) and the population health data have already been inserted. The first task of Exercise 2 is to estimate βs for lung cancer, asthma, and bronchitis. The formula to estimate β in Excel is $= LN(RR)/10$ an example has already been provided in J4 (mortality all causes). The third task of this exercise consists of quantifying the health outcomes associated with the different interventions using a 4-year time horizon (including year 0 before any intervention). For each health outcome estimate γ by multiplying the population size by the prevalence of the disease/percentage of incidence in the target population. An example has been provided for all-cause mortality cell M11 which is equal to the total number of inhabitants (50,000) multiplied by the mortality rate in the target population.

Once γ has been estimated for each of the four health outcomes considered, it is possible to quantify the number of health outcomes attributable (AC) to industrial pollutant at year 0 (before any intervention). AC is estimated using formulas reported above. For simplicity the industrial pollutants concentration for each health outcome, by year, have already been inserted using Step 1 results.

The final task of Step 2 consists of estimating the number of health outcomes (PC) that can be averted by removing the industrial pollution. For each intervention, PC is estimated with the following formula:

$$PC_{yia} = X_{a0} - AC_{aiy} \tag{11.3}$$

where PC_{yia} is the number of preventable cases for a given year y, intervention i and health outcome a, X_{a0} are the number of cases observed at in Year 0 (without any intervention) and AC_{aiy} are the cases attributable for a given year y, intervention i, and health outcome a. The analysis has already been conducted for all-cause mortality and leukemia.

11.3.3 Step 3: Assigning a monetary value to the health benefits

11.3.3.1 Step 3 methodology

The third step of our practical exercise consists of assigning a monetary value to the health outcomes quantified in Step 2.

11.3.3.2 Value of statistical life

As explained in Chapter 4, Monetary analysis of health outcomes, assigning a monetary value to health benefits arsing from a reduction in environmental pollutants is not the same as placing a monetary value on a human life. What is being evaluated in this study, in monetary terms, is the willingness to pay for reducing the risk of dying associated with pollution exposure.

Ideally all the monetary values used in this case study should be elicited as close as possible to the policy site (soil remediation in Mexico). Whenever this is not possible, a benefit transfer procedure can be used. Details on how the values are used to populate the model are provided below. For further details on assigning a monetary value to health outcomes in CBA, see Chapters 4 and 5. Table 11.3 summarizes results from the literature review of estimates of value of statistical life (VSL). We favor studies that provide estimates for Mexico, and of these there are few primary studies that estimate VSL using either stated or revealed preference approaches for Mexico. There are also benefits transfer studies that use primary data from Mexico. Using the results provided in Table 11.3, we used a VSL ranging between US$211,000 (lower bound) and US$1.75 million (upper bound). These values are derived from the most recent report of the Secretaria de Medio Ambiente y Recursos Naturales (SEMARNAT) and the Instituto National de Ecologia y Cambio Climático (Instituto Nacional de Ecología y Cambio Climático, 2016) on health impact estimations in

Table 11.3 Value of a statistical life (VSL) estimates for Mexico found in the literature review.

Authors	Year	Context	Region	Organization	Methodology	IE	VSL	Details
Hammitt and Ibarrarán	2002	Health risk reduction air pollution	Mexico City	Academic	CV (reduce risk of flu and chronic bronchitis)	—	US$500,000	
Hammitt and Ibarrarán	2002	Health risk reduction air pollution	Mexico City	Academic	Hedonic model. Wages and perceived occupational health risks for blue collar workers in Mexico	—	US$150,000	
Cesar et al.	2002	Improving air quality in Mexico City	Mexico City	World Bank Report	Benefit transfer from European VSLs	0, 0.4, 1	US$4.28 million, 3.06 million, 1.85 million	2010 values
Cifuentes et al.	2005	Improving air quality in Mexico City	Mexico City	IADB Report	Takes Cesar et al. (2002) VSL values	0, 0.4, 1	US$4.28 million, 3.06 million, 1.85 million	2010 values
López et al.	2005	Health impact from power plant emissions	Veracruz	Academic	Benefit transfer from Hammitt and Ibarrarán (2002)	1, 4	US$280,000	
Hammitt and Ibarrarán	2006	Economic value of fatal and nonfatal occupational risks in Mexico City	Mexico City	Academic	Hedonic model (wage-risk). Actual risks from Labor Stats. Perceived fatal and nonfatal occupational injury risks were elicited using survey	—	Actual risk: US $235,000– US$325,000. Perceived risk: US$235,000	2002 values
INECC	2014	Economic valuation of health benefits from reducing $PM_{2.5}$	Mexico City, Monterrey, 0and Guadalajara	Government Report	Benefit transfer from US study (Kochi et al., 2006) US VSL US$5.4 million (2000 prices)	0.5 and 2	US$1.65 million	2010 values

Source	Year	Title	Location	Type	Methodology		Value	Values
LSE and INECC	2015	The value of statistical life in Mexico: a contingent valuation study	Mexico City	Government Report	Stated preference—WTP (using payment card) for reduced number of fatalities (risk) from a policy change. Adapted from Alberini et al. (2003) and Krupnick et al. (2002)	—	US$211,000 ($1,687,037 MXN)	2011 values
Rocha de Lima	2016	PhD Thesis (LSE)—Nonmarket Valuation for Environmental and Health Policy in Mexico	Mexico City	PhD Thesis				
SEMARNAT and INECC	2016	Estimation of health impacts from air pollution in the central region	Mexico Central Region (inc Mexico City)	Government Report	Uses LSE and Instituto Nacional de Ecología y Cambio Climático, London School of Economics and Political Science (2015) values as a local and main value. Uses Instituto Nacional de Ecología y Cambio Climático (2014) as a comparator	—	US$211,000 local value. US $1.75 million for comparison	2014 values

(Continued)

Table 11.3 (Continued)

Authors	Year	Context	Region	Organization	Methodology	IE	VSL	Details
Mexico City Government and Harvard School of Public Health	2018	Historical Analysis of Population Health Benefits Associated with AQ in Mexico City	Mexico Valley Metro Area	Local Government Report	Benefit transfer from unknown US study	—	Mean VSL Mexico City: US$5.1 million. Mean VSL Mexico Valley Metro Area (minus Mexico City): US$1.9 million. Population weighted mean VSL Mexico Valley Metro: US$3.3 million	
Robinson et al.	2018	Valuing mortality risk reductions	Worldwide Mexico	×ion	Benefit transfer from US value of $9.4 million	1, 5	US$1.47 million	
Barham	2011	Investigating whether cash transfers can reduce infant mortality	Rural Mexico	Journal of Development Economics	Benefit transfer from a US VSL of US$4 million	0.6, 1.25	US$0.53 million to US$1.5 million	2005 values
Instituto Nacional de Ecología y Cambio Climático (INECC)	2017	Estimación del valor de una vida estadística en México: un estudio de valoración contingente	Mexico (3 major metropolitan areas: Mexico City, Guadalajara, Monterrey)	Government Report	CV (WTP for reduced mortality risk)	—	2,797,808 MXN or US $352,813	2014

IE, Income elasticity used in the study.

Mexico's Central Region, which includes Mexico City. This report calculated VSL estimates from local studies and used benefit transfer estimates as comparators. The lower estimate of US$211,000 comes from an earlier 2015 London School of Economics and INECC report which carried out a stated preference study (Contingent Valuation) in Mexico. The upper estimate of $1.75 million comes from a 2014 INECC report that used benefit transfers from a US study (Kochi et al., 2006) with a US VSL of US$5.4 million. There are three other local studies, two of which were authored by Hammitt and Ibarràn (2002). They estimate VSLs of US$500,000 (using a contingent valuation approach) and US$280,000 (using hedonic modeling of wages). A 2017 INECC contingent valuation study conducted across the three major Mexican metropolitan areas found an average VSL of $352,813. All three values fall within the proposed range.

11.3.3.3 Morbidity
Table 11.3 reports the morbidity estimates for Mexico. The majority of WTP studies used benefit transfers from international studies. In the case study, we decided to use local study estimates, the majority of which used a cost of illness approach. The value of reducing the risk of bronchitis was retrieved from a contingent valuation study conducted by Hammitt and Ibarrarán in 2002. The average monetary estimate quantified by the study is US$30,000 per case of chronic bronchitis. In Northeast Mexico, the annual cost for consultations of children asthma, using a cost of illness approach, is US$225 per patient (Gallardo Martínez et al., 2007). Unfortunately, there are no studies estimating the willingness to pay to reduce the risk of lung cancer from pollution exposure in Mexico. Using a cost of illness approach, the cost per cancer is US$21,300 (Reynales-Shigematsu et al., 2006). According to a cost of illness study conducted in 2006 by Santos Padron, the mean cost of treating an adult patient with (myeloblastic) leukemia is US$42,276 (in 2004 prices).

11.3.3.4 Excel exercise 3
Open the Excel worksheet *Step 3* and enter the input values in the green cells. Once you have monetary estimates to populate the analysis, it is essential to report all of them at the year in which the analysis is conducted (2014) using the inflation formula below:

$$\text{Adjusting for Inflation} = (((CPI_1 - CPI_0)/CPI_0) * WTP) + WTP$$

$$(11.4)$$

Table 11.4 Annual US Consumer Price Index.

Year	CPI
2002	180
2002	184
2003	189
2004	195
2005	202
2006	203
2007	207
2008	215
2009	214
2010	218
2011	225
2012	230
2013	233
2014	237

Source: IC Consumer Price Index, 2019. Link to the website: <https://www.ecb.europa.eu/stats/macroeconomic_and_sectoral/ hicp/html/index.en.html> (IC Consumer Price Index, 2019).

where CPI_0 is the Consumer Price Index of the year in which the study was conducted and CPI_1 Consumer Price Index of the year in which our CBA is carried out (e.g., 2014). The mean annual values of Consumer Price Index from 2000 to 2014 are reported in Table 11.4.

11.3.4 Step 4: Quantifying the costs

11.3.4.1 Step 4 methodology

It is difficult to estimate a priori the cost of remediating a contaminated site. Site-specific geologic, geochemical, and contaminant conditions significantly affect the cost of different remediation technologies. Given the impact of soil characteristics and pollution history on the cost of remediation technologies, it is also not possible to transfer cost estimates from one site to another.

Among the different technologies, the largest uncertainty is for estimating the cost of in situ processes that are more affected by site's characteristics. For ex situ technologies, technology providers typically report costs in terms of dollars per volume treated (e.g., cost/volume: $/m^3$; or cost per weight of contaminant treated or removed: $/kg). This information is supplemented by percent reduction in contaminant concentration or mobility achieved. For in situ technologies this approach to cost reporting is less common than making a direct comparison between remediating alternatives challenging.

In the United States, the Federal Remediation Technologies Roundtable has developed a guide to documenting the costs of remediation projects carried out by federal facilities (National Research Council, 1997). The guide provided a very useful breakdown of costs items that have been adopted as a starting point in the financial cost analysis of the present case study. As observed in Table 11.5, in the first 3 years, the cost will significantly differ between the alternative interventions. After year 3, the cost for the two interventions is assumed to be equal to be zero, while the cost for the no intervention alternative will remain constant over the entire time horizon. At year 10, if remediated, the site will be sold to a private investor who offered $150,000 to convert the site into an amusement park.

As explained in greater detail in Chapter 7, Discounting benefits and costs, the financial dimension is concerned with the net costs to the public sector of the adoption of a given intervention. Given that the perspective adopted for the analysis is a societal perspective in addition to the financial costs for the public sector, the social costs incurred by households, individuals, and environment should also be included. Moving from a financial analysis to an economic one allowing us to include in the cost-evaluation additional costs (and benefits) items. In addition to the health outcomes associated with industrial related pollution accounted for in the benefits evaluation, there exists negative externalities associated with an industrial site such as visual disamenities, odor, and noise. As suggested by the EC Guidelines for CBA, the negative externalities associated with a landfill site do not vary with the amount of disposal waste. The same approach is applicable to an industrial site. Depending on the intervention, these disamenities can remain stable (e.g., in the case of no intervention), increase for a short term (e.g., in the case of ex situ remediation) or decrease (e.g., in situ remediation). In this case study, we also account for the increase in real estate prices of the houses located in proximity to the industrial site by 7%. This increase is equal to an additional monetary benefit of US $50,000 that will be achieved in the case of site remediation (both in situ and ex situ) in the third year.

11.3.4.2 Excel exercise 4

Open the Excel worksheet *Step 4* and complete the last two green rows by making the sum of the input values for the three alternatives considered. As seen, the cost remains constant for the no-intervention over the

Table 11.5 Financial cost analysis.

Capital cost	Year 1			Year 2			Year 3		
	In situ	Ex situ	No intervention	In situ	Ex situ	No intervention	In situ	Ex situ	No intervention
Site preparation									
Site clearing	50,000	30,000		50,000	30,000		50,000	30,000	
Site access	5000	5000	500	5000	5000	500	5000	5000	500
Heath, gas, electricity	15,000	7000	2000	15,000	7000	2000	15,000	7000	2000
Structures	1000	1000		1000	1000		1000	1000	
Building	1000	1000	700	1000	1000	700	1000	1000	700
Equipment	30,000	10,000		30,000	10,000		30,000	10,000	
Process equipment									
Costs of technologies	50,000	12,000		50,000	12,000		50,000	12,000	
Materials and supplies	25,000	7000		25,000	7000		25,000	7000	
Nonprocess equipment									
Safety equipment	2500	2500		2500	2500		2500	2500	
Utilities	10,000	10,000		10,000	10,000		10,000	10,000	
Operating costs									
Labor costs	85,000	50,000		85,000	50,000		85,000	50,000	
Materials	15,000	3000		15,000	3000		15,000	3000	
Transport	400	26,000		400	26,000		400	26,000	
Disposal		50,000			50,000			50,000	

entire time horizon, while for the two alternative interventions, the total cost will fall to zero after year 3 (in the excel spreadsheet for simplicity is reported only year 10). For each year, estimate the revenues by intervention type and insert the value in row 26. The no intervention will bring no monetary benefits, while for the two alternative interventions, there will be an additional 50,000 that will be achieved in the case of site remediation in the third year and the $150.000 revenue in year 10.

11.3.5 Step 5: Discounting costs and benefits

11.2.5.1 Step 5 methodology

As in Guerriero et al. (2011), the formula used to estimate the present value of the health benefit arising from the reclaiming of polluted waste sites is the following:

$$PV_a = WTP_a * PC_{ai} * 1 - 1/(1+d)^t)/d \qquad (11.5)$$

where PV_a is the present value estimated for each health outcome a and PC_{ai} is the estimated annual number of health outcome a for each intervention as an annuity lasting t year. In the formula, it is assumed that the number of PC does not vary by year, so this assumption will be relaxed in the analysis. This is reexpressed as a present value using the discount rate d. The time horizon t should be the same for all the interventions considered. In the baseline scenario, t is assumed to be equal to 50 years. Two one-way sensitivity analyses are conducted for a 100 and 30 year-time horizon. The discount rate is assumed to be either 4% or 2%.

11.3.5.2 Excel exercise 5

Open the Excel worksheet Step 5. To facilitate the estimation and prepare the ground for subsequent one-way sensitivity analyses, the formula to estimate PV_a has been decomposed in three components: (1) $WTP_a \times X_a$, (2) $(1 - 1/(1 + d)^t)/d$, and (3) $WTP_a \times X_a \times (1 - 1/(1 + d)^t)/d$

1. $WTP_a \times X_a$: The analysis for mortality has already been done to provide an example. Complete the analysis for the other health outcomes filling the green cells.
2. $(1 - 1/(1 + d)^t)/d$: The analysis has been set for three possible time horizons (t): 100, 50, and 30 years and two different discount factor: 4% and 2%. Keep in mind to consider the difference in health outcomes prevented between in situ and ex situ intervention during the first 3 years. In the example provided for mortality, we first estimated

the present value for the first 3 years after the intervention for each of the intervention. Then we quantified the remaining benefits assuming three different time horizons (97, 47, and 27 years). Complete the analysis for the 2% discount factor (green cells).

3. Once the two components of the PV formula have been estimated, quantify the PV for each health outcome by adding the present value of the monetary benefits for the first 3 years and then for the remaining years of the time horizon.

4. The last part of Step 5 worksheet estimates the present value of costs and non-health benefits arising from the three different interventions. Keep in mind that the annual cost of no intervention is constant for the entire time horizon considered, while for ex situ and in situ remediation, the cost of remediation occurs only in the first 3 years (and as consequence will be the constant independently from the time horizon considered). As described in Step 4, the revenues are zero for the no-intervention scenario. For ex situ and in situ remediation, there will be an increase in real estate price occurring at year 3 and the revenue of $150,000 in year 10. Both values need to be discounted. The analysis is already completed for a 4% discount factor, while estimates still need to be calculated for a 2% discount (green cells).

11.3.6 Step 6: Comparing costs with benefits

11.3.6.1 Step 6 methodology

The objective of Step 6 is to compare the present value of the benefits with the present value of the cost. The main condition for the adoption of an intervention is that the present value of the benefit (including nonhealth benefits) exceeds the present value of the cost or that the net present benefit (NPB) is larger than 0. The NPB rule is usually adopted to decide whether to accept or reject an option, to rank different projects, and to choose between mutually exclusive projects. An equivalent feasibility test is the benefit cost ratio (BCR) test: present value of benefit (PVB)/present value of cost (PVC) > 1. Both these measures will be estimated in this case study for the different interventions proposed.

11.3.6.2 Excel exercise 6

Open the Excel worksheet *Step 6* and complete the analysis. Add the present value of the monetary health-related benefits to the present value of revenues estimated in Step 5. For each intervention estimate the NPB and the BCR using the following formulas:

$$NPB = PVB-PVC$$
$$BCR = PVB/PVC$$

(11.6)

11.3.7 Step 7: Dealing with uncertainty
11.3.7.1 Step 7 methodology
Sensitivity analysis explores how the outcome of CBA changes with the variation in inputs, assumptions, and/or framework used for the analysis.

If the objective of sensitivity analysis is to assess the degree of uncertainty associated with single-model parameters, deterministic sensitivity analysis, specifically, one-way or multiway sensitivity analyses, can be used.

As the name suggests, one-way deterministic analysis assesses the sensibility of the NPB to changes of a single variable in the model. One-way sensitivity analyses have already been performed in the previous steps to account for different time horizons (100, 50, and 30 years) and discount factors (2% and 4%).

The one-way sensitivity analysis used in this step is a Tornado Diagram that allows to assess the relative importance of variables in one visual display.

The second approach to assess uncertainty in the CBA results is PSA and Monte Carlo simulation. Both are routinely used in cost-effectiveness analysis to account for parameter variability and uncertainty.

PSA consists of assigning a probability distribution to the input parameters of the analysis. The choice of the distribution depends on the characteristics of the variable (e.g., bounds of the variable and symmetry of the distribution) and the available information (Briggs et al., 2006). Briggs et al. (2006) suggests the adoption of a Beta distribution for binomial data, such as proportion and probabilities, as these are naturally bounded between 0 and 1; Gamma or Lognormal distributions are the perfect candidates to use for simulating uncertainty in the cost parameter while relative risks can be assigned a Lognormal distribution. Due to the central limit theorem, the normal distribution is a good candidate for any parameter and does not fall in the aforementioned categories (Briggs et al., 2006). Once the distribution has been assigned to each parameter, using Monte Carlo simulation random values are drawn from each distribution (usually 1000 draws). The costs, benefits, and the expected net benefit are calculated for each simulation according to the following formula: expected net benefit = EB − EC.

The Monte Carlo simulation results can be plotted graphically using cost-benefit acceptability curves (CBAC). In pure health-care decision-making, cost-effectiveness acceptability curves indicate the probability that an intervention is cost-effective compared with the alternative(s), given a range of λ willingness to pay values (e.g., for an additional quality of life year gained). In the case of CBA of EHIs, both cost and benefits are reported in monetary values. Thus, the condition for the pollution control policy to be implemented is the following:

$$NPB = PVB - PVC > 0 \qquad (11.7)$$

where NPB is the net present benefit and PVB and PVC are the present value of benefits and costs associated with the intervention.

11.3.7.2 Excel exercise 7
11.3.7.2.1 Deterministic sensitivity analysis
Open the worksheet *Step* 7. The objective of this first part of exercise 7 is to present the results of several one-way sensitivity analyses using a Tornado Diagram. This type of graphical display illustrates the model parameters having the greatest effect on the analysis results. The tornado diagram has already been completed for in situ remediation. Fill in the green cells for ex situ.

11.3.7.2.2 Probabilistic sensitivity analysis
To perform PSA, a different Excel file "CBA PSA" has been created and is availbale online for download at the following link: is: https://www.elsevier.com/books/cost-benefit-analysis-of-environmental-health-interventions/guerriero/978-0-12-812885-5.

The objective of this part of exercise 7 is to transform a deterministic CBA model into a probabilistic one. Open the "CaseStudyProbabilistic.xsl". As you can see the case study has been simplified to only one health outcome: all-cause mortality assuming a 50 years' time horizon and a 4% discount rate (these assumptions can easily be relaxed by making the parameters probabilistic). When opening the file, you will notice that a new worksheet called "parameters" has been added. All the parameters of the study (epidemiological data, demographic data, and cost data, etc.) have been included in a column named "live values." While the cell B3

Table 11.6 Parameters distribution for probabilistic sensitivity analysis.

Distribution	Parameters	Excel command
Normal	Mean and standard deviation	NORMINV(.)
Beta	α and β where alpha is the number of events, while beta is the exposed population minus the number of events.	BETAINV(.)
Gamma	α and β	GAMMAINV(.)
Lognormal	Mean and standard deviation and lv	EXP(NORMINV(.))

switches from a deterministic mode (if the value is 0) to a probabilistic one (if the value is 1), you can switch a value from column C to D.

The first step to perform PSA is to assign the parameters a probabilistic distribution. The relative risk of all-cause mortality associated with $PM_{2.5}$ is 1.07 (95%1.04−1.09). Using this information, it is necessary to estimate the natural logarithm of the mean: = LN(D6) and the natural logarithm of the standard error: = (LN(1.09) − LN(1.04))/(1.96 × 2) (See Table 11.6). Once these two values have been included, the probabilistic values will be obtained with the following formula: = EXP(NORMINV(RAND(); F35; G35)). The Beta distribution is defined by two parameters: β and α where α is equal to the number of events of interest while β is the sample size minus the number of events. From the data provided in the text, we know that for every 1000 individuals living in the target population, there are 10.3 deaths. Using this information, α and β can easily be estimated. Once these two values have been inserted in cells H7 and I7, the probabilistic following function = BETAINV(RAND(); H7;I7) can be used to produce random draws. The last four values are assigned a Gamma distribution. The formulas to use to estimate α and β parameters for the Gamma distribution are: = mean^2/SE^2 and = SE^2/mean, respectively, where mean is the mean cost and SE is the standard error.

The second task to conduct PSA requires usage of a simple Macro "MCsimulation" to produce 1000 probabilistic trials of the model. Open the "Simulation" worksheet and enter in the green line the "live" values for each of the parameter and estimated results. Once this task is complete, go to Visualize > Macros > MCsimulation > Run. The Macro will automatically copy and paste the results of 1000 simulations. To estimate the probabilistic results of CBA, simply calculate in cells K1006:S1006 the mean values across the 1000 trials of the model and copy the estimated numbers to the probabilistic result table provided in the worksheet Step 6.

The final task of PSA consists of "building" the CBACs (one for each intervention considered).

In this exercise the CBACs show the probability that a reclaim policy is cost-beneficial for a range of clean-up intervention costs. In cell V2, insert the cost of the remediation from AB5. Using the remediation cost inserted in V2, estimate in the cells U5 and V5 the NPB for in situ and ex situ remediation using the 1000 simulated present benefit values. In columns AC (for in situ) and AD (for ex situ), use the IF(...) function to generate a binary variable taking the value of 1 when the net-benefit is positive, and zero when the net-benefit is negative. In the cells X4 and Y4 estimate the mean of columns X and Y, respectively. These two means show the proportions of the simulated trials in which the net benefit is positive given the clean-up cost. Once you have done these preparatory actions, it is possible to run the CBAC Marco: go to Visualize > Macros > CBAC > Run. The Macro will automatically copy and paste different values of remediation costs in V2 and estimate the corresponding means for the proportions of the simulated trials in which the net benefit is positive. The CBACs for the two interventions are shown in the worksheet "CBACcurve." For a practical example of PSA using CBAC, see Guerriero et al. (2011). Another possible application of CBAC is to show the incremental net benefit of remediation in situ and ex situ compared to the no-intervention scenario.

Incremental   net   benefit $_{insitu} = PVB_{insitu} - PVB_{donothing}/$ $PVC_{insitu} - PVC_{donothin}$

11.4 Conclusion

The objective of this chapter was to provide a step-by-step guide to perform CBA of EHIs. The EHIs described in the chapter are two mutually exclusive remediation approaches and a no-intervention scenario; however, the flexibility of the model described and the use of Excel allow to easily adapt the model to other types of EHIs such as interventions targeting water pollution and/or air pollution.

References

Alberini, A., Boyle, K., Welsh, M., 2003. Analysis of contingent valuation data with multiple bids and response options allowing respondents to express uncertainty. J. Environ. Econ. Manag. 45, 40−62.

Barham, T., 2011. A healthier start: the effect of conditional cash transfers on neonatal and infant mortality in rural Mexico. J. Dev. Econ. 94 (1), 74−85.

Briggs, A., Sculpher, M., Claxton, K., 2006. Decision Modelling for Health Economic Evaluation. Oxford University Press.

Cesar, H., Borja-Aburto, V.H., Cicero-Fernandez, P., Dorland, K., Muñoz Cruz, R., Brander, L., et al., 2002. Improving Air Quality in Metropolitan Mexico City: An Economic Valuation. World Bank. Retrieved from: <http://documents.worldbank. org/curated/en/607361468777295667/pdf/multi0page.pdf>.

Cifuentes, L.A., Krupnick, A.J., O'Ryan, R., Toman, M., 2005. Urban Air Quality and Human Health in Latin America and the Caribbean. Inter-American Development Bank. Retrieved from: <https://www.cepal.org/ilpes/noticias/paginas/5/22145/Cifuentes%20et%20al.%20reporte%20-%20IADB.pdf>.

EC, 2014. Guidelines to cost-benefit analysis of investment projects. Economic Appraisal Tool for Cohesion Policy 2014-2020. European Commission. Available from: https://ec.europa.eu/inea/sites/inea/files/cba_guide_cohesion_policy.pdf.

Guerriero, C., Bianchi, F., Cairns, J., Cori, L., 2011. Policies to clean up toxic industrial contaminated sites of Gela and Priolo: a cost-benefit analysis. Environ. Health 10, 68. Available from: http://www.ehjournal.net/content/10/1/68.

Hänninen, O., et al., 2014. Environmental burden of disease in Europe: assessing nine risk factors in six countries. Environ. Health Perspect. 122 (5), 439—446.

Hammitt, J.K., Ibarraràn, M.E., 2002. Estimating the Economic Value of Reducing Health Risks by Improving Air Quality in Mexico City. Newsletter on Integrated Program on Air Pollution, 2.

Hammitt, J.K., Ibarrarán, M.E., 2006. The economic value of fatal and non-fatal occupational risks in Mexico City using actuarial-and perceived-risk estimates. Health Econ. 15 (12), 1329—1335.

IC Consumer Price Index 2019. Link to the website: <https://www.ecb.europa.eu/stats/macroeconomic_and_sectoral/hicp/html/index.en.html>.

INECC, 2017. Estimación del valor de una vida estadística en México: un estudio de valoración contingente. Informe final. Instituto Nacional de Ecología y Cambio Climático (INECC). México. Retrieved from: <https://www.gob.mx/cms/uploads/attachment/file/436696/Informe_final_VEV_vf.pdf>.

Instituto Nacional de Ecología y Cambio Climático, 2014. Valoración económica de los beneficios a la salud de la población que se alcanzarían por la reducción de las PM2.5 en tres zonas metropolitanas mexicanas. Secretaría de Medio Ambiente y Recursos Naturales, Distrito Federal, México. Retrieved from: <https://www.gob.mx/cms/uploads/attachment/file/195224/2014_CGCSA_Beneficos_econ_micos_al_reducir_PM2.5.pdf>.

Instituto Nacional de Ecología y Cambio Climático, London School of Economics and Political Science, 2015. The Value of Statistical Life in Mexico: A Contingent Valuation Study. Distrito Federal, México. Retrieved from: <https://www.gob.mx/cms/uploads/attachment/file/191446/Disponibilidad_a_pagar_por_reducir_riesgo_de_muerte.pdf>.

Instituto Nacional de Ecología y Cambio Climático, 2016. Estimación de impactos en la salud por contaminación atmosférica en la región centro del país y alternativas de gestión. Secretaría de Medio Ambiente y Recursos Naturales, Distrito Federal, México. Retrieved from: <https://www.gob.mx/cms/uploads/attachment/file/208105/INECC_CAME_Final_14022017.pdf>.

Kochi, I., Hubbell, B., Kramer, R., 2006. An empirical Bayes approach to combining and comparing estimates of the value of a statistical life for environmental policy analysis. Environ. Resour. Econ. 34 (3), 385—406.

Krupnick, A., et al., 2002. Age, health and the willingness to pay for mortality risk reductions: a contingent valuation survey of ontario residents. J. Risk Uncertainty 24 (2), 161—186.

Martínez, G.G., Cruz, A.A., Díaz, S.N.G., Rodríguez, G.G., 2007. Costos derivados de la atención médica del asma en un grupo de niños del Noreste de México. Revista Alergia México 54 (3), 82—85.

National Research Council, 1997. Innovations in Ground Water and Soil Cleanup: From Concept to Commercialization. The National Academies Press, Washington, DC. Available from: https://doi.org/10.17226/5781.

Reynales-Shigematsu, L.M., Rodríguez-Bolaños, R.D.L.Á., Jiménez, J.A., Juárez-Márquez, S.A., Castro-Ríos, A., Hernández-Ávila, M., 2006. Costos de la atención médica atribuibles al consumo de tabaco en el Instituto Mexicano del Seguro Social. Salud Pública de México 48 (S1), 48−64.

Robinson, L.A., Hammitt, J.K., O'Keeffe, L., 2018. Valuing mortality risk reductions in global benefit-cost analysis. J. Benefit-Cost Anal. 1−36.

Rocha de Lima, M., 2016. Non-Market Valuation for Environmental and Health Policy in Mexico (doctoral dissertation). Retrieved from: <http://etheses.lse.ac.uk/3424/1/Lima_Non-Market_Valuation.pdf>.

Santos Padrón, H., 2006. Relación entre la pobreza, iniquidad y exclusión social con las enfermedades de alto costo en México. Revista Cubana de Salud Pública 32 (2), 31−45.

World Health Organization Expert Meeting, 2014. <http://www.euro.who.int/__data/assets/pdf_file/0010/263629/WHO-Expert-Meeting-Methods-and-tools-for-assessing-the-health-risks-of-air-pollution-at-local-national-and-international-level. pdfWHO2000> (http://www.euro.who.int/document/e71922.pdf) IC 2019: Source: <https://www.usinflationcalculator.com/>.

World Health Organization Regional Office for Europe, 2013. Health Risks of Air Pollution in Europe − HRAPIE Project: Recommendations for Concentration − Response Functions for Cost−Benefit Analysis of Particulate Matter, Ozone and Nitrogen Dioxide. http://www.euro.who.int/__data/assets/pdf_file/0006/238956/Health_risks_air_pollution_HRAPIE_project.pdf?ua = 1.

Further reading

Hamra, G.B., Guha, N., Cohen, A., Laden, F., Raaschou-Nielsen, O., Samet, J.M., et al., 2014. Outdoor particulate matter exposure and lung cancer: a systematic review and meta analysis. Environ. Health Persp. 122 (9), 906−911. Available from: https://doi.org/10.1289/ehp/1408092.

Lopez, M.T., Zuk, M., Garibay, V., Tzintzun, G., Iniestra, R., Fernandez, A., 2005. Health impacts from power plant emissions in Mexico. Atmos. Environ. 39 (7), 1199−1209.

Secretaría del Medio Ambiente de la Ciudad de México, School of Public Health Harvard, 2018. Análisis Histórico de los Beneficios en la Salud de la Población Asociados a la Calidad del Aire en la Ciudad de México entre 1990 y 2015. Distrito Federal, México. Retrieved from: <http://www.data.sedema.cdmx.gob.mx/beneficios-en-salud-por-la-mejora-de-la-calidad-del-aire/descargas/analisis-espanol.pdf>.

World Health Organization Regional Office for Europe, 2014. WHO Expert Meeting. Methods and Tools for Assessing the Health Risks of Air Pollution at Local, National and International Level. Copenhagen. <http://www.euro.who.int/__data/assets/pdf_file/0010/263629/WHO-Expert-Meeting-Methods-andtools-for-assessing-the-health-risks-of-air-pollution-at-local-national-and-international-levelpdf?ua = 1>.

CHAPTER 12

Conclusion

Carla Guerriero[1] and John S. F. Wright[2]
[1]Department of Economics and Statistics, University of Naples Federico II, Naples, Italy; Centre for Studies in Economics and Finance (CSEF), Naples, Italy
[2]Institute for Public Policy and Governance, University of Technology Sydney, Sydney, NSW, Australia

Contents

In the context of complex policy problems and a scarcity of resources available for their redress, cost—benefit analysis (CBA) provides a transparent and potentially important source of evidence for policy makers in prioritizing interventions. However, in both developed and developing countries, CBA has rarely been used to prioritize environmental health interventions (EHIs). The objective of this book is to provide a comprehensive guide to CBA of EHIs using an interdisciplinary approach. Each chapter of the book summarizes existing evidence on a specific issue of CBA, including the monetary valuation of health outcomes, the different discounting approaches, and the management of uncertainty in the results of economic evaluation.

The aim of this final chapter is to outline two areas in which further research is needed to enhance the utility of CBA to policy making: the importance of accounting for equity in CBA and, related to this issue, the inclusion of child welfare estimates in the valuation of costs and benefits.

12.1 Why equity should be considered in cost—benefit analysis

As mentioned in the introduction section of this book, CBA is based on the Kaldor and Hicks efficiency criterion: there is a net gain if gainers could, in principle, compensate the losers, whether or not they do actually compensate them. This criterion depends on the assumptions that the marginal utility of money is constant and that the utility different people attach to money is comparable.

The Kaldor—Hicks criterion is unsatisfactory because it assumes that money has the same utility to everyone, and, as consequence, CBA evaluates governmental policies by aggregating the monetary equivalents of very different individuals. In short, CBA is insensitive to distributional issues. It ignores that the value of money is different to people at the top and the bottom of the distribution curve and that the effectiveness of interventions is different for people who belong to specific minority groups. Distributional analysis is a term used to define the assessment of the impacts of an intervention on different groups in society. Interventions may differ in their effects according to the income level, geographical location, race or age group.

To take an example of why distributional issues pose a problem for CBA, imagine a policy for the reclamation of several toxic waste sites in and around a major city. The reclamation of the sites naturally involves a range of costs and benefits to the citizens of the city. But the policy for reclaiming the sites does not affect one group of people in the city disproportionately. All citizens of the metropolis benefit from the reclamation of waste sites regardless of their place on the income distribution scale. But, following the clean-up, all citizens pay for goods and services at higher prices to accommodate the costs of the clean-up and the wider improvement in the city's quality of living. Following the reclamation of the sites, the city is more pleasant for all citizens. And superficially, CBA captures the important aspects of the policy in terms of benefits to their health status and happiness. However, citizens at the lower end of the city's income distribution pay disproportionately more, in terms of monetary outlay, to gain the same benefit as those at the top of the distribution. Because citizens at the lower end of the distribution have less money, the money that they have is much more valuable to them. Further, those at the top end of the income distribution pay less in terms of monetary outlay and may even gain disproportionately more from the clean-up in terms of health and quality of living benefits. Under the Pareto effect, property prices rise and rents increase, advantaging the wealthier and disadvantaging those at the bottom of the income scale exponentially. In short, benefit value expressed by traditional CBA does not capture the cost and value of money to those who have less of it, and it does not capture the compounding "welfare gains" that the reclamation policy has for those at the top end of the distribution. In this situation, distributional impacts become a highly relevant consideration.

There is an ongoing debate regarding the appropriate approach for accommodating equity concerns in CBA. According to Fleurbaey et al. (2013), a possible solution is to take social preferences and priority setting into account. For example, in a city in which residents are deeply concerned about environment health, and much less with other goods and services, might simply prioritize policies for the reclamation of waste sites. In such a case of revealed social preferences, distributional impacts are absorbed within the citizens' collective decisions about issues directly affecting them and their own constructions of what is valuable. However, critics suggest that a preference-based approach is more or less an aggregation the preferences of individual citizens, who engage in a competition for services and resources, and who will likely disagree on public priorities. In such case, it is not possible to aggregate preferences at societal level. By extension, practitioners also debate the nature of individual preferences, contesting the suggestion that they derive from rational choices, arguing that they do not express the deeper convictions of individuals, and are subject to informational and decision-making limitations (Samson et al., 2018). These objections constitute the thin edge of larger wedge of problems associated with the task of adding distributional weights to CBA. The academic challenge is to develop a means for considering distributional weights without relying on individual preferences that fall into the difficult area of subjective welfare. And at this point, considerations of the social welfare function (SWF), interpersonal comparison, and the equivalent income approach (EIA) have become relevant to contemporary thinking regarding measures for accommodating equity issues in CBA. These two approaches and their limitations will be discussed in the two following sections.

12.1.1 The social welfare function and interpersonal comparison

SWF is about making policy based on a definition of the distribution of utilities within a ven population. Specifically, it aims to improve CBA through the concept of expressed utility preferences. In this sense, SWF assumes that utilities are comparable on an interpersonal basis. It suggests that a single vector involving different rankings and values can express the outcome of a policy choice for every individual who will be affected by the policy (e.g., remediation of polluted city) (Adler, 2016). And so, invariably, the SWF function requires practioners to settle on a definition of "utilities." The problem is that there is no basis for settling the specific vector on which the outcome of the citizen's policy choices can be expressed. Equally, there is no firm basis for deciding the values on which outcomes along the vector are ranked. To some extent, CBA attempts to escape the need to define the vector and values for expressing utilities within a population by quantifying the societal willingness to pay (WTP) for the social benefit of reducing environmental pollution (e.g., cleaning up the city waste sites). But, with money having a different value for different individuals within the city, the measure is deeply flawed. And as such, welfare economists have been critical of measures like WTP for some time (Adler, 2016). For the future, the continued relevance of CBA to policymaking depends upon practitioners developing a reasonable way for thinking about distributional weighting and avoiding perverse results described in the polluted city. For some practitioners, thinking reasonably about sensitizing CBA means adopting a preference-based approach that adjudicates the relative costs and gains associated with diverse groups within the area affected by the policy. Along this line of thought, CBA needs to confront the issue of distributive justice in order to serve as a reliable foundation for policy-making (Fleurbaey et al., 2010).

For welfare economists, resource trade-offs are decided based on individual preferences. But where economists use measures like WTP, they implicitly give larger weight to the preferences of the rich people compared with those of the poor (Fleurbaey et al., 2010). Alternatively, other economists argue that the ethical preferences of the population affected by the policy are the only reliable basis on which to assign utility vectors and values to outcomes that are interpersonally comparable (Bergson, 1948, 1954; Samuelson, 1947; Harsanyi, 1977; Adler, 2016, 268). Sensitizing CBA with appropriate distributional weights is about structuring the analysis in relation to ethical views. But CBA must consider individual interests without synthesizing the political views of citizens into a subjective and collectivized doctrine (Fleurbaey et al., 2010). Advocates suggest that there is close connection between an individual's welfare and their ethical preferences (Adler, 2016, 268). And the pay-off of finding such a basis is that it allows practitioners to recognize that money has greater value for the poor than for the rich (Fleurbaey and Abi-Rafehy, 2016, 287). Indeed, within any community, there is a wide variety of ethical views regarding preferences for the distribution of social benefits. But the role of economists is to engage with these preferences, derive weights from basic ethical principles in order to sensitize CBA, and then to carry out CBA in such a way that respects individual preferences (Fleurbaey et al., 2010).

To date, practitioners of CBA have been reluctant to engage in this kind of work. But ignoring the need to weight CBA outside WTP is suboptimal approach to weighting. Broadly, practitioners have experienced difficulty addressing the issues of distributional weights in CBA on the basis that there is no reliable basis from which to apply the SWF. However, the key to solving the problem is recognizing the necessity of solving the problem. On this basis, practitioners remain aware that choosing utility vectors and values is a contentious issue, especially in a preferentially heterogeneous population, but there is a requirement to avoid using an unweighted CBA and settle upon an interpersonally comparable vector utility (Fleurbaey and Abi-Rafehy, 2016). Finding a basis for interpersonal comparisons is not particularly difficult, some suggest, so long as practitioners remain transparent about the underlying assumptions that their efforts to sensitize CBA make (Fleurbaey and Abi-Rafehy, 2016). In any one polity, citizens are likely to exhibit some personal preferences that are relatable on a comparative basis. In this case, distributional weightings based on ethical principles are relatively straightforward. But even where they are heterogeneous, an application of appropriate concepts can help the SWF operate effectively (Adler, 2016).

12.1.2 The equivalent income approach

The EIA is an increasingly popular means for drawing the difficult issue of allocating distributional weights to CBA without falling prey to welfarism and the subjective determination of utility preferences. To some extent, EIA functions as a context to conduct analyses of WTP. Subjective utility is an awkward basis on which to adjust CBA for distributional impacts. Measuring subjective utility is difficult. And there is also the question of whether subjectively expressed utilities are comparable on an interpersonal basis. Indeed, the act of comparing subjective utilities involves the implicit assumption that the object of human life is the satisfaction of utilities, that there is a meta-vector and meta-values along which these utilities might be expressed and compared. Individuals do not pursue collectivized or a higher order of goals in life, rather goals that are relevant to their own existence, in particular (Rawls, 1982). Further, individuals also adapt their preferences according to the demands of the situation in which they find themselves. In this sense the comparison of stated utility preferences of those that the top and the bottom of the income scale is also unreasonable (Sen, 1992). In both these senses, subjective utility is an inappropriate measure with which to account for distributional weights.

The notion of equivalent income avoids the pitfalls associated with comparisons of subjective utilities. In short, individual income is a variable, but also a nonsubjective utility, which can be ranked and deployed as a distributional weight when associated with other concepts of social benefit outcome, such as "one year of perfect health." Not unlike the process in the adjacent field of health economics for determining the effectiveness of different medicines in quality-adjusted life-year (QALY), making an assessment of the individuals WTP relative to equivalent income for a particular benefit allows interpersonal comparison of valuations in the same way the QALY allows comparisons of health gain across different diseases areas (Weinstein et al., 2009). For these reasons, practioners have enthusiastically embraced equivalent income as a means for weighting CBA in a nonwelfarist way. Analysts collect a representative sample of the population associating weights for different levels of income and social benefit categories, calculating the WTP for gains on the basis of a ratio to income levels. The EIA, therefore, is not subject to criticisms of meta-preferences and adaptation. As such, equivalent income offers an ethically attractive and nonwelfarist means for adding weights to CBA. The main challenge of conducting CBA, from the perspective of the EIA, is to determine the preferences of people concerning income and areas of social benefit. Via the inclusion of EIA, CBA becomes a method of economic evaluation that is sensitive to distributional issues. Still, determining preferences should not be done in relation to specific policies, but to generalized ethical concerns for social benefits (Fleurbaey et al., 2010). Whereas efforts to sensitize CBA on the stated utility preferences are subject to various biases both material and hypothetical, the methodological issues involved with equivalent incomes are tractable and not far removed from issues associated with QALYs. Improving the estimation of individual preferences should be one of the first priorities on the research agenda (Fleurbaey et al., 2010).

12.1.3 Cost–benefit analysis and distributional considerations

For some time, practitioners have sought to use distributional weights to sensitize CBA to the social preferences of individuals on higher or lower incomes. While distributional weights have seen some limited application in Europe, they are rarely applied in the United States (Adler, 2016). Distributional weights are contentious. In a world of heterogeneous preferences, some doubt the possibility of making the objective interpersonal comparisons necessary to distributional weighting (Adler, 2016). The EIA approach suggests that individual budgets may be an appropriate basis for examining the relative consumption of social benefits. However, a drawback of this approach is the assumption the monetary income expresses the total value of all income that individuals gain. For example, nonmarket sources of income, such as networks and social capital, maybe equally valuable to individuals in assessing WTP. Further, income is also situational. It does not exist in a vacuum. Individuals on lower incomes typically exist within suboptimal environments that affect their determinations of preference. Other attempts to sensitize CBA to distributional impacts have included impersonal comparisons of happiness and wellbeing which are subject to the same objections as the EIA approach. Arguably, the EIA approach is less subjective than the surveys of happiness and wellbeing. Surveys of nebulous topics such as happiness and well-being might ignore unobserved variations in the status of individuals, the aspects of their lives relevant to happiness and wellbeing. EIA does "monetize" interpersonal comparisons, which some might consider morally unacceptable. But equally, money is simply a concept, a convenient measure that aggregates a wide variety of social advantages and disadvantages into a single statistical value. In this light, income is simply a convenient leading indicator common to all individuals. But perhaps the point is that both the decision to use distribution weights and the decision not to use them both involve ethical judgments. And the role of practitioners is to make such decisions. While heterogeneous personal preferences certainly complicate distributional weights, they are not intractable. Concepts and methodologies already in use in the adjacent field of health economics may make the problem of interpersonal considerations much more tractable.

12.2 The inclusion of children's welfare estimates in the valuation of costs and benefits

Related to the issue of accounting for distributional effects in CBA is the inclusion of children's welfare estimates in CBA. The US Executive Order 13045 "Protection of Children from Environmental Health Risks" states that "Each Federal Agency shall make a high priority to identify and assess environmental health risks and safety risks that may disproportionately affect children; and shall ensure that its policies, programs, activities and standards address disproportionate risks to children that result from environmental health or safety risks" [Environmental Protection Agency (EPA), 2006].

Children are a life stage group that is characterized by peculiar psychological, physical, and behavioral attributes [Environmental Protection Agency (EPA), 2003]. They are different from adults with respect to their risk, exposure, and susceptibility to environmental hazards (OECD, 2006; Alberini et al., 2007). Epidemiological evidence has shown that exposure to environmental hazards during the gestational period increases the risk of congenital malformations (Dolk et al., 1998; Geschwind et al., 1992). During their first years of life, children are also more vulnerable to environment-related risks than adults because their bodies are still developing and are less able to protect themselves from the effects of pollutants (Wigle et al., 2007; Prüss-Üstün and Corvalán, 2007). In addition, their faster metabolism exposes them to higher doses of food, water, and air per unit of body weight (Wigle et al., 2007).

Perhaps the most difficult challenge to including benefits for children in the economic evaluation of EHIs is the monetary valuation of their health benefits (OECD, 2006). In particular, Alberini et al. (2010) highlight three key methodological issues associated with the valuation of child health benefits: the elicitation of child preferences, the context of the valuation, and the difficulties related to age, latency, and discounts.

According to previous authors, the main obstacle in the evaluation of child health benefits is that children do not possess the necessary cognitive abilities to formulate preferences for their own health risk reductions (OECD, 2006; Alberini et al., 2007; Harbaugh, 1999). Further, children are also not able to understand health risk and have no control over financial resources. Excluding the child perspective, previous studies have used three other types of perspectives to elicit child WTP estimates: the societal perspective, the adult as a child perspective, and the parental perspective

(OECD, 2006; EPA Environmental Protection Agency, 2003). The societal perspective consists of asking a representative group of the society (parents and nonparents) the amount they are willing to pay for child health risk reduction (OECD, 2006). The second perspective asks adults to imagine themselves as children and to assign a value to the health risks they faced when they were children (OECD, 2006). The third, and most commonly adopted perspective, asks parents how much they are willing to pay for child health risk reductions. According to Alberini et al., the adult as a child perspective is the most challenging perspective. Respondents are required to reflect on their own childhood and value the risks they were facing as a child. Of the three, the parental perspective might seem the most workable given that parents are the most reliable proxies for their children and have the child's best interests at heart (OECD, 2006; Alberini et al., 2007). However, all three approaches have major limitations: first, they violate the principle of consumer sovereignty by failing to elicit WTP estimates from the individual who is actually facing the risk; second, adult individuals show greater risk aversion toward risks faced by children than toward risks faced themselves, and thus place greater value on risk reductions for child health compared with adults health; and third, altruism toward children may substantially increase WTP estimates and lead to a higher than efficient provision of safety compared with other goods (Bloomquist et al., 2010; Dickie and Messman, 2004).

Another relevant question when valuing child health benefits is whether WTP should be adjusted for the characteristics of the child, in particular, for their age (OECD, 2006). Existing economic evaluations of the relationship between child age and parental WTP offer contrasting findings. According to Dickie and Messman (2004) and Hammitt and Haninger (2010), parental WTP for child health risk reduction decreases as children grow older. However, Alberini and Scansy (2011) investigated parental WTP for child mortality risk reductions in Italy and the Czech Republic to find that WTP did not change with age in Italy, and that it increased as children grew older in the Czech Republic.

Finally, there are two other important elements to take into account in valuing children's health benefits, namely, latency and discounting (EPA Environmental Protection Agency, 2003). The majority of the health benefits arising from EHIs occur in the future. Exposure to some hazards during childhood, such as heavy metals, will display effects only later in life when the child has become an adult (OECD, 2006).

Challenges associated with discounting child health benefits are also related to the issue of latency. If the EHI displays benefits over a period of time longer than 1 year, the future health benefits should be reexpressed in terms of present value (OECD, 2006). There is limited research on parental and child discounted future health benefits, and also regarding the rate (fixed or variable over time) at which future health benefits should be discounted (EPA Environmental Protection Agency, 2003). A study conducted by Alberini et al. (2007) investigating individual WTP for reductions in mortality risk associated with remediation policies found a discount factor of 7%. However, a subsequent study conducted on parental estimates of the WTP for reducing the mortality risk for themselves, or for one of their children, found a 0% discount rate (Alberini et al., 2007). In conclusion, despite the important role that economic evaluation can play in guiding decision-making, there are still many troublesome issues associated with methodology and the availability of economic benefit values that limit its use.

Despite the higher vulnerability of children to environmental hazards, few resources are invested to prevent child exposure to these hazards (Cairns and van der Pol, 1999). Possible reasons for this are the lack of epidemiological and economic data are the methodological issues associated with eliciting WTP estimates to value children's health benefits (Dolk et al., 1998; EPA Environmental Protection Agency, 2003). When EHIs affect children's health, the availability of child-specific monetary value is essential to assess the intervention cost-effectiveness.

12.3 Ways forward for cost–benefit analysis

In the 21st century, policy problems are complex, and the resources available for their redress are limited. In this context, CBA has the potential to function as a useful tool for policy makers in prioritizing interventions. In order to serve in this capacity, however, CBA must face up to some serious challenges, especially those involving the issues of distribution and equity, which includes consideration of the children of today and for future generations. To be sure the consequences of climate change on the earth's ecosystem will affect children disproportionally. And as the inspiring campaign of Greta Thunberg demonstrates, children not only want to be included in discussions about climate change, but they seek a greater voice in deciding the issues that will shape the future of the planet. And in any case, societies are rarely homogenous. They comprise different ethnicities and age groups, which themselves comprise individuals with different levels of wealth, education, health, and opportunity. EHIs will benefit and cost these different sections of society differently. In using CBA to make policy interventions within heterogeneous societies, the role of practitioners is to make a decision regarding these different impacts. These decisions are necessarily subjective. But making these kinds of decisions is about demonstrating reflexivity, understanding the assumptions involved in the weighting of equity, age, and distributional concerns.

The 2015 Paris Agreement gathered the 195 member states of the United Nations and successfully committed them to tackling the common problem of climate change. Following the 1950 Great Acceleration, the human imprint on the environment has played a central role in changing the earth's geology and ecosystem; this process began with the conclusion of the Second World War and continues to accelerate to this very day. CBA can play a central role in prioritizing interventions that target climate change. This book summarizes the guidelines in use in different countries with a view to offering a common interdisciplinary framework for understanding and gauging the issues critical to the evaluation of EHI.

It is not our part to master all the tides of the world, but to do what is in us for the succour of those years wherein we are set, uprooting the evil in the fields that we know, so that those who live after may have clean earth to till. What weather they shall have is not ours to rule.

J.R.R. Tolkien.

References

Alberini, A., et al., 2007. Paying for permanence: public preferences for contaminated site clean-up. J. Risk Uncertainty 34 (2), 155–178.

Alberini, A. (Ed.), 2010. Valuation of Environment-Related Health Risks for Children. OECD.

Alberini, A., Scansy, M., 2011. Context and the VSL: evidence from a stated preference study in Italy and the Czech Republic. Environ. Resour. Econ. Manage. 48 (4), 511–538.

Adler, M.D., 2016. Benefit–cost analysis and distributional weights: an overview. Rev. Environ. Econ. Policy 10 (2), 264–285.

Bergson, Abram, 1954. On the concept of social welfare. Quarterly Journal of Economics 68, 233–252.

Bloomquist, G.C., Dickie, M., O'Conor, R.M., 2010. Willingness to pay for improving fatality risks and asthma symptoms: values for children and adults of all age. Resour. Energy Econ. 33 (2), 410–425.

Cairns, J., van der Pol, M., 1999. Do people value their own future health differently from others' future health? Med. Decis. Making 19 (4), 466–472.

Dickie, M., Messman, V.L., 2004. Parental altruism and the value of avoiding acute illness: are kids worth more than parents. J. Environ. Resour. Manage. 2004 (48), 1146–1174.

Dolk, H., et al., 1998. Risk of congenital anomalies near hazardous-waste landfill sites in Europe: the EUROHAZCON study. Lancet 352 (9126), 423–427.

Environmental Protection Agency, 2003. Handbook of Valuing Children's Health. < https://www.epa.gov/environmental-economics/handbook-valuing-childrens-health >.

Environmental Protection Agency (EPA), 2006. Guide to Considering Children's Health When Developing EPA Actions: Implementing Executive Order 13045 and EPAs Policy on Evaluating Health Risks to Children. Available online at: <https://www.epa.gov/sites/production/files/2014-05/documents/epa_adp_guide_childrenhealth.pdf>.

Fleurbaey, M., Luchini, S., Muller, C., Schokkaert, E., 2010. Equivalent Income and the Economic Evaluation of Health Care. Center for Operations Research and Econometrics Discussion Paper.

Fleurbaey, M., Luchini, S., Muller, C., Schokkaert, E., 2013. Equivalent income and fair evaluation of health care. Health Econ. 22, 711–729.

Fleurbaey, M., Abi-Rafehy, R., 2016. The use of distributional weights in benefit–cost analysis: insights from welfare economics. Rev. Environ. Econ. Policy 10 (2), 286–307.

Geschwind, S.A., et al., 1992. Risk of congenital malformations associated with proximity to hazardous waste sites. Am. J. Epidemiol. 135 (11), 1197–1207.

Hammitt, J.K., Haninger, K., 2010. Valuing fatal risks to children and adults: effects of disease, latency, and risk aversion. J. Risk Uncertainty 40, 57–83.

Harbaugh, T.W., 1999. Valuing Children's Health and Life: What Does Economic Theory Say About Including Parental and Societal Willingness to Pay. University of Oregon Economics Working Paper 1999.

Harsanyi, J., 1977. Rational behavior and bargaining equilibrium in games and social situations. Cambridge: Cambridge University Press.

OECD, 2006. Economic Evaluation of Environmental Health Risks to Children. OECD Publishing, Paris, 2006.

Prüss-Üstün, A., Corvalán, C., 2007. How much disease burden can be prevented by environmental interventions? Epidemiology 2007 (18), 167–178.

Rawls J., 1982. Social unity and primary goods. In Utilitarianism and Beyond, Sen AK, Williams B(eds.). Cambridge University Press: Cambridge.

Samson, A.-L., Schokkaert, E., Thébaut, C., Dormont, B., Fleurbaey, M., Luchini, S., et al., 2018. Fairness in cost-benefit analysis: a methodology for health technology assessment. Health Econ. 27, 102–114. 2018.

Samuelson, P.A., 1947. Foundations of economic analysis. Cambridge, MA: Harvard University Press.

Sen, A., 1992. Commodities and capabilities. Amsterdam: North-Holland.

Weinstein, M.C., Torrance, G., McGuire, A., 2009. QALYs: the basics. Value Health 12 (1), 5–9.

Wigle, D.T., et al., 2007. Environmental hazards: evidence for effects on child health. J. Toxicol. Environ. Health B: Crit. Rev. 2007 (10), 3–39.

Further reading

Cairns, J., 1994. Valuing future benefits. Health Econ. 3 (4), 221–229.

Dickie, M., Gerking, S., 2007. Altruism and environmental health risks to health of parents and their children. Environ. Resour. Econ. Manage. 2007 (53), 323–341.

Viscusi, W.K., Magat, W.A., Huber, J., 1987. An investigation of the rationality of consumer valuations of multiple health risks. RAND J. Econ. 18 (4), 465–479.

Index

Note: Page numbers followed by "*f*" and "*t*" refer to figures and tables, respectively.

Printed in the United States
By Bookmasters